MW00572522

57 SF activities for facilitators and consultants:

Putting Solutions Focus into action

57 SF activities for facilitators and consultants:

Putting Solutions Focus into action

Edited by

Peter Röhrig and Jenny Clarke

solutions books

First published in Great Britain in 2008 by
SolutionsBooks
26 Christchurch Road
Cheltenham
GL50 2PL
United Kingdom
www.solutionsbooks.com

Originally published in 2008 in German as 'Solutions Tools' by
managerSeminare Verlags GmbH
Endenicher Str. 282
D-53121 Bonn
Germany
www.managerseminare.de

German edition compiled and edited by Peter Röhrig.
Compilation and editorial material in English edition Copyright © Peter Röhrig
and Jenny Clarke

ISBN 978-0-9549749-6-1

Cover design by
Cathi Stevenson

Design, typesetting and production by
Action Publishing Technology Ltd, Gloucester

Contents

Acknowledgements

We would like to thank all the contributors whose generosity made this book possible: Jane Adams, Yasuteru Aoki, Liselotte Baeijaert, Stephanie von Bidder, Annie Bordeleau, Klaus Botzenhardt, Kirsten Dierolf, Madeleine Duclos, Ben Furman, Bert Garssen, Carey Glass, Wilhelm Geisbauer, Dominik Godat, Michael Goran, Josef Grün, Michael Hjerth, Felix Hirschburger, Paul Z Jackson, Björn Johansson, Alan Kay, Susanne Keck, Loraine Kennedy, Hans-Peter Korn, Christine Kuch, Annette Lentze, Thomas Lenz, Mark McKergow, Alasdair Macdonald, Daniel Meier, Gesa Niggemann, Eva Persson, Armin Rohm, Gabriele Röttgen-Wallrath, Klaus Schenk, Lilo Schmitz, Lina Skantze, Insa Sparrer, Anton Stellamans, Peter Szabó, Frank Taschner, Janine Waldman, Penny West, Barry Winbolt and Inge Zellermann. We are grateful to Matthias Varga von Kibéd for his thoughtful – and thought-provoking – preface.

Our thanks also go to Dr. Susanne Angerhausen, Ingo Bräu, Susanne Hohenschild, Jochen Kehr, Ulrike de Kruijf, Melanie Niestroj, Gabriele Röttgen-Wallrath and Stefan Schmidt for test-driving the activities and to Carey Glass and Veronica Hughes-Friederichs for polishing broken English.

We would also like to thank all our friends and colleagues from the SOLWorld community for advancing the art and practice of applying solution focused ideas in new fields.

We all stand on the shoulders of Steve de Shazer and Insoo Kim Berg whose writing and teaching led us along the solution focused path. We miss them and remember them with gratitude.

We have relied heavily on the skill, patience and customer focus of Miles Bailey and his team at Action Publishing Technology in the production of the English version of this book. Thank you.

Peter Röhrig and Jenny Clarke
March 2008

Preface

Matthias Varga von Kibéd

Do you have 15 minutes to spare? Then I'd like to invite you to have a quick look at this book. But beware! If you only have 15 minutes, you might miss your next appointment, as even a quick glance through these pages will give you so many interesting new ideas that you might forget the passage of time as you start to think about how to use these ideas in your own professional life.

57 SF Activities is the most thorough collection of solution focused activities available. There is a wealth of new exercises using the approach developed by Steve de Shazer, Insoo Kim Berg and the Milwaukee school which they founded with their colleagues and co-workers. These activities are designed for the world of teams and organisations, coaching and training, project planning and vision development, conflict resolution and team development, leadership training and organisational development issues. They have all been tested in workshops.

The SOLWorld Conferences, initiated in 2002 by the Bristol Group[1], contributed greatly to bringing international attention to the solution focused approach and its near universal applicability. Since 2005, the annual SOLWorld Summer Universities have continued the tradition of developing and sharing new applications.

Steve de Shazer and Insoo Kim Berg both left us a short time ago, only 16 months apart. This book honours their dedication and genius, their human kindness and their sharp minds, their clarity and their brilliant practice. We are indebted to them for the solu-

---

[1] In 2002, the Bristol Solutions Group consisted of Jenny Clarke, Kate Hart, John Henden, Paul Z. Jackson, Mark McKergow and Harry Norman.

tion focused approach; their ideas and practice now extend beyond the original realm of therapy. The SOLWorld community has greatly contributed to this, this book being one of the fruits of that tree.

As the solution focused approach presents a pragmatic methodology developed over decades rather than the classical architecture of a theory, it is consistent with its basic tenets to develop it further by new forms of practical applications. In addition, Ludwig Wittgenstein's philosophy is one of the most important foundations for the method especially for Steve de Shazer. This can be seen as a foundation a posteriori as he did not build his form of practice on Wittgenstein – but he might have! Solution focused work certainly comes from a systemic and (de)constructivist point of view. Steve sometimes used to remark to me how happy he felt finally to have found somebody in Wittgenstein who thought in a similar way.

I'd like to remind you of just one of the central ideas of the late Wittgenstein here: according to Wittgenstein's late work, the Philosophical Investigations, regular behaviour – so called rule following – cannot be split up into the rule in question on one side and the following of it on the other. As Wittgenstein[2] stresses, such a case of rule following already reaches 'bedrock, and my spade is turned'.

Both problematic human behaviour and behaviour after the miracle are of course examples of rule following. The radical shift in the usual point of view prompted by Wittgenstein's ideas on rule following thus becomes a provocative source of inspiration for all fields concerned with changes of human behaviour.

Today we find many forms of analysis of so called behavioural patterns and belief sentences; seen from a Wittgensteinian perspective as well as from a solution focused one, these at best can be regarded as misleading ways of speaking. The mistake here lies in the ultimate impossibility of finding 'the' rule in an instance of rule following.

When we bring our attention to the many and creative formats in this book, developed in part by some of the most experienced pioneers of the solution focused approach and in part

---

[2] Wittgenstein, Philosophical Investigations 217: 'How am I able to obey a rule?' – if this is not a question about causes, then it is about the justification for my following the rule the way I do. If I have exhausted the justifications I have reached bedrock, and my spade is turned. Then I am inclined to say 'this is simply what I do.'

by some colleagues who with a fresh wind joined the crew a short time ago, we should remember the point about following a rule.

The descriptions of the many activities in this book may at first sight give the impression that the solution focused consultants, trainers and facilitators had forgotten about the irreducibility of following a rule to rules, writing just as if they could describe some new rules and patterns of proceeding.

From a Wittgensteinian point of view however, as well as seen from Steve de Shazer's perspective, and incorporated by Insoo Kim Berg when you observed her working, such exercises should be seen rather as as-if constructions. You might decide to try one or other suggestion in your own professional work, following the instructions like rules. This might result a new form of rule following in a hopefully useful way for the clients. In practising these formats with increased proficiency, new applications slowly emerge as if by themselves. After some time you may be surprised to notice that you are doing something-effective and useful but something no longer in accordance with the original rules.

Say 'Hello and welcome' to these changes! Because rule following really never was just a combination of the rule (a theory or method) and following it (an action); useful new forms of application for the solution focused approach will arise from changing the instructions.

In the same way, according to the communication theory embedded in the solution focused approach, the meaning of a question is not fixed in a dialogue until it has been answered. And similarly, Steve and Insoo thought that whatever a client did that made his life better, after having been given an experiment, the client could be seen as having successfully done the experiment. And for the same reason Steve and Insoo never regarded the miracle question as the same question they had already asked before but always as a new question.

To preserve the power and inner unity of this approach, it is important to see work focused on good practice, like this book, against the background of a synopsis and philosophical foundation as given by the fundamental theoretical and philosophical observations in the writings of Steve de Shazer and by Gale Miller ('Becoming Miracle Workers'). Both observed the solution focused practice of Insoo Kim Berg and Steve himself; furthermore by the common and evolving ground appearing in Steve de Shazer's and Yvonne Dolan's joint book[3] 'More than Miracles' (which was to become Steve's last work); by Günter Lueger developing suitable new principles and forms of measuring the effects of solution focused interventions applicable in the organisational field; by Insa Sparrer's Solution Focused Structural Constellations (in her book 'Miracle, Solution and System') and our joint idea of a transverbal solution focus which might bring a new form of coherence to the background of the solution focused approach; and by Mark McKergow together with Gale Miller (in their work on 'Simple Complexity or Complex Simplicity') analysing the whole solution focused approach in a fresh way.

Without such a foundation, the solution focused approach would be blind, like experiences without concepts according to Kant, while without the continuation and development of new forms of practice, these foundations would stay empty like thoughts without content.

So, please enjoy changing your own way of acting, your own practice, your own form of rule following, inspired by coming into contact with the many creative ideas from the contributors of this book!

The job of editor is certainly not easy. Peter Röhrig and Jenny Clarke have produced an unusual and special book, carefully and professionally. It should find wide distribution and careful attention; so if it proves useful for you, please tell others – and if you have ideas for improvement, please tell them!

Steve and Insoo certainly would have been happy to see how well their gift to mankind is growing and evolving!

Matthias Varga von Kibéd
Munich, February 2008

---

[3] (with dialogues and comments from and with Insoo Kim Berg, Harry Korman, Terry Trepper und Eric McCollum)

About *Prof. Dr. Matthias Varga von Kibéd*

– SySt-Institute Munich

Cofounder with his wife Insa Sparrer of the Systemic Structural Constellations approach & SySt-Institute Munich; University teacher (Logic & Epistemology, Department of Philosophy, University of Munich;) Special fields: paradoxes, Wittgenstein, philosophy of language; teaches systemic consultants; business consultant, coach & trainer; regular seminars on systemic & SF work for 4 years at the SySt-Institute and in Germany, Austria, Switzerland, Italy, Hungary, Netherlands, France, Greece, Slovenia

Address: Leopoldstrasse 118, D 80802 Munich, Germany
Phone/Mobile: +49-(0)89-363661 (SySt-Institute); +49-(0)89-38346973 (secretary)
e-mail: Matthias.varga@gmx.de; sekretariat.varga@syst.info
info@syst.info
www.syst.info

CHAPTER 1

What's this book about?

An interview with Peter Röhrig by Jenny Clarke, co-editor
of the English edition

*Jenny Clarke: What is the essence of the solution focus approach
for you?*

Peter Röhrig: For me 'essence' is a very big word. The very special
thing for me is that solution focus means a focus on effectiveness.
And it's a very friendly and respectful way of consulting by encouraging clients in their belief that they can master change by and for
themselves. Solutions and ideas emerge in a dialogue, in the interaction between the client and the consultant, instead of through the
traditional way of giving advice.

*So tell me a little bit more about things emerging in conversation.
How do you think that works?*

I think it works by looking first at things that work instead of at
things that don't work. Even in the midst of gloom you can
discover success. I have had workshops with people who were
really desperate about their working situation – and still they found
some little diamonds, some things that functioned or at least functioned from time to time. By looking at things that work you will
always find ways to broaden the perspectives and the possibilities
of clients. (For instance with the exercise 'What's in it for me?' by
Björn Johansson and Eva Persson.)

What's the most surprising success story that you can think of?

There is a story that refers to my own development. When I started
consulting and training, I worked a lot with medical doctors. They
are clever people and they don't have much time for their own

training. They expected for instance that they could learn every-thing about leadership within three hours on a Wednesday afternoon.

Of course, because they are diagnosticians, they like diagnosis.

Yes – and they like recipes. They expected detailed instructions on how to work with their nurses in a more efficient way. So when I started that, I had to decide what I could pack into these three hours of leadership training that was absolutely necessary for doctors to know. I had a lot of stress and still it was never enough! After three hours the doctors said *Well, that was interesting but I still have so many very important questions to be answered, for instance 'How can I be a leader?'*

So when I discovered the solution focused approach, I started to change my attitude and my behaviour as a facilitator and trainer. I thought much more about responsibility – what I was responsible for and what the participants were responsible for. I started to sit back and ask them what they knew already and what they wanted to learn. There was always a lot they already had in their repertoire and behaviour. So I could build on that – which made it much easier for everybody. In three hours we could work on their own situations and they went away with very practical and tangible ideas fit for their own practice.

That made a great difference. I was aware of the difference espe-cially in the way I felt after workshops. I felt relaxed and satisfied and that was quite opposite to what I had felt before.

In this short story you gave examples of three out of six SIMPLE principles developed by Jackson and McKergow: 1. The solution not the problem, in other words: concentrate on what they want not what they don't want. Why not ask them? 2. Make use of what's there. Take what they already know and build on that. 3. Every case is different. Every one of these doctors and their partic-ular staff is in a very different situation, which only they know about. And I think the other three principles are probably in it as well. In fact everything you said about interaction and dialogue is a principle: things happen inbetween people, in conversations.

My next question is about how you discovered the ideas of solution focus and what attracted you.

To cut a long story short: by chance I discovered a workshop by Lilo Schmitz who offered an introduction to solution focused consulting. When I read the headline 'Solution focused consulting', I thought *'Well, that's what I am doing already. At least, it's what I want to do. I should know more about that.'* I went there and discovered a new way of thinking and acting as a facilitator. I gladly worked with Lilo for years, first as a student with a wonderful teacher who had a lot of confidence in my abilities. She really walked her talk. One of her favourite sentences was *'Just try it out!'* Through her confidence and trust, she gave me so much confidence that we succeeded in doing things we would not have thought ourselves capable of. That's how it started for me.

Lilo worked mainly in the social sector. So we started to translate solution focused ideas into management and training. We developed solution focused leadership training and did that successfully with many people.

How did you make that translation from therapy to things more appropriate to your own context? How did you go about it? It is not easy; we took ages to do that.

Actually I just did what Lilo said: I tried it out. I get the best ideas from my clients, from their questions and the things they want to achieve. I work a lot in quality management and development. And people always wanted a more simple way to work with ideas of quality management, away from the idea that it is very bureaucratic, a lot of extra work and documentation. So I tried to support them with a simple approach. For instance I started workshops by asking people to think about the qualities in their personal work and write them down. And then to write down qualities in their organisation. So we had some initial ideas we could put on the wall and have a look at them together to in order to learn something about quality. (See my exercise 'Quality mirror'.)

This was a completely different approach to what they were used to. Usually they started by looking at problems, deficits and weak-

3

nesses: *'What are the urgent things we have to fix? How can we keep or raise our standards?'* These were their usual questions. So I offered them quite a different way of entering into that field. And actually it was not my idea but the client's idea.

Again, because who would know best – them or you? This reminds me of another example of the first principle: solutions not problems. And I do not know if this is true in German as it is in English. I suspect it is: that word 'solution' to ordinary people tends to mean What do we have to do? For us it means What do we want? What is the Future Perfect or the miracle situation? It amazes me how rarely we ask the question – even to our clients – What do you want?

It's very similar in German. The word solution – Lösung – implies action, some way of doing something, rather than possibilities. And my work is much more about possibilities. I work with my clients in a 'possible world', supporting them to make it very colourful and with many interesting details so that ideas emerge about how they could follow these possibilities. And then there might emerge solutions in that common meaning of the word. First tiny steps set in a general direction.

And then the world is different. You used the phrase 'broadening perspectives' earlier. It's like having a buffet – a choice. Because usually people come to us when they are stuck and from their perspective there are no possibilities.

Or too many possibilities or sometimes just two – yes or no – and there are always more in between. That reminds me to tell you something about the field in which I work with the solution focus. Very often it is teambuilding, which means they feel stuck, because co-operation and mutual information isn't working the way they wanted. Another very important field is conflict resolution. And also strategic work on questions like 'How can we master the future?'

Given the world the way it is, given that we can't master the future.

That's the nice thing about planning: the harder you plan, the more you are struck by chance.

4

Yes, that's right! And somebody said 'Just because the plan is no good, it doesn't mean that planning is pointless.' That brings us neatly to the book. You have given three or four activities about quality development, kinds of situations in which you found solutions focused work useful. In the book there are many others. How do you want people to use this book?

I can only talk about how I like to use collections of methods. For me they are a kind of treasure chest: collections of different ideas from different people who share their experience. These are colleagues who work in different fields who have developed good ideas about how to do things even better. I can look at these ideas and find out how appealing they are for me, how I could try to use them, which methods could fit to my personal style of facilitating etc.

Good point about the personal style. What I like enormously about this book is exactly that: so many different voices here, so many forms of experience. It is very generous of them and you to bring all this together.

The book is laid out in a way that may imply some kind of process. Would you like to say something about that?

No, I think it's self-explanatory. Actually I had some resistance to structuring it at all. My very first idea was to present it simply in alphabetical order of contributors or contributions. Then I thought that might be a bit too strange.

I think the structuring you did was helpful.

And I have another idea how people could use this book. You know how to travel on a globe? You spin it around, close your eyes, put a finger on it and find an interesting place. So working with the book could be just flipping through it and stopping at an interesting page and finding a random idea about how to work next time.

I agree with that. I think it could be worth doing exactly that, just flip through it and wait until it opens at a page. The titles of many of them, of course, let you know what you could find.

Yes, the titles of many. And sometimes the titles are a bit mysterious to make readers curious.

Tell me a bit about who the authors are, what kind of work they do, what kind of a range there is.

Most of them come from the SOLWorld network (www.solworld.org). That makes it different to other collections where contributors write down all the activities they collected, saying 'I gathered them from here and there and this is how I do it!' I asked all the experienced colleagues I know – and I am glad to know so many people who do solution focused work all over the world who have accepted the invitation to contribute an activity. Our annual conferences have a strong spirit of sharing. So I have seen a lot of them working there. And the cooperation is even more intense in the SOLWorld Summer Universities that we organise.

You must have had some criteria for deciding what is and what isn't solution focused. So can you say something about what they have in common, something that makes them qualify for inclusion in this book?

I only asked facilitators or process consultants who are experienced solution focused practitioners. They have all tried their activities out, they know what works and they have something to share. That was my first and most important criterion. The second is a bit softer. I asked for descriptions of methods that make it more or less obvious that these colleagues work with a solution focused attitude, that they work with solution focused principles, not only with solution focused tools.

These principles are what you stated so nicely at the beginning of our conversation: for instance belief in the client, the emergence of ideas, finding little diamonds and so on?

I had to reject some contributions because of that criterion. That was not easy. And I still found it a good experience because it made me think about how to express good reasons for rejection. So in the end, the people whose contributions I had to reject all accepted it.

I would just like to pay tribute here to the way you do that. This friendliness and the encouraging nature of the way you do your work. And I can imagine how carefully you thought about good reasons. Good reasons meaning acceptable reasons.

One very crucial point which was not so easy for me was that some people sent me contributions which were clearly about training. I had asked for contributions about workshops. Of course there is an area where workshops and training go together. In fact, most of my 'training' nowadays is workshops in which I work interactively and on participants' issues with minimal input. But many contributions were on training solution focused ideas – and that's something different.

So the book addresses facilitators, consultants, managers and allied trades? And it is not a training book, although trainers might find interesting stuff in it?

Exactly.

What else should I be asking you about?

This is a question I am not prepared for! Actually I would like to talk about the benefits of the book.

I thought this was obvious because it has got Peter Röhrig's name on it! So why should people use the book? What are the benefits?

I think it is a very practical book. All the activities are described in detail. You can easily use them in your own practice. And – on the other hand – it is not a recipe book. The activities are described in their proper context. So you can think about adapting them if you have an idea about a context where you want to do something different. Most contributions describe not only what happens but also how the interventions are staged, how they work, what the background is, what is special about them. I really like the fact that that most contributors wrote something about their personal preferences, about how they like to work with that activity, their own experience, what surprised them.

And it is a book written by over 40 people from all over the world, which provides a big variety of facilitation methods. These professionals have very different experiential backgrounds and still stand side by side and complement each other. They all work in a solution focused way and speak to us in various ways. Some address your brain, some your heart, others your gut; some write humorously, some more seriously. So what they write about is really very personal.

That's lovely. And this brings me back to the universality of the approach. Sometimes people say it is very North American, very positive and I think they haven't got it. It is about the clients, where they are coming from and what they want. That means that it can't be culture specific. All that we can do is encourage that dialogue that you talked about in the context of the person you're talking to and support them in finding new possibilities. I am sure that this book can contribute a lot to this.

Reference:

Paul Z Jackson and Mark McKergow, '*The Solutions Focus: Making Coaching and Change SIMPLE*', Nicholas Brealey, 2nd edition, 2007.

About the editors

Dr. Peter Röhrig

– ConsultContor · Consulting and Coaching

Peter is an SF organisational consultant, facilitator and executive coach, born 1948, with two children.

- *Formal education as an economist and social psychologist*
- *Advanced training in epidemiology, organisational development, total quality management (EFQM) and solution focused consulting*
- *11 years as general manager of service companies*

- *Many publications, mainly about self-management, leadership and quality development*
- *Partner of ConsultContor, consulting and coaching, in Cologne, Germany*

Renate Kerbst, one of his co-partners at ConsultContor, says about Peter:

Zeal for solutions is the name of an SF training series initiated by Peter, and this is a strong impulse for his professional functioning. His focus on practical resources and his attentiveness to simplicity are a solid foundation for his consulting and facilitating work. With subtle persistence he helps his clients to find surprising and progressive solutions.

As a recovering former manager he supports people whole-heartedly in challenging leadership positions – and people who want to create effective teamwork. One of his main working areas is quality development, with a special emphasis on the health and social sector.

Peter is committed to the international SOLWorld network and faculty member of the SOLWorld Summer University. He offers advanced training in SF consulting and workshop design.

Mark McKergow says about him:

The biggest quiet style – a giant with velvet hands.

Address: Balthasarstsse 81, D 50670 Cologne, Germany
Phone: + 49 (0)228 34 66 14 Mobile: + 49 (0)179 523 46 86
e-mail: : peter.roehrig@consultcontor.de
www.ConsultContor.de

Jenny Clarke

– The Centre for Solutions Focus at Work (sfwork)

Jenny Clarke is the co-director of sfwork with Mark McKergow. She is an SF consultant and coach with wide functional experience in industry, including strategic and business planning, dealing with Government and regulatory issues, public inquiry management and administration. Her strengths are in communication, presentation, consultation and negotiation. These, allied with a facilitative style, enthusiasm and human insight make a vital contribution to meeting her clients' objectives. All her work is informed by the philosophy and attitudes of Solutions Focused thinking. She delights in finding new applications, new activities and new friends through the international SOLWorld network, of which she is a founder member.

Address: 26 Christchurch Road, Cheltenham, GL50 2PL, UK
Phone: +44 (0) 1242 511441
e-mail: jenny@sfwork.com
www.sfwork.com

CHAPTER 2

Before the workshop begins

Compact contracting   *Wilhelm Geisbauer, Austria*

Mission impossible?   *Klaus Botzenhardt, Germany*

Getting going before the workshop   *Alan Kay, Canada*

Change is happening all the time. Why wait until the workshop begins, when you can get the participants to start harnessing useful change beforehand? These activities get the ball rolling.

Compact contracting

Nothing ends the way it began …

Wilhelm Geisbauer, Austria

At the beginning of a consulting relationship, we often find ourselves caught between the client's expectations and demands on the one hand and the limited scope of consulting (and our own abilities) on the other. Together with Ben Furman, the creator of the Reteaming method, I have developed and refined a simple, clear outline for the frequently difficult and sometimes lengthy initial interview, in which the scope of the consultation is mapped out at the start of solution oriented consulting processes. My aim here is to help consultants to identify the scope of the assignment in complex situations and to formulate a contract for the work.

Setting

1 to 1.5 hours maximum.

Context and purpose

At the start of every consulting process – in this context, I will focus on individual and team coaching – it is necessary to define the scope of the assignment (the goal of the consulting process) and the expectations of both parties.

The aim of Compact Contracting is to work with the client to define the scope of the assignment (global goal) and an appropriate environment (Who should be involved? How long should it take?). It helps the consultant to avoid wasting time with a poorly defined goal and loss of autonomy, and to guide the client into a firm and constructive consulting process.

Detailed description

Consultants are usually called in when people find themselves confronting a problem which they experience as unsettling or even threatening. When a client focuses too hard on a problem, they can find themselves in a problem trance or a stuck state, in which they feel overwhelmed by the size of the problem and limited in their choice of options for addressing it. In this state, they are often incapable of seeing goals and solutions.

At this point, a deeper analysis of the problem would tend to exacerbate the situation, as the people involved lose face, feel attacked or look for someone else to blame. The solution oriented approach dispenses with this deeper analysis and looks for the client's goals, not information about the problem.

The following rules and attitudes help to promote dialogue:

- *Show respect for the people involved*
- *Acknowledge the issues that are perceived as problems*
- *Ask solution oriented and pertinent questions*
- *Refrain from (immediately) seeking a solution*
- *Acknowledge past efforts to solve the problem*
- *Identify a question (a global goal) as a point of departure and framework for future efforts*

An ideal example of a compact contracting process
The client speaks first in the interview. He will want to make the consultant fully aware of the problem and may convey a great deal of information in the process. The consultant listens patiently with the following focus: 'What strengths can we identify at this point?'

The consultant then asks permission to ask questions. This is a crucial phase of the interview as it is the point where the consultant assumes control of the conversation and starts the actual consulting process.

Here are some key questions and follow-up questions:

1. *What do you want to achieve, what is your goal?*
   - What would happen if you don't do anything about the situation?
   - What are the advantages of the status quo, and who benefits from it?

- If you break down your (very ambitious) goal into stages, what would your first partial goal be?
- On a scale of 1 to 10, how high would you rate your desire to change the situation?

2. *How would you be able to tell that the consulting process was successful or useful?*
   - What would be one of the first signs that told you that things were improving?
   - What would be your criteria for recognising the success of the consulting process?

3. *How would you know that I was useful as a consultant?*
   - What role do you want me to play?
   - What services do you want me to provide?

4. *What would be the benefit for you/others?*
   - Who would benefit, and in what way, if you reach your goal?
   - Who would benefit, and in what way, if the conflict remains unsolved?

5. *What have you tried so far to solve the problem?*
   Hint: In problematic situations, one frequently overlooks the fact that the client is already making efforts to contribute to the solution. These efforts should be acknowledged.

6. *What might be a motto (global goal) for our work together?*
   Hint: It is always best if the client finds the motto himself. The client knows the language of his system and knows what would motivate him and his team members. The motto must not have a constricting effect, but should indicate a general thrust for future efforts.

7. *Who should be involved, and how will you inform your employees?*
   - Who can make a contribution to the solution?
   - What is the smallest possible system that requires consulting?
   - Who can be left out without ill effects?
   - Who must not be left out under any circumstances?
   - What time frame should we set for ourselves?

- Who are the people who influence the system (organigram)? Hint: Involve as few people as possible, but without omitting important people.

8. *Is there any important question that I haven't asked?*

9. *Other things to clarify:*
   - What the consultant wants or expects from the client (for example, time for discussions with the client, access to key personnel, sufficient time for the project, access to important information, willingness to co-operate, willingness to implement necessary measures).
   - Services offered by the consultant (subject and goals of the consulting process – technically, methodologically and personally; evaluation of the results of the consultation).
   - Fees and payment methods, contract confirmation (including general terms and conditions of business).

What happens next

Once the motto (*global goal*) has been accepted by all participants, an SF process such as the Reteaming approach can be implemented. This includes a description of the desired state (ideal scenario); identification of target; fostering awareness of the benefits of reaching the goal; acknowledging recent positive developments; recruiting supporters; preliminary plans for taking specific action; creation of an action plan; acknowledging the challenge; finding reasons for optimism; promising individual contributions; monitoring the rate of progress; finding strategies to counter possible setbacks; celebrating successes.

Comments

In my view, it is important for the consultant to be aware of his gut feelings during compact contracting, as the body is the best supervisor. When a consultant feels any kind of physical discomfort, this is usually a sign that important questions have been left unasked.

In the case of team coaching, I point out to the client at the end of the compact contracting phase that this interview and the *global goal* represent a preliminary start point which must be discussed

15

again at the start of the actual consulting (*is the global goal correct?*). This point can be skipped, of course, if the Compact Contracting was carried out with the entire team.

Acknowledgements / Further reading

Simon & Rech-Simon, (1999): Zirkuläres Fragen, Carl Auer Systeme Verlag, Heidelberg, pp. 270–272

Merl, (2006): Über das Offensichtliche oder: den Wald vor lauter Bäumen sehen, Verlag Krammer, Vienna

Furman & Ahola, (2007): TwinStar – Lösungen vom anderen Stern, Teamentwicklung für mehr Erfolg und Zufriedenheit am Arbeitsplatz, Carl-Auer-Systeme Verlag, Heidelberg, 2nd ed.

Geisbauer (Ed.), (2006): Reteaming – Methodenhandbuch zur lösungsorientierten Beratung, Carl-Auer-Systeme Verlag, Heidelberg, 2nd ed.

About *Wilhelm Geisbauer*

Born 1952, Master's Degree in psychosocial counselling, educationalist, systemic management counsellor/coach, teacher trainer & coordinator for Reteaming coaches' training in Germany, Austria, Switzerland; Supervisor of ÖVS. Was manager of a leading Austrian medium-sized enterprise for many years. Since 1997: independent consultant & coach at the Institut für OE, Scharnstein; international networking; methods trainer for Reteaming at several universities.

Address: Promenade 9, A-4644 Scharnstein, Austria
Phone: +43 7615 30283
e-mail: reteaming@geisbauer.com
www.geisbauer.at

Mission impossible?

How an internal consultant can run a successful assignment

Klaus Botzenhardt, Germany

There are special challenges for internal consultants in companies. As well as clarifying what your client wants (see Wilhelm Geisbauer: Compact contracting), you also have to clarify your own role and position in the project. This activity helps you to maximise your effectiveness in this situation. It provides orientation, encourages you and enhances your work. [I am using the word 'internal' in two senses here: internal to the organisation and internal as self-reflection.]

Setting

This takes 30–45 minutes to do, either on your own or with a colleague or external coach. Make sure you that you will be uninterrupted and that you can use the time to focus on yourself and not on your client. You will be ready to discuss the assignment with your client and purchaser after this activity.

When doing this, please take your own preferences into consideration. Where and when do you have a chance to stop to think? What kind of media do you prefer – blackboard, notepad, flip-chart, laptop?

Context and purpose

As an insider you know your company better than any external consultant. You know the formal and informal rules, the interpersonal relationships and different moods of your company; you know its financial situation, and you know the strengths and weaknesses of the various players. However, as an employee of the company, you will be under greater pressure than an external contractor to succeed and you might have more to lose. There is a risk that both you and your client will get caught up in a problem induced trance.

This tool helps you to assess these risks adequately, to keep a clear mind and to stay on a solution focused track even when you are on a 'mission impossible'. It is to be used before and after contract negotiation with the internal client.

Detailed description

1. Create an organisation chart of your company. Where do you, your director and your department fit? Include the networks and relationships which are important in your assignment as well as relevant resources, conflicts, tensions and dependencies.
2. Assess your resources using the questions in the table below. In the first column you will find eight questions to score on a scale from 1 to 10. They will help you to identify typical challenges in your assignment. Then for each of the eight questions, ask yourself questions A – E. They will enable you to deal with the challenges in a solution focused way.

Questions to score on a scale from 1 to 10	Your assets and resources
1. How confident are you in your ability to deal with the pressure to succeed?	A. How come you scored x and not 1?
2. How confident are you that you will deal adequately with critical information you receive?	B. Who (including yourself) and what helped you reach x and not 1?
3. How confident are you in your assessment of how dependent you are (financially and otherwise) on your company?	C. Imagine what the situation would be if you had scored 10. What is different?

4. How confident are you that you will be able to communicate adequately with people at different levels in the hierarchy?	D. What do you think is the minimum score necessary (y) to carry out the contract successfully?
5. How confident are you that you will find a solution oriented way out of a problem induced trance?	
6. How confident are you that you will recognise hidden, messy aspects of your contract?	E. What can you do to reach y or higher?
7. How confident are you that you will be successful in the contract negotiation?	
8. How confident are you that you will manage your contract well?	

It is quite a lot to answer 40 solution oriented questions. Be relaxed when working this through. Find out where the critical points of your internal contract might be and what questions and resources you should focus on.

What happens next

You are now in a good position to discuss with your customer, clients and your director the special features of the contract. It shows that you have reflected on what you have been asked to do and that you have thought carefully about the particular circumstances of your company.

Comments

From my experience you can't always attain 100% clarification of your contract. Therefore it is even more important to be prepared for some typical risks and adverse events. I made this tool for my own self-reflection. Although it is time and energy consuming, I like to prove my ability to go beyond my routine work and the resource matrix works as an early warning system. It draws attention to potential hazards and helps me to keep a solution oriented track.

I am willing to take risks and I am happy about every single internal contract I deal with. Positive feedback is a great motivation for me.

Acknowledgements and references

I designed the matrix in order to negotiate my own internal assignments. These were my main sources:
Schmitz, Lilo: Lösungsorientierte Gesprächsführung, x-Lösungen, 2002
Thomann, Christoph: Klärungshilfe 2, Rowohlt Taschenbuch Verlag, 2004

About *Klaus Botzenhardt*

I have worked in the Complaints Management Department in the University Clinic of Cologne for four years. It might sound terrible to deal with criticism all the time but on the contrary, in many cases I have amazing success. I give communication training to staff members in the Clinic and appreciate the effectiveness of working in a solution oriented way.

e-mail: kbotzenhardt@web.de

Getting going before the workshop

A pre-workshop warm-up

Alan Kay, Canada

In our workshops we help the client notice that a) more is working than they realise, b) they have some good ideas about what they want to happen in the future, c) they really don't need to talk about the problem any further.

Why not give them the pleasure of this knowledge before the workshop and speed up the workshop process and outcomes?

Setting

Try to get everyone who is coming to the workshop to participate via e-mail. Also, interview a few of the key participants.

I give an example as a template. You can develop your own template and adjust it to each client's workshop goals and desired outcomes.

Context and purpose

In general this is useful for every workshop or facilitation task. It is particularly helpful for teams with diverse interests, where there is high emotion and considerable lack of alignment. It is very helpful for strategy planning.

The purpose is to allow the team to be more efficient and effective at the workshop itself. By noticing strengths and developing ideas about the future beforehand, we can have people arrive in a more helpful frame of mind and thus speed up the future alignment process. We have seen teams with seemingly entirely opposed perspectives arrive at the workshop wondering what their previous 'annoyance' was about.

Detailed description

There are two forms of pre-work: a customised e-mail that goes to all participants and 30 minute telephone interviews with a small group of participants, usually 4–6 people.

In both cases we want participants to think about

- what's already working in the organisation/team
- what they want to see done differently/changes they might want to work on
- what success will look like sometime after the workshop

During the *project contracting phase* sell your client the idea of pre-work on the basis that it will make the workshop activity quicker and more effective. Clients appreciate this as a benefit. Explain that the pre-workshop effort is not a research tool and that the client can use the feedback for their preparation, but that it is not necessary. You can offer to do an analysis of the feedback, but only as an option.

Once the client has agreed to the contract and project design, develop the e-mail questionnaire (see example). Base it on the goals and needs of the client and participants. A standard template questionnaire may work, but you will probably want to customise the questions.

Ask the client leader to issue the questionnaire e-mail with a covering note explaining the request. Set a completion date close to the main event giving the client time to review the responses.

Example: Covering letter from client to participants

We are looking forward to getting your input at our strategy planning meeting on [time and date] at [venue].

The goal will be to develop teamwork, a shared understanding and a commitment to an overall integrated brand framework by the mangers and partners team.

We have had a great start in this country and a great global story – a solid foundation on which we can build.

I would like to seek your support before the meeting. Your input to the planning process is vital and so I would like you to complete the attached document and return it to me by [date] so that the external facilitator [name] and I have time to digest your ideas before the meeting.

Thank you for your support.

Attachment:

In thinking about the FUTURE of [company or project name], please

Name 3 strengths of the organisation:

Name 2 ideas/strategies to grow the business in the next 12 months:

What 3 areas of [project name] can we focus on in the next 12 months?

Imagine it is [date ~ 12 months ahead] and we are now successful in [project]

What do you see us doing for our customers now?

What actions did we take as a team which made us so successful?

In addition, make the phone call interviews to the identified workshop participants. Ask for two types of participants – change agents and traditionalists. The conversation should follow the same approach as the e-mail template: strengths, desired differences and outcomes. Begin by asking the person for a sense of their business goals. In this case it is appropriate at the start of the conversation to ask the participants for a *brief* description of what they see as the main business obstacles to success. This gives you a broader context and sense of the audience than the client leader can give you – their briefing process can never fully explain the situation. Move quickly to solutions with an emphasis on how the workshop can be of particular help to them, the team and any other stakeholders, for example customers.

As the paperwork comes back to the client (don't necessarily expect 100% participation), you may have to remind them that an analysis is unnecessary. Do ask them to highlight some of the more interesting and insightful comments as an acknowledgement to the participants at the start of the workshop.

Your client may want an informal de-brief on the phone interviews. Again, only the more interesting and insightful comments are useful. After all, we don't want the client to start fishing for problems. If they show particular interest in problems, tell them briefly what was said and then go back to the solutions stated by the interviewees.

At the workshop, have the leader thank and acknowledge the team for the pre-work, read aloud a few of the insights and then hand the session over to you as the facilitator. By having the client state the insights, the group hears itself talking solutions from the very start of the session.

What happens next

It is suggested that the consultant should return some time later (4–6 weeks) to ask *What's different?*

Comments

- Much of this thinking comes from two observations
  - Change management basics stress lots of communication in advance of any change activities. The pre-input and phone interviews are a form of communication that says *we are interested in your perspective.*
  - Since we are going to talk about solutions (not the problem) in the workshop, why not begin before the event. It not only helps the participants, but also the client leader.
- Teams that are already well aligned on the need for change will respond to the pre-work quite well. Teams that have deep divisions in outlook, philosophy and practice will find it very helpful. On one occasion, a highly frustrated and divided board group arrived at the pre-workshop dinner and hardly noticed their differences. Halfway through the evening, several noted with surprise how positive the atmosphere had become. It had also helped the two team leaders notice before the workshop that the team was in better shape than they realised.
- The recommended approaches outlined above need not necessarily be followed in detail. You may find the client has a good survey method and you can adapt it to focus on solutions. You may also want to invest in more interviews depending on the task, especially if it is a large group requiring more than one workshop.
- Finally, a client who had successfully used the approach in a previous year decided the following year to change the pre-work to problem focused questions. The client then noticed the pre-work had not gone as well. However, at the workshop we focused on solutions.

Acknowledgement of sources

Acknowledgement goes to all the many fine people who developed and researched solution focus.

About *Alan Kay*

Alan Kay is president of The Glasgow Group, a consulting firm focusing on solution focused strategic planning and branded customer experience implementation. His Canadian, US and UK clients range from banks to industrial to not-for-profit organisations. Until the early 1990s, he managed an advertising agency business. Alan also teaches executives at Schulich School of Business, York University, using a highly interactive action-learning teaching style.

Address: 179 Douglas Avenue, Toronto, Ontario, M5M 1G7, Canada
Phone: + 01 416 401 3588
e-mail: akay@glasgrp.com
www.glasgrp.com

CHAPTER 3

Off to a good start

Time spent building a solid platform is time well spent.

Resource telephone

The affirming whisper circle

Dominik Godat, Switzerland

Resource telephone is an affirming and playful activity that can be used at the beginning of a workshop, in the middle to loosen up or at the end to create even more positive energy. Standing in a circle, the participants whisper into their neighbour's ear his resources, strengths, abilities and positive characteristics. After one round, it is fun to do it again, changing direction and changing position.

Setting

- Time needed: 5–30 minutes depending on the size and energy level of the group.
- Optimal number of participants: 6–10 people in a circle. If there are more participants, build several small circles.
- You need plenty of space for the participants to form one or more circles.

Context and purpose

In groups that know each other, this activity can easily be used at the beginning of the workshop, during the workshop to loosen up or at the end as affirmation and confidence building. No preparation time is needed and so it can also be spontaneously introduced at any time. If the participants don't know each other at the beginning, it is better used during the workshop or at the end.

The aim is to focus the attention of the participants on their resources, abilities and positive characteristics in a playful way. Everyone gets affirming, constructive and motivating feedback. That's why this activity creates a good platform for the workshop. If you use the exercise at the end of a workshop, you can increase the participants' motivation and confidence and with that the probability of success in everyday life.

Detailed description

The facilitator starts by asking participants to form a circle. In workshops with more than ten participants, it is good to form several circles.

Now the facilitator can introduce the exercise as follows:

You probably all know the game called Chinese Whispers or Telephone, where each successive participant passes on to the next a phrase or sentence whispered to them by the preceding participant. By the end of the round, there is usually a very different message.

This is a bit different: the Resource Telephone.

Please think of a resource, a strength, an ability or a positive characteristic of your neighbour, and whisper it into his ear. For example 'I am very impressed how you can ... do this or that (e.g. how attentively you can listen to others)' or '... how ... you are (e.g. how patient you are' or '... how you do this or that (e.g. how well you accomplish your projects)', etc. The beneficiary listens to this compliment, thanks his neighbour and then whispers a different affirming message to the next person.

Continue until everyone has given and received an affirming message. Depending on the group and the fun they have, you can keep going, change direction spontaneously or change the position of the people in the circle.

What happens next

If there is plenty of time left, it is useful to have a break after this activity, so that the participants have time to write down their affirming messages, to reflect on them or to share them with others. After that you can continue with the workshop.

Comments

- Resources, strengths, abilities, positive and useful characteristics and affirming feedback are pivotal in solution focused work. They are often door openers in difficult situations. Unfortunately, in everyday life, we are not used to focus explicitly on them, or to receive and accept compliments readily. That is why I looked for a playful intervention that focuses on resources and in which every participant has to give and receive affirming messages.
- The Resource Telephone has been very useful for me, because it can be applied very flexibly, can be altered very easily, and no preparation time is needed.
- This activity can also be played out loud, so that the participants get a public feedback. If you do it like that, really fast positive group dynamics usually evolve and the participants are inspired by the messages of the others to think of more resourceful feedback. In addition, the publicity and the participants' ability to share what they have heard increase the effect of the messages even more.
- Often, the participants have fun in sharing the feedback they have given and received and anything that surprised them during a break.
- If the participants don't know each other at the beginning, this is better done during or at the end of the workshop because it is easier for the participants to come up with resources after they got to know each other. However, if you want to use it at the beginning, the participants can make hypothetical compliments. (*I have only known you for a few minutes, but I think you can do this or that very well … (e.g. that you can listen very attentively), that you are like … (e.g. that you are very patient) etc.*)
- If the group struggles to focus on the resources of the others at the beginning, it is useful to give them some time to prepare and think of possible compliments that they can give to the other group members.

Acknowledgement of sources

I was inspired by several playful workshops, including those at the SOLWorld Conference in Interlaken, and developed this method from the Chinese Whispers game which is often played in schools.

About **Dominik Godat**

As an economist, HR specialist and founder of Godat Coaching, Dominik Godat invented Random Coaching in 2006. He works mainly in Switzerland as a coach with profit and non-profit organisations helping them to implement solution focused management ideas. He also trains and coaches individuals, managers and teams who are looking for success in their private and business lives.

Address: Hechtliacker 44, 4053 Basel, Switzerland
Phone: +41 76 420 19 18
e-mail: coaching@godat.ch
www.godat.ch

Team spirit

Resources and opportunities to work together as a team and to activate the team's potential

Josef Grün, Germany

Team spirit is an ideal introductory exercise for team development and team workshops. The team has the opportunity to acknowledge and discuss the moods, atmosphere and collaboration within the team. Just as in sports teams, team spirit is equivalent to having an extra player. If the spirit plays along, it boosts the team's potential and performance.

Setting

- Between 30–40 minutes depending on group size.
- For teams between 10 and 20 members. Ideally between 10 and 15 people.
- Flip chart, post-its and marker pens.

Context and purpose

An opening exercise to allow the participants to acknowledge and develop the team's potential. The participants talk about the atmosphere, the behaviours and attitudes which contribute to the team's present success.

Detailed description

The participants sit in a circle and an extra empty chair is placed in the middle.

The facilitator introduces the exercise by elaborating on a common observation:

In any sport, we see again and again that teams are not as successful as we'd expect them to be given the individual athletes' skills. In these cases, the absence or shortage of team spirit explains the gap between expectations and actual performance. Some teams have such a strong team spirit that they exceed the sum of the players' potential of and win more often than expected. According to this understanding of team spirit, please describe your current team situation or your team's spirit. When possible, use metaphors, imagery and/or associations with fairy tales and mythology.

For example: our current team spirit could be described as a friendly ghost, an evil ghost, a poltergeist, a genie in a bottle, a witch, a good fairy, like the Ghost of Christmas Past in 'A Christmas Carol' or even Gandalf in 'The Lord of the Rings'.

The team then describes the spirit that they imagine sitting in the empty chair in the middle of the circle. The description can begin with: *The spirit sitting on that chair is ...*

Every team member portrays the team spirit or spirits as vividly as possible.

The facilitator writes the most important aspects of the description (name, characteristics and effects) on post-its and places these on the empty chair. If necessary the facilitator can help the team find an appropriate name for their spirit.

After this round, every participant is invited to add some of the spirit's particularly useful skills or magical abilities. The facilitator writes these down and adds them to the other post-its on the chair in the middle of the circle.

All of the post-its are then clustered onto a flip chart in two groups: the characteristics that are helpful for the team and the ones that are rather disturbing for the team.

This is then photographed and can be used in future team meetings to assess and discuss how the team spirit is doing at the moment.

Another approach

After each round, ask the participants:
Looking at the various spirits that live in your team, which ones would you want to continue to shelter and which ones would you want to drive away?

What happens next

The actual team development work begins after this introductory exercise.

Comments

- This exercise is an easy introduction to a team development workshop or seminar. Talking about the team spirit in the third person allows participants to speak more freely and more easily about their team situation. They are not pointing the finger at other team members or at themselves but at the good or bad spirit who alone is responsible for the team situation.
- Also in difficult situations, the team members do not feel attacked or blamed when the spirit is described as annoying, disturbing, sly or evil. It can also be interesting for the facilitator to ask, in a second round, what other spirit could help drive this bad spirit away.
- The more time is spent describing the useful spirit (by asking 'what else?'), the more helpful characteristics and magic abilities are exposed. The participants can also be asked to give examples of when these characteristics have contributed to the team's performance.

About **Josef Grün**

I have been working as a consultant and coach for profit and non-profit organisations since 1989. My main focus is on individual and collective learning in organisations: to clarify goals and structures and to support individuals in their roles at work. Key topics include developing guidelines and strategies in small and medium sized organisations, as well as team building and leadership coaching.

Address: Balthasarstr. 81, 50670 Cologne, Germany
Phone: + 49 221 973130 20
e-mail: josef.gruen@consultcontor.de
www.consultcontor.de

34

What's in it for me?

(or The Björn as some people call it)

Björn Johansson and Eva Persson, Sweden

This is a good starter exercise in situations where people know each other fairly well. An inspiring way of getting people together, creating curiosity and having fun.

Setting

- Time: 15 minutes plus 5–15 minutes for reflections.
- Number of participants: 9-200.
- You need a projector or white board or flipchart with the instructions.

Context and purpose

Insoo Kim Berg used to say *always address the person in her/his resources*. The first question in the exercise gives the facilitator and participants the opportunity to find out about their strengths and skills – to meet participants in their resources.

It also gives a very positive start to an event, gathers ideas for the agenda and makes people conscious of their responsibility for their own goals and interests.

It is applicable in many contexts: team development, workshops and seminars.

Detailed description

Invite the participants to stand up. Divide them into groups of three. Show the A-B-C pattern and ask them to decide who will be A. If the number of participants is not divisible into three, a group of four is better than pairs.

The exercise follows a structured pattern where A asks the first question you give them to B. B answers and asks the same question to C. C answers and asks it of A. Ask the groups to let you know when they have finished the round.

When most of the groups have finished the first round, repeat the pattern with the next question.

Before the fifth round when it is time to give compliments, ask for attention. Be really clear about what they have done and refer to their listening skills, which they have just been using.

Both A and B give compliments to C; B and C compliment A and C and A compliment B.

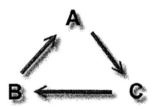

1. *Of all the things you do in your work, what would you say you are most satisfied with?*

2. *What else?*

3. *So, in view of all that, and all the other things you do in your work, what is the most interesting thing to develop during (this course/ period/project...)?*

4. *What will be the first small sign that tells you that you had come one tiny step further?*

5. *Give compliments.*

Debrief

There are a lot of options for debriefing depending on the purpose and the group. Some examples:

- *What did you discover during this activity?*
- *What did you find out about yourself and your colleagues?*
- *In what way was it useful?*
- *In what way can these questions be relevant at work?*
- *What did you find out about your goals for this workshop?* (Draw up the agenda.)

Comments

Participants will meet each other in their strengths and resources and will find ideas about their own development within the current context. Even colleagues from the same workplace – for example training groups, workplace development, co-operation, team development seminars etc – will probably discover new things about each other.

We have used this exercise for 3 or 4 years and it is still one of our favourites. It can easily be applied to many different contexts and can clarify relevant individual goals within organisational change, training etc. It gives a fresh start to seminars and works best with 20 participants or more. We are also impressed by the way this format and this kind of question can easily be varied, for follow ups, learning reviews etc.

Acknowledgement of sources

This exercise has developed from some ideas about the circulating format we first met in a workshop with Evan George several years ago. It is a format we have found very useful and active in various group settings. The questions have developed from an idea which was originally about appraisals in a workshop with Gale Miller. We are happy to share this activity with you and would appreciate any reflection or development.

About *Björn Johansson and Eva Persson*

CLUES – Center för Lösningsfokuserad Utveckling

Björn and Eva are experienced trainers and coaches working with organisational change. Together with their colleagues they run a centre in Karlstad, an arena for creativity, training and development of solution focused approaches. Their curiosity and their engagement has led to wide international work. They have conducted several controlled studies regarding the effects of solution focused approaches (in group settings, leadership and organisational development).

Address: Box 4034, 650 04 Karlstad, Sweden
Phone: +46 73 6872710
e-mail: bjorn@clues.se & eva@clues.se
www.clues.se

Large group warm-up

Too many to shake hands?

Alasdair J Macdonald, United Kingdom

This is a rapid and largely non-verbal exercise to start working with groups. It establishes interest among participants and prepares them for work focused on resources and competencies. The facilitator gains some information about the group's knowledge of and interest in solution focused approaches.

Setting

- Allow 5–6 minutes.
- Any number from five to several hundred, as long as you can see all of them.
- Use after individual introductions by participants if the group is small enough. With large groups, you can use it before or after introducing yourself.

Context and purpose

This was originally devised for large groups with too many people for any form of individual introductions. However, the exercise is equally effective for small groups. It can be used in settings with fixed seating.

The exercise is best suited to first contacts. If you use it for a second meeting with the same group then you will need to find different questions. It is not useful with groups who meet regularly, because the participants will know one another already.

Identifying competencies helps the participants to see that you recognise their individual ability and to recognise it themselves. This leads easily to subsequent exercises and conversations focusing on compliments, strengths and resilience. Their curiosity about each other encourages joining and social interaction with each other.

Effect: People smile, appear proud, look at one another, whisper questions: '*What kind of pet?*'! The act of raising a hand opens body posture and breaks up closed body language. This increases the potential for participation in the work that follows.

Detailed description

The facilitator asks the following questions, pausing to see responses each time:

I would like to know some more about you all.
Please raise your right hand if you have had training in solution focused work.

Please raise your left hand if you have a brother or sister.

Please raise your hand if you live in (town the workshop is in).

Please raise your hand if you drove yourself here today in a car.

Please raise your hand if the solution focused approach is your preferred way of working with people.

Please raise your hand if you are a parent.

Please raise your hand if you work with children and young people.

Please raise your hand if you have a pet.

Please raise your hand if your pet is not a dog or cat.

Please raise your hand if you can play a musical instrument or if you sing in a choir.

Please raise your hand if you have a teenage child.

Please raise your hand if you can play a team sport.

Please raise your hand if you can speak more than one language.

These abilities are relevant to what we are doing here today because they all require knowledge of communication skills in complex circumstances. They all require an ability to interact and co-operate effectively with others, whether through the use of speech or with other methods.

Make eye contact with some of them as they raise their hands. Nodding, smiling and looking impressed are helpful! You may choose to write a note of the number of hands raised as they reply. This shows that you are taking their responses seriously, but is not essential. The directly useful information is the proportion of the audience who know something about solution focused ideas, and the proportion for whom it is their preferred way of working. This information will assist you in carrying out the activities of the workshop. If a significant proportion play a musical instrument or sing, then you can use music metaphors during the workshop.

What happens next

Next, you move on to your plan for the day and begin the formal work. This exercise has opened the topics of existing skills and of interest in solution focused work. You may have found abilities such as music or childcare to which you can link activities during the workshop.

Comments

- I developed the exercise when an organiser and I had misunderstood each other. I faced an audience of 100 when I had prepared for 30. I could not say *Two-thirds of you have to go home* so I had to modify my exercises very quickly. Since then I have chosen to use this version in almost every workshop. In my opinion, the exercise directs attention to skills and compliments from the moment that you begin the day.
- This activity speaks directly to people's strengths and competencies, which they may not have recognised or shared previously. If you have chosen your questions well, almost every delegate will have raised a hand in response to one or more questions. They will begin to feel a connection with you, and you with them.

41

- Some believe that the dominant (usually right) hand is the conscious/controlled side of life, and that the non-dominant (often left) hand favours the unconscious/spontaneous aspects of the person. Hence the first two questions ask for a specific hand in order to include both sides. This also encourages attention to the wording of the subsequent questions. Thereafter, to save time, the wording need not specify a choice of hand.
- Questions may be added or removed, according to the focus of the workshop or the professionals concerned. Keep the topics general, for example *Please raise your hand if you work for a big corporation* is less provocative than *Please raise your hand if you work for Microsoft*. Do not have too many questions or the exercise will take too much time and will lose its novelty.
- Questions about age, marital status and family size appear to provoke anxiety and therefore are best avoided. If the audience are all from a single firm or organisation, then there may be personal issues around such topics which people do not wish to expose.

Acknowledgement of sources

To the best of my knowledge, I invented this exercise as a response to a crisis. However, I have seen work by many outstanding solution focused practitioners, so if I have unintentionally claimed someone else's idea then please tell me.

About **Dr Alasdair J Macdonald**

– Consultant Psychiatrist

UK consultant psychiatrist for 25 years, registered family therapist and supervisor. Brief therapist for 25 years, solution focused therapist since 1988. Research into psychotherapy outcome and other interests. Past President, European Brief Therapy Association. Former Medical Director; now freelance trainer and management consultant.

Address: 3 Beechwood Square, Poundbury, Dorchester DT1 3SS, UK
Phone: + 44 7738 938376
e-mail: macdonald@solutionsdoc.co.uk
www.solutionsdoc.co.uk

What do we have to get right?

Turning the corner from problem to solution

Mark McKergow, United Kingdom

Sometimes people seem to love to talk about problems. This exercise allows them to do so, while staying solution focused.

Setting

- This activity can take from 15–30 minutes, depending on the context. There are many variants which can take more or less time.
- It works well for any number of people from one upwards.
- You need a flip chart and participants need pens and paper.

Context and purpose

In workshops and team coaching sessions, participants often want to talk about what's wrong. Closing this discussion down too quickly can lead to people feeling they are not being taken seriously. However, leading the group into a discussion of what they must get right in moving forwards (the essentials and/or non-negotiable elements) lets them discuss issues and at the same time turn from 'what's wrong' to 'what do we want' – the crucial distinction between problem and solution.

This is an excellent activity to get things moving in a workshop. Having agreed on the project or endeavour to be tackled, this activity can add a lot of detail to the solution whilst giving people the chance to raise the issues as they see them.

Detailed description

There are many ways to use this basic idea. This is one format I use with teams, following the classic think-pair-share sequence.

Having generated a good working atmosphere and established the issues the team wants to work on, I make sure that everyone has a pen and paper and announce:

Next, we're going to think about the issues relating to this topic. I would like each of you to take a few moments to think quietly about this question. 'What do we have to get right in moving forward with this?' Write down as long a list as you can of the things we must get right. Three minutes. Go.

Everyone thinks hard and writes fast – some lists will be longer than others, and that's OK. Then I ask people to pair up – possibly with the person next to them, or by some other means. If there are people from different departments or different levels in the hierarchy, I might ask groups from the same department or level to work together. I give them five minutes to discuss their lists and combine them, and start to prioritise the items. The time for this phase is extendable, of course, if the discussion seems particularly productive.

I then start to gather the items by going around each group and getting an item from the top of their priority list. I write the item on a flip chart, taking great care that the words match what was said. If an issue is presented as a problem, I can turn it around by saying something like *Yes, that's an important issue. So, what do we have to get right in relation to this?*

Move fairly quickly around the groups so that everyone gets a turn. I like to get all the items on to the list if possible, so that no-one thinks that anything has been ignored. The flip chart is then displayed on the wall.

What happens next

Once that has been done, it's usually time to move to a Future Perfect activity or some such. This can be framed as *What would happen supposing we were indeed to get all these things right?* This allows all the factors identified in this exercise to be combined together into a working description, leaving the individual issues behind. It adds a lot of potential detail to the next steps, as well as kick-starting the thinking about 'life with the problem vanished' – the solution in solution focus.

Comments

- I developed this activity during a team workshop. The team wanted to discuss the 'hot topics' facing them in relation to a reorganisation. I rephrased the question from what the problems were to what they wanted to be right, and it turned out to be very effective, bringing lots of ideas into view as well as being a great base on which to develop a Future Perfect.
- I think it is important that people don't feel pushed from problem to solution. If they come up with problem talk, I think to myself that it is not that they have got the activity wrong – it is just that they haven't finished it yet.
- The answers do not have to be specific – the specifics are usually generated in the next stage. So, if people say that communication between the managers and the team has not been good, and therefore communication needs to be better, that's fine. Going into more detail (as we might do in a Future Perfect or Counters exercise) may lead to disagreements about the nature of the better communication – not usually what's wanted at this stage. This activity is a part of building the platform.

Acknowledgements

I generated this activity while playing around with the ideas in Daniel Meier's book *Team Coaching with the SolutionCircle*. His 'Hot Topics' process inspired this variation, which looks not at the hot topics but at the surrounding issues and concerns, partly relating to process as well as content.

About *Dr Mark McKergow*

– The Centre for Solutions Focus at Work (sfwork)

*Dr Mark McKergow is co-director of sfwork –
The Centre for Solutions Focus at Work. He is
an international consultant, speaker and
contributor. Many people around the world
have been inspired by his work in Solutions
Focus – presented with his inimitable blend of
scientific rigour and performance pizzazz. He
has written and edited three books and dozens
of articles; was instrumental in the founding of
the SolWorld organisation (www.solworld.org), and founded
SolutionsBooks with Jenny Clarke in 2005; their most recent
book is the case study collection Solutions Focus Working (2007).
He has presented on every continent except Antarctica, and is an
international conference keynote presenter.*

Address: 26 Christchurch Road, Cheltenham, GL50 2PL, United
Kingdom
Phone: +44 (0) 1242 511441
e-mail: mark@sfwork.com
www.sfwork.com

Sparkling moments

Finding and building on many tiny aspects of success

Mark McKergow, United Kingdom

This exercise comprises three stages: identifying what made a particular 'sparkling moment' sparkle (using 'what else?'), offering Affirms and identifying small steps based on the positive qualities and strengths identified. People work in pairs.

Setting

- About 15–20 minutes for the whole thing, with 5–10 minutes to debrief if you wish.
- I have run the exercise with groups ranging from two people to three hundred people – it is very good for large events as each of the three sections is short and can be described in clear detail. Find a way of evening up the numbers – it's much harder to do in a group of 3.
- Everyone needs paper and a pen.

Context and purpose

I use this three-part exercise near the start of team coaching sessions and workshops, and also as an introduction to SF ideas. It is very simple to do (as long as the instructions are clearly given) and people are often amazed at how many things they can find that might be useful. The idea of affirming is also introduced in a very usable way.

It quickly and powerfully brings several SF elements into a conversation. It leads to a very resourceful conversation, without getting drawn into psychological musing and is a great way to encourage 'staying on the surface'. People are often amazed at how the 'what else?' question helps them to quickly pile up potentially useful stuff, and how well the Affirms based on the first part of the exercise fit. It also shows that affirming is not a difficult skill – it can be done on the basis of a very short and focused piece of listening. The third part develops small steps to build on what's working – there are a variety of ways to do this, depending on the context.

Detailed description

The facilitator sets the scene, perhaps by announcing that

We're going to start off by exploring some small but significant moments – 'sparkling moments'. Please find a partner to work with, and decide who will be Person A and who will be Person B first. It doesn't matter who does what, we will be doing it both ways around – you just need to decide who is Person A first. Also make sure you have a piece of paper each, and at least one pen between you.

You may want to provide pens and paper – these are used in an interesting way, as we shall see. Once the people have found partners, you continue to brief the first part of the activity:

Part 1 – Sparkling moments
This is the first part of a three part activity. Person A asks Person B to describe a 'sparkling moment' at work during the past few weeks or months – when you felt best about being here and were really getting what you wanted. This is a sparkling MOMENT, not a sparkling month! A small instant will be enough to work with.

Then Person A asks Person B 'How come that moment was sparkling? What was it about that moment that made it sparkle for you?' Person B thinks and tells Person A what made it sparkle. Person A writes it down, smiles and nods encouragingly, and gently asks 'What else?' And Person B thinks again and tells of another thing that made that moment sparkle. Person A again writes it down and asks 'What else?'

You will have three minutes to get as long a list as possible of the things that made this moment sparkle. And then we'll change over and do it the other way around. It's important that you write down what your partner says – you'll need that in a moment. Any questions ... OK, go!

I like to be very specific about the time. After precisely three minutes, signal the change over by (for example) ringing a bell and saying *OK, time to change over!*

At the end of another three minutes, ring the bell again and gently bring the group's attention back to you.

Part 2 – Spotting strengths and qualities

You should now both have a list of what made your partner's moment sparkle – do you have a list? (Check that people are nodding and waving their lists). *OK, for the second part of this three part process I want you to think about this: what do you now know about your partner's useful qualities and strengths, based on what they have just told you? In a moment I will give you sixty seconds of silent thinking time to have a go at identifying two strengths you think your partner must have, based on what they said. Then, you will tell them about these two qualities and strengths using a form of words like this:*

'Based on what you just said, it seems to me that maybe you are a ... person.'

(inserting the relevant quality or strength), and perhaps expanding a bit on how that came across to you. And WATCH FOR THE REACTION. If they think about it, smile, nod and say 'Thank You', we can take that as an acceptance that, yes, they admit that they may indeed have a little bit of that quality. That's what we are hoping for.

There is another very slight possibility – they may vehemently deny that this quality is anything to do with them. That's OK too – you are basing this on a very short discussion and will be guessing a little bit. If that happens, just apologise, say you are a great optimist and have a go with the other strength! So, you have sixty seconds to think of two strengths that your partner has – based on what they just said ... OK? Your sixty seconds start now.

I make sure that the above sentence is visible on a screen or flip chart, so people can refer to it easily. People will usually write the strengths on the piece of paper, alongside the sparkling moment factors – encourage them to do this.

Time sixty seconds, then say gently:

OK ... when you and your partner are both ready, go ahead. Tell your partner your view of two strengths, and see how they respond. Then swap over and do it the other way around. You have about three minutes in total. Off you go.

I like to watch how things are going at this point – looking for the smiling and nodding responses that signal that an affirm has 'landed' and been accepted. Wait until everyone has finished both ways – check around if necessary – and then debrief:

OK, how did you get on? Let's see ... if your partner found at least one strength or quality that you were able to say 'Thank you' to, please raise your hand. (Most, if not all of the hands go up.) *Excellent! Well done. It's amazing what you can do based on three minutes careful questioning, isn't it?*

Part 3 – Small steps

This part of the exercise is very flexible and can be adjusted to fit the context. The version I use most often is to find small steps based on the strengths identified. This is both an introduction to the power of small steps and a nice extension of building on strengths rather than just on the sparkling moment (another possibility).

So, we now know about the things that made your partner's moment sparkle, and you have discussed two of their strengths. Let's build on that to find some small steps which might increase the chance of more sparkling moments happening in future. Again in pairs, Person A asks Person B:

If these qualities were to play an even greater part in your life at work, what would you notice?

What else? (x2)

What small signs might your colleagues notice?

Then A asks B to suggest a couple of small actions for himself to take in the next few days, building on everything that's been discussed. Again, note down what your partner says. You have four minutes each way this time. Ready ... go!

Again, ring the bell after four minutes to signal the change-over.

At the end of the exercise, ask people to swap their pieces of paper with their partner – that way, everyone ends up with detailed notes of their sparkling moment, strengths, small signs and actions. I like to make a little ceremony out of this, with people thanking their partners.

The action step can also be omitted, or left until later.

What happens next

There are various possibilities for finishing the activity depending on the context:

- Ask everyone to note their actions in their diaries, so that they remember to do them.
- Debrief the whole exercise – what was useful about it? What was interesting? What surprised people about how it all worked?
- Use the identified strengths in some way – perhaps by listing them all on flipcharts for reference as the workshop continues.
- (In a team context) – give the opportunity to name and discuss the sparkling moments. Other members of the team may be surprised about what was well regarded.

Comments

- This activity is a little unusual in that it jumps straight to a sparkling moment from the recent past, rather than first identifying what people want. This makes it a good candidate for use in the opening stages of a workshop, to find useful things which are already happening. I based it on an activity from narrative practice used by Evan George of BRIEF in London, and added the affirming and small action sections as time went on.
- The conversations are all set up to be interactional – about visible signs in the world rather than in the head. You may note that even though the strengths are described rather as if they are individually based, they are postulated interactionally (in conversation) and are agreed or not in terms of language-in-use.
- This is a great activity to get everyone working together. It is energetic and quick fire, and raises the energy in the room very rapidly.
- A period of reflection might follow (perhaps a coffee break) to allow people to reflect on their experience.
- Be firm and confident in the briefing. I have never found anyone without a sparkling moment of some kind (although there are sometimes ironic laughs when I announce the exercise, and people may mutter about how there aren't any). Very occasionally someone does not raise their hand (showing their partner

didn't find any strengths they agreed with) in Part 2 – I pass over this without comment, as the vast majority of hands are raised, and no-one has complained that they had nothing to work with in Part 3.

- I tell people to listen carefully and make notes in the first part, but don't tell them at the start that they will be affirming later on. I think that it helps to keep minds clear in the first part, without worrying about what will happen next.

Acknowledgement of sources

I first did something like the first part of this exercise with Evan George of BRIEF in about 1999. I have adjusted the wording and added the other two sections since then, and used the exercise all over the world.

About **Dr Mark McKergow**

– The Centre for Solutions Focus at Work (sfwork)

Dr Mark McKergow is co-director of sfwork – The Centre for Solutions Focus at Work. He is an international consultant, speaker and contributor. Many people around the world have been inspired by his work in Solutions Focus – presented with his inimitable blend of scientific rigour and performance pizzazz. He has written and edited three books and dozens of articles; was instrumental in the founding of the SolWorld organisation (www.solworld.org), and founded SolutionsBooks with Jenny Clarke in 2005; their most recent book is the case study collection Solutions Focus Working (2007). He has presented on every continent except Antarctica, and is an international conference keynote presenter.

Address: 26 Christchurch Road, Cheltenham, GL50 2PL, United Kingdom
Phone: +44 (0)1242 511441
e-mail: mark@sfwork.com
www.sfwork.com

Structured goal chat

Defining personal goals

Daniel Meier, Switzerland

The structured goal chat helps the participants of a workshop to become aware of their personal goals for the event. They become custodians of their own goals and can focus on their success right from the beginning.

Setting

- 10 to 30 minutes.
- Suitable for any number of participants.
- Flipchart with the respective questions for the groups.

Context and purpose

Usually workshops have an overall topic such as improved collaboration. However, the participants who meet to discuss the given topic also come with their own individual goals about it. Learning is enhanced if these personal goals are attended to – if they are taken into account, the workshop will become a personal highlight.

The exercise is designed for the beginning of the workshop, giving participants the opportunity to come into contact with one another and focus their awareness on their goals very early on. They reflect on the question of what would actually need to happen in the workshop to make it worth taking part. It also helps them to take responsibility for their own learning and stay committed to reaching their own learning goals.

Detailed description

The participants form groups of four and decide who will be A, B, C and D.

As facilitator you prepare a flipchart with three (maximum four) questions about the topic or their personal goals.
The following questions have proven very useful:

- *What is fascinating for you about the topic X?*
- *What should happen here today concerning the things you just mentioned to make it worth your while being here?*
- *What would be a first sign during the workshop that shows you that you are on the right track to reach your goals?*

A starts by asking the first question to person B who quickly answers it. B then poses the same question to person C, then C to D and finally D to A which finishes the first question round. You need approximately 8 minutes for this.

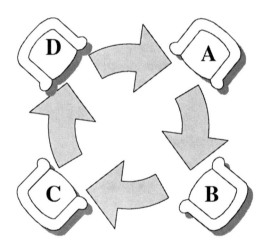

You continue with the second question: A ask B, B asks C, etc.

Every one of the questions is asked and answered in turn. It really helps if the facilitator indicates the end of each round of questions with a gong or another sign.

You can end the exercise after the questions. If you still have some time, there is a nice and effective addition: the resource chat:

B, C and D chat about person A (who in turn listens with interest). *What resources did you detect in A's statements that make you confident that A will be able to reach his or her goals?* Signal the end after two minutes of chatting and then allow 2 minutes each for chat about B, C and D in turn.

What happens next

After the exercise it is helpful to ask the following question of the whole group:

Is there anything arising from this exercise that is important for me as facilitator to know about, something that has a direct influence on the design or programme of the workshop?

Comments

This exercise is useful in helping you to see the needs of the participants in their daily lives and at the same time to acknowledge them as the experts for their goals and their learning. The highly structured procedure produces an intensive work atmosphere very quickly and helps focus.

The participants get to know one another by talking about the topic, their goals and their resources rather than about their function or position in the organisation.

The exercise can be used again in longer workshops (2 to 3 days), when the same groups meet again at the end to evaluate their own learning.

Acknowledgement of sources

I first encountered this exercise at the SOLWorld Conference in Stockholm 2004. It was introduced by Björn Johannson from Sweden.

About *Daniel Meier*

– Solutionsurfers

Daniel is the co-founder and managing partner of the international Brief Coach training institute Solutionsurfers®, based in Switzerland. He is the Director of the German speaking part of this association. Solutionsurfers® offer solution focused Coach Training in different countries and different languages, leading the trainees to a certificate by the International Coach Federation. Daniel has been coaching managers and teams in a solution focused way since 2001. His latest book is Team Coaching with the SolutionCircle, SolutionsBooks, 2005.

Address: Waldstätterstrasse 9, CH – 6003 Lucerne, Switzerland
 Phone: + 41 (0)41 210 3973
e-mail: daniel.meier@solutionsurfers.com
www.solutionsurfers.com
www.weiterbildungsforum.ch

The miracle at work

Getting to know resources in the workplace

Lilo Schmitz, Germany

This exercise offers a two-fold opportunity to see resources: the participants get to know each other's resources at work and at the same time they experience basic features of resource and solution focused interviewing.

Setting

- This exercise will take between 100 and 120 minutes including a short introduction.
- You can do it with groups of any size from three. I once tried it with a group of 200 participants and it was extremely successful.
- You need a worksheet for everybody (see below).
- Space for the subgroup activities. When the weather is fine, subgroups may conduct their interviews walking around slowly outside.

Context and purpose

- For getting to know each other in groups with participants from different work areas.
- Suitable for a first short introduction to the basic elements of the solution focused approach.

Detailed description

Split the participants into groups of three from different work areas. (If the numbers aren't right, join in or have one or two pairs.) Give everyone a worksheet.

58

Depending on your personal working style and what the people you are working with are used to, you can either tell everyone where they can find you if they have any questions or stroll past them and observe quietly.

The Miracle at Work Worksheet

In each group of three you change position three times: everyone is interviewed about her/his workplace for a maximum of 30 minutes. The other two conduct the interview. Where there are groups of two, then one person will interview the other and there is more time for the interview.

Please conduct the interview using the words we suggest below, taking turns to ask the questions. When you are being interviewed, please respond naturally and truthfully and don't invent answers.

THE INTERVIEW

1. *Suppose when this workshop is finished you do your usual things, go to sleep and overnight a miracle happens: at work everything has become wonderful, just the way you always wanted it. But as you were asleep you do not know that the miracle has happened. What is the first thing on Monday (or your next working day) that will tell you that a miracle must have happened?*
2. *How will your miracle day on Monday continue?*
3. *What else will be different and will tell you that a miracle has happened?*
4. *Now think about this scale. If 10 stands for the miracle at work and 0 (zero) for the extreme opposite, the worst day you ever had at work, where are you between 0 (zero) and 10 (ten) usually?*
5. *Tell me about someone apart from you who helped you to be at x on the scale and not at zero.*
6. *Tell me about something good at work that helped you to be at x on the scale and not at zero.*
7. *Now tell me something you have done that helped you to be at x on the scale and not at zero.*

Say thank you to the partner who was interviewed, send him/her away and spend three minutes discussing the things you like and admire about how he/she works, things you can really and sincerely appreciate. Select two things, call your partner and tell him what you appreciate.

After that change roles!

59

Next steps

Debrief the exercise in the full group – *What was interesting? What thoughts do you want to share with everyone?*

If there are more than 15 participants you can ask for feedback from a few participants who would like to give comments.

Give the participants time for a longer break after this activity.

Comments

This activity introduces solution focused coaching without addressing a specific concern or problem. Instead it assumes a universal desire that most people have: they want to feel good at work. Participants become aware of their own and others' resources, working styles and work environments.

Acknowledgements

This exercise is inspired by the miracle question devised by Insoo Kim Berg and Steve de Shazer.

About *Dr. Lilo Schmitz*

– University of Applied Sciences Duesseldorf

Family roots: blacksmiths and farmers*
Scientific roots: Social Anthropology and
Educational Sciences * Roots in counselling:
Person-centred approach (Carl Rogers),
Solution Focused approach (Berg/ de Shazer) *
Main focus in teaching and research:
Transculturality and solution focused
counselling, Burnout-Prevention * My home regions: Rhineland,
Turkey, Greece* My hobbies: Yoga, percussion, accordion.

Address: Kaiserstrasse 42, D – 50321 Bruehl, Germany
Phone: + 49 2232 149864 & + 49 211 8114647
e-mail: lilo.schmitz@fh-duesseldorf.de
www.liloschmitz.de

The solution onion

A classical starter exercise spiced with solution focus

Lilo Schmitz, Germany

With this exercise at the beginning of a workshop you bring participants together and invite them to small talk – you will see how the faces of people change and how the atmosphere becomes friendly and active.

Setting

Depending on the number of participants, you will need 15–20 minutes for this starter exercise. The maximum number of participants depends on how many people you can reach with your voice – if you have a microphone, you can bring hundreds of people to talk to each other at the same time.

The room must be big enough for participants to stand in two concentric circles.

Context and purpose

When starting in a new group, it is very difficult for people to get acquainted with lots of people. But they can easily manage to make contact with a few. You can organise this with the classical onion exercise.

Detailed description

In the classical onion, you have an inner and an outer circle of people. The inner circle faces outwards and the outer circle faces inwards, so that everyone is facing someone in the other circle.

The facilitator explains the exercise. After a given signal, each pair talk about a topic given to them by the facilitator. In the solution focused onion, people talk about solution focused topics for about 2 minutes. After this short conversation, the inner circle stands still while the outer circle moves clockwise to the next person. With their new partners people talk for 2 minutes about the next topic.

The following resource and solution focused topics have proved very good for new groups:

- *What was the most interesting thing you saw on your way here?*
- *What is your favourite hobby? Show it with a pantomime / by gesture without words to your partner and guess each other's hobbies.*
- *Where would you be today if you were not here at this workshop?*
- *What did you do well at your workplace so the people there can manage without you for a couple of days?*
- *What do you already know about the topics of this workshop?*
- *What do you think can you learn best from this workshop?*
- *What could you do tonight to give someone you like a treat (do something nice for him/her)?*
- *What could you do tonight to give yourself a treat/do something nice for yourself?*
- *If you had to select another country to work in for a year, which country would you choose and why?*
- *If you were working in another country for a year, what would your colleagues miss most?*
- *If by chance you got an extra paid holiday for two months, how would you spend this time?*

What happens next

The workshop starts after this warm-up!

Comments

During the solution onion exercise, half of the people in the room are talking – an incredibly activating experience! As facilitator you see and hear your participants in action and get a feeling for the style and the voice of the people.

Acknowledgements

I do not know who first invented the onion method – if readers know more please let me know! It is as old as social group work, probably dating back to the 1920s. The moves are reminiscent of partner changing in folk dancing.

About *Dr. Lilo Schmitz*

– University of Applied Sciences Duesseldorf

Family roots: blacksmiths and farmers*
Scientific roots: Social Anthropology and
Educational Sciences * Roots in counselling:
Person-centred approach (Carl Rogers),
Solution Focused approach (Berg/ de Shazer) *
Main focus in teaching and research:
Transculturality and solution focused
counselling, Burnout-Prevention * My home
regions: Rhineland, Turkey, Greece* My hobbies: Yoga,
percussion, accordion.

Address: Kaiserstrasse 42, D – 50321 Bruehl, Germany
Phone: +49 2232 149864 & +49 211 8114647
e-mail: lilo.schmitz@fh-duesseldorf.de
www.liloschmitz.de

CHAPTER 4

Containing problems and conflicts

A container for problems   *Carey Glass, United Kingdom*

Getting co-operation when teams are in conflict   *Lilo Schmitz, Germany*

Successes   *Barry Winbolt, United Kingdom*

Three in one   *Inge Zellermann, Germany*

Being solution focused doesn't mean being problem phobic. These activities allow participants to voice problems without dwelling on them.

A container for problems

... one with no cracks!

Carey Glass, United Kingdom

This activity enables a group of people to move speedily and wholeheartedly from problem talk to solution talk. They have the opportunity to say as much as they need to about the problem. They can then move on to solutions without the problem interfering with their ability to move forward.

Setting

- This usually takes between 20–60 minutes – the participants decide how long they need to do it.
- It is suitable for 2 to 25 people.

Context and purpose

Insoo Kim Berg often said that 'being solution focused does not mean that you are problem phobic'. In SF, analysing problems is not seen as useful in finding solutions, so an SF facilitator does not enquire into problems that are being expressed. However, in SF it is also recognised that when people bring up problems repeatedly it is often because they have felt prevented from expressing them to the extent that they wish and have not felt heard. So in SF work the facilitator does not avoid problems but shows that they are actively listening to whatever the individual chooses to express, without making enquiries into the problem. The approach respects people's desire to be heard without becoming problem focused.

This activity is designed to give people permission to talk about the problem as much as they want and ensures that they are heard. It provides a contained space and time in which to express the problem. The effect is that people are ready to focus on solutions earlier and in a practical and productive way. The problem no longer leaks into the process of solution building. As a side benefit it serves to confirm or re-create a sense of connectedness amongst the group and models an approach in which the group has an opportunity to express the problem but also takes on the responsibility for finding solutions.

The exercise is especially useful with teams struggling emotionally with a difficult situation that they are facing as a group or with an experience that has happened to them, especially if this experience keeps intruding into their attempts to move forward.

It is best used after their hopes and goals for the day have been considered but before the solution building phase of the work.

Detailed description

This activity is worked into a team workshop designed to find ways forward. Before the workshop the facilitator is likely to be aware that there is a problem disturbing the group and preventing them from moving towards solution building. For example this often happens to a group following a major restructure, after heavy financial losses, when a division is placed under close observation or has to hit seemingly unattainable targets. Please note that the facilitator can also introduce it into a workshop on the spur of the moment if he can see that the group is continuously troubled by the problem.

The activity is introduced as part of the agenda for the day so that the group knows that they will have an opportunity to talk about what has happened or is happening to them. It is helpful to say explicitly that you would like to have a session early in the workshop to allow people to express their thoughts and feelings about the problem.

In order to keep the focus on solution building as the main purpose of the day, it is important that the group does an exercise to consider their goals and best hopes before this exercise. This ensures that the main purpose of the day remains evident.

Step 1: Individuals consider what they would like to express to the group

Introduce the activity and say that the first step is for individuals to have an opportunity to think about what they would like to say to the group. If the group has up to 6 people, ask them to spend 5 minutes quietly considering their thoughts and feelings about the problem and what they would like to say about it. With larger numbers it is best to work in pairs and ask the pairs to spend 15 minutes discussing their thoughts and feelings about the problem together. Participants are welcome to jot down their thoughts.

Step 2: The group shares their thoughts and feelings about the problem

After Step 1, ask the whole group how long they would like to spend sharing their thoughts and feelings and accept the time frame that they suggest. Accepting their time frame is essential to the success of the activity so that individuals do not feel prevented from having adequate time to express themselves.

Ask them to gather together in a circle at one end of the room or in another room if available. This can work well quite informally, with participants deciding whether they will drag a chair along, lean on tables etc.

Go around the group inviting individuals to take turns to express their thoughts and feelings. Use a fairly fluid style, allowing others to add their reflections to somebody's thoughts. As necessary, reflect back what is being said so that individuals know that they are being heard. You can go around a second time if listening to others has sparked further thoughts.

Half way through the allocated time ask the group if that time frame is still OK and adjust it if necessary. At the end, check again that they are ready to leave this activity and move on. My experience is that the group usually needs less time than they have said.

When the group has finished expressing their thoughts it is helpful to take a short break to separate the focus on the past from a focus on the future after the break.

What happens next

When people have left the past behind them through this activity, it is good to move directly into an activity that marks this shift such as the preferred future, the miracle question etc.

Comments

I developed this activity to provide a symbolic way to enact movement from the past to the future, from problem to solution in SF terms. In SF, problems are seen as part of the past and solutions as part of the future. In this activity, different spaces are used to symbolise the past and the future, with participants choosing to leave the space where they have talked about the past when they are ready and moving into the space where they will talk about the future and build solutions.

There are three keys to this activity. The first is for the facilitator to give permission to the group to talk about the problem by building time into the agenda. Once individuals know that they will be heard, their anxiety to be heard wanes and they no longer continuously search for ways to bring up their feelings about the problem.

The second is to ensure that the group is in control of the time chosen to share these thoughts. In SF, if people talk about the problem as much as they want to and no more than that, then giving the group control over the time ensures that this happens. In practice, once people are not fighting to be heard, the time required for this activity often tends to be less than estimated.

The third is to have a symbolically different space in the room or another room so that the group can physically leave the past behind them after this activity. The problem is fully placed into a container in one space and no longer needs to leak into the other space.

Acknowledgement of sources

This activity offers a way for a group to actualise Steve de Shazer and Insoo Kim Berg's perfectly balanced way of understanding and accepting people's needs to express their feelings about a problem without becoming problem focused. People talk about the problem as much as they want, and no more.

About **Carey Glass**

– The Human Centre

Carey Glass, Business Psychologist and Director of The Human Centre, works with leaders who want to shine from the UK's largest private sector and public service organisations, to foster success in their teams. An Aussie, who herself managed massive change as Director of Planning and Development of one of Adelaide's largest health service organisations, Carey now loves seeing the magic that occurs as she helps chairs, managers and teams transform organisations into communities of action and achievement.

Address: 13 Street Lane, Leeds, LS8 1BW, UK
Phone/Mobile: + 44 113 226 2738 + 44 7703 460 812
e-mail: carey.glass@thehumancentre.co.uk
www.thehumancentre.co.uk

Getting co-operation when teams are in conflict

Lilo Schmitz, Germany

When you are called in because teams or departments are in dispute, you are always in danger of being caught between two fronts. With the following humorous solution focused activity, you normalise conflict, improve the atmosphere and support first steps to better communication.

Setting

- Depending on the size of the group you will need 3–5 hours (well invested) plus time for a break.
- For 6–40 participants.
- You need 2 rooms for large groups and break-out rooms for small groups.
- Working sheet with the three questions.
- Moderation cards or posters for the results.
- Coloured sticky dots.
- Pinboard.
- 3 final posters.

Context and purpose

Conflicts between teams are part of everyday life at work and can even be useful sometimes. They enhance cohesion in one's own group and can be motivational and exciting. But when tension is too high, this humorous and solution focused moderation activity comes into its own.

It is very useful when two opposing groups, teams or departments have hardened their positions to such an extent that the effectiveness of the whole organisation is jeopardised. The clear structure of the activity provides the facilitator with a clear framework to normalise the situation, relieve the tension and restore the organisation's effectiveness.

A precondition is that most of the participants acknowledge that there is a conflict between two teams and that everyone is willing and able to stay for the whole activity. The best way to do this is to arrange a meeting away from the usual working place.

Detailed description

Phase 1: Normalising
Give a little speech and normalise the conflict. Explain how exciting and motivational conflicts can be. Stress that usually there is no absolute right or wrong, but just conflicting opinions – each right depending on one's perspective.

Most people participating in conflicts have very good reasons for doing so. However they have to come to reliable working arrangements if the organisation is to be effective. Invite the participants to spend a couple of hours finding ways forward.

Phase 2: Playing with stereotypes
Each group has a room for itself. Each group should appoint a moderator and someone to write down a short summary of their results for the full group meeting. Give them posters or flip charts to write on.

Give the groups 30 minutes (bigger groups 40 minutes) to discuss the following three questions (provide the questions on a sheet of paper) and to bring the answers to the questions to the plenary session. The questions are:

1. *Despite all difficulties, what works quite well in the other team/department?*
2. *What would the other team/department have to do to make the situation worse?*
3. *What do you think the other team will say when asked what the most awful and difficult things are about our team?*

After that both groups meet in a plenary session. The person who wrote down the results presents the answers of her/his group to the three questions. The answers to question 3 usually cause laughter and a humorous atmosphere. After that there is a short break.

Phase 3: Gather topics for clarification

Gather topics on a flip chart by asking the full group:

If we want to work together in a better way, what topics do we need to clarify?

Cluster similar topics together. Then give every participant three coloured sticky dots. Everyone puts their sticky dots beside the topics she/he considers the most important and urgent – if someone thinks a topic is vitally important, they can stick all three dots on that topic. In the plenary, count the points and find the three most important topics. Ask the participants to write these topics down.

Phase 4: Small group session

Now by random selection, form small groups consisting of people from BOTH teams. These small groups have an hour in which to find suggestions for improvement in the three most important topics.

Phase 5: Final plenary

The small groups present their solutions and suggestions for improvement topic by topic. Keep the discussion short and vote on the solutions. Record the most popular solutions on one of the following posters you have prepared:

A: We agree on ... This is what we can do at once (sections: who/when/what?). Include here only solutions that everybody agrees with, i.e. the participants vote either *We agree* or *We don't mind*.

B: We cannot come to an agreement today, but this topic has to be clarified soon (sections: who clarifies this/when/how/where?). Record here all the subjects which remain controversial, but need clarification soon. Make sure that the subjects belong to Poster B by asking: *Do we HAVE to come to an agreement? What would happen if we didn't?'*

C: This remains controversial for now, but we do not have to be unanimous on this topic.

Please try to include here as many of the controversial topics as possible in order to normalise and respect diversity in the organisation.

Agree how and when the concrete next steps of the posters A and B need to be revised.

Thank everybody for their participation.

What happens next

This powerful model is usually a single intervention.

Comments

You create a light and easy atmosphere and people hold their positions less strongly through humour and playing with the stereotypes. The resourceful first questions invite the participants to look ironically and self-critically at their own group and to retain respect for the other group. By forming the mixed small groups which are competing for the best solutions you create new lines of co-operation, new group boundaries and new perspectives.

The normalisations reinforce multi-perspectives in a solution focused and systemic way:

- In your first statements you say that conflicts are normal and sometimes helpful.
- In the opening speculation *What bad things are the others saying about us?* you normalise gossip and humorously exaggerate it.
- In the third Poster C – *This remains controversial for now, but we do not necessarily need to be unanimous* – you normalise different perspectives and appreciate diversity.
- By splitting into small mixed groups you create new solidarities. If a small group's suggestion is followed, that small group is reinforced. Even if a suggestion is rejected there is solidarity.

Acknowledgement

Some elements of this activity were created by the clever organisational consultants Burns and Stalker in the 1960s. Burns, T. and Stalker, G.M.: The Management of Innovation. London 1961

About **Dr. Lilo Schmitz**

– University of Applied Sciences Duesseldorf

Family roots: blacksmiths and farmers*
Scientific roots: Social Anthropology and
Educational Sciences * Roots in counselling:
Person-centred approach (Carl Rogers),
Solution Focused approach (Berg/ de Shazer) *
Main focus in teaching and research:
Transculturality and solution focused
counselling, Burnout-Prevention * My home
regions: Rhineland, Turkey, Greece* My
hobbies: Yoga, percussion, accordion.

Address: Kaiserstrasse 42, D – 50321 Bruehl, Germany
Phone: + 49 2232 149864 & + 49 211 8114647
e-mail: lilo.schmitz@fh-duesseldorf.de
www.liloschmitz.de

Successes

Barry Winbolt, United Kingdom

A solution focused way to help people discover that they already possess skills they did not know they have.

Setting

- 20 minutes with 10 minutes for debrief.
- Teams of four or five, overall group size 20–25.
- Enough space for the teams to discuss in comfort.
- A flipchart or whiteboard for the facilitator, marker pens.

Context and purpose

People know more than they think they know. For example, we all know how to manage conflict, but we remember only the failures, when conflict goes out of control. This exercise helps participants identify a significant success they have had and learn something about their natural conflict management skills.

This activity can be used at any time during the workshop. I use it to reinforce learning at the end of my Solution Focused Conflict Resolution workshops. It can be used with any topic, not just conflict. For example, we all know how to manage stress, but we remember only our failures, the times we find stressful or where we respond badly.

Detailed description

Organise the group into teams of four or five. For debriefing, you will need a range of responses, so it is good to ensure that you have at least four or five teams. If the overall group size is small, adjust the team numbers. So, if you only have 12 in the group, make four teams of three.

Ask each person in the team to remember a time when they were in an uncomfortable situation when it looked as if a real conflict might develop, but it didn't. Not only was there no conflict, they ended up with the other person with whom the conflict might have occurred thanking them. In other words, they avoided a tricky situation by something they did (do not ask them how they did it at this stage). Everyone has examples of this. Using small groups makes it easier for them to remember their successes and talk about them.

Give them 15–20 minutes to think of an example and share it with the team. When they have confirmed that they have all done this, move to the next stage.

Now ask for volunteers to share their team's success stories with you. You only need only two people to give you examples. This is where the team approach pays off. Some people will be too shy or modest to talk about their successes, but their team mates will be happy to boast for them. Then

- Ask for a brief description of their success.
- Summarise your understanding of this.
- Congratulate them.
- Now focus on the real purpose of the exercise. Ask them *What were the special qualities that you brought to this situation that helped produce this positive outcome?* In a potential conflict situation they will say things like *I listened to them; I could see they were angry, so I didn't argue; I could understand why they were upset.*
- Summarise these comments as single words on a flip chart: 'Listened'; 'Observed'; 'Understood', etc.
- You may have to help them to draw out some of this detail. In some cultures, people are very modest and feel uncomfortable talking about success as it sounds like bragging.
- When you have done this, thank and compliment them, then move to the second volunteer. Repeat the exercise, summarise the points on the flip chart.

The debrief

The points on the flip chart will match the key skills in conflict resolution (listening, empathising, objectivity, seeking to understand, etc). This is why I do it to reinforce learning at the end of my conflict resolution workshops. Take each respondent in turn through their list, affirming how able and creative they were, repeating from time to time *How did you do that?* In my workshops, I tell them in the morning that, by the end of the day, I will demonstrate that they have all the skills they need to handle conflict.

This exercise reinforces the learning from the day. Remember, you only need to debrief two or three people. The others in the group will be reflecting on their own skills as you debrief the exercise.

Thank the contributors, affirm their special qualities and point out that we all have hidden talents.

What happens next

Allow the group time to share and acknowledge each other's successes once the exercise is over. I either make this the last activity of the day, or break for coffee right after the exercise.

Comments

- This is a naturalistic SF exercise because everyone can manage conflict, we just forget to use the skills sometimes (or refuse to).
- After all, if we are learning new skills (playing the piano, golf, painting), we do not use our practice sessions to repeat our failures, we aim to build on, and repeat, our successes!
- It is a very affirming exercise. I have taught groups in the Social Services to use this process, and share their successes, at their weekly team meetings.
- The facilitator may have to help a little with the language when writing up the summary. Make sure that it 'fits' the points covered during the day.
- Occasionally, someone will share a story that is not the right kind of success (for example, a chance occurrence interrupted their conflict). Simply thank them, congratulate them for sharing, and move on to a stronger example.

Acknowledgement of sources

Originally developed by Barry Winbolt, at a workshop in Hull, UK, 2001

About **Barry Winbolt**

Barry Winbolt MSc. provides Solution Focused training in conflict management, communication skills, Brief Therapy and Mediation. He is also Programme Coordinator for the Advanced Certificate in Conflict Resolution and Mediation Studies at Birkbeck College, University of London. He travels widely in his work and is a fluent French speaker.

Address: 4200 Nash Court, John Smith Drive, Oxford, OX4 2RU, UK
Phone: +44 7980 66 53 49
e-mail: info@barrywinbolt.com
www.barrywinbolt.com

Three in one

With six eyes you will see more

Inge Zellermann, Germany

Three in one aids the understanding of difficult or conflict situations and it shows new possibilities of responding. Seeing the situation from different points of view offers new ideas of the others' positions and individuals' own roles in the conflict situation become apparent.

Setting

- Between 20–30 minutes.
- For groups of up to 16. The room should be big enough for everyone to find space – and the facilitator should be able to see everyone.
- Provide paper or cards and marker pens for everyone.

Context and purpose

One of the fundamental rules of SF work is 'If something doesn't work, don't try harder, but try something different!' People in conflict situations often think that it's up to the other people to change their behaviour. The aim of this activity is to shine the light on people's own behaviour and then to find different ways of dealing with the situation. Seeing different points of view helps people to recognise and to understand other people's behaviour and shows a way out of the difficult situation.

The activity is very helpful and practical in situations where conflicts are seen as someone else's fault. It is also suitable when people feel themselves helpless and incapable of acting (for example, problems with colleagues, difficult clients, team conflicts etc). The best time to do this is some time into a workshop when participants have worked together and got to know each other.

Participants must have a serious desire to change the situation and a willingness to reflect on their own role, based on the following question: *What has to happen next time this happens so you feel you have handled it in a constructive and satisfying way?*

Detailed description

The facilitator invites the group to join an experiment:

The following activity gives you the opportunity to reflect upon a conflict situation you have had in the past. This will give you new perspectives which may lead you to a better understanding and ideas about how to respond next time such a situation arises.

You will experience the situation in three different roles: your own (A), the role of the other person/s (B) and as an impartial observer (C).

First, look around the room and find somewhere to stand for the next 20 minutes. You need enough space to be able to swing your arms around. Take three cards and a marker with you.

Now, write A, B and C on the cards (one on each) and lay them down in front of you in a triangle with sides about a metre long. You should be able to see all three cards from where you're standing.

The facilitator makes sure that the participants all have enough space around themselves without disturbing others. It is very important that positions A, B and C are well separated.

First step
The place where you are standing now is your starting point. Move to position A and stand on the card. This is the position where you will experience the conflict situation from your own point of view. It may be easier for you to remember with your eyes closed.

Second step – Position A (me):
The facilitator now speaks softly and slowly, with many pauses, helping the participants recall the experience in a trance-like way.

Now, as you are once more in this difficult situation, notice what and whom you see around you, in front of you, beside you ... watch the face of the other person, eyes and mouth, the visual impression ... notice how far away or close to you the other person is, how he's standing or sitting ... and you may hear voices, loud or soft, the sound, the tempo ... you hear what the other person says and you hear yourself, what you are saying and how that sounds ...

- *What do you want from the other person?*
- *What good reasons or intentions or motivation ... do you have for that?*
- *What are you doing to avoid escalating the situation?*
- *What helped you to do this?*

And now it's time to leave this situation and this place, open your eyes and go back to your starting-point. Think about the parts of the experience in position A which may be helpful next time you're in a conflict situation.

The facilitator must make sure that all participants really leave position A and go back to the starting-point.

Third step – Position B (the other)
The facilitator asks the participants to stand on card B and helps them again to remember the same situation, this time from the other person's perspective.

Now, you're wearing the other person's shoes. Try to stand and to look like the other person does; and wearing these shoes, notice what and whom you see around you, in front of you, beside you ... (as for second step)

- *What do you want to hear or to get from the other person in this situation?*
- *What good reasons do you have for attending to that?*
- *What are you doing to avoid escalating the situation?*
- *What helped you do this?*

And now it's time to leave this situation, open your eyes and go back to your starting point. Think about the parts of the experience in position B that may be helpful next time you're in a conflict situation.

Fourth step – Position C (impartial viewer)

The facilitator now asks the participants to move to card C and to experience the situation as an observer or witness; once more he helps them to remember:

Imagine that you happened to be there when these two had this conflict situation – what did you see ... hear ...? etc.

- *What do they each want to get from the other one?*
- *What good reasons do they have for that?*
- *What are they doing to avoid escalating the situation?*
- *How are they succeeding in doing it?*
- *Do they have similar needs or wishes?*
- *What ways forward or beginnings of ways forward can you see from your perspective?*
- *If the two of them asked you for advice, what would you advise them to do?*

Fifth step

The facilitator asks everyone to go back to the starting point again saying:

And now it's time to leave this position, open your eyes and come back to your starting point. Think about parts of the experience in position C that may be helpful next time you're in a conflict situation.

Give the participants some time reflect on their experiences. After a while, the facilitator asks them to pick up their cards A, B and C and to go back to their seats.

Sixth step – closing

- Ask everyone to write down their three most important insights.
- Form small groups of two or three and ask them to discuss: *Looking into the future, what could you do (more of, less of, or something completely different) to experience similar situations in a more constructive, satisfactory and helpful way?*

What happens next

This activity encourages understanding different perspectives of the same situation and is a good starting point workshop in, for example, customer service, negotiation, team work etc.

Comments

This activity is one of my favourites in coaching sessions and I wondered how it may be helpful in group situations. I tested the idea while training in communication and conflict situations in customer relationship and the participants found it very helpful.

People often are not aware that they already know the solution. A trip around a situation from different perspectives, assisted by asking for resources (for example *What are you doing to avoid escalating the situation?*) helps them become aware of their strengths – and to use these resources in the future.

It also has the advantage that nobody has to talk about his feelings to the others – the work is done in silence.

Acknowledgement of sources

This activity has been adapted from the NLP Perceptual Positions Model.

About **Inge Zellermann**

– Consulting and Coaching, Cologne

Educated in economics, social work and consulting, I have been working as a consultant and coach since 1997. I specialise in time management and organisational effectiveness, also in communication and presentation skills.

Address: Balthasarstr. 81, 50670 Cologne, Germany
Phone/Mobile: + 49 (0)221 973130 30
e-mail: inge.zellermann@consultcontor.de
www.ConsultContor.de

CHAPTER 5

Looking at resources

SF facilitators focus on what helps their clients get what they want – not on what gets in their way!

Ubuntu

One step forward with your network

Liselotte Baeijaert and Anton Stellamans, Belgium

Ubuntu is a revealing exercise in which the participants discover how their personal growth is tightly linked to other people, and explore how they can develop themselves further by relying on (new) personal networks.

Setting

- Allow 50 minutes for the exercise and 15 minutes to debrief.
- The activity is suitable for 5 to 20 people.
- Have one flip chart paper and one pencil per participant, and three different kinds (different shapes or colours) of post-it notes (at least 20 post-it notes of one kind and at least 10 of the other two). Adhesive tape to post the flip charts on the wall (optional).
- We advise you to show a completed flip chart as an example.
- You need enough room (on tables or on the floor) for the participants to work on their flip charts.
- We play some music before the start of this exercise and when the participants are mapping.

Context and purpose

- When working with people looking for a new job or for another role or function within their organisation.
- To help human resources consultants develop an interactional view of competence management: competencies are developed in interaction with other people and new interactions can lead to the development of new competencies.
- When training coaches to show the importance of using the client's personal network as a resource.

The purpose of this exercise is to let your participants:

- Look back on the skills, attitudes and knowledge they have already developed.
- Acknowledge the role other people played in their personal development, introducing new networks, new activities and new competencies.
- Imagine how other people might play a role in the next steps of your personal growth.
- Wonder about the coincidences and lucky encounters which led up to where they are now.
- See how they can make use of this serendipity to develop themselves further.
- Realise that they too could be a key person in other people's development.

Detailed description

The facilitator explains the spirit of Ubuntu:

Ubuntu is the African belief that we are what we are thanks to the people around us. It is recognising the contribution that others have made to the person we are today. This exercise will help you to look back on your personal development and become aware of the people who have played a key role at different stages.

The aim of the exercise is to discover

- *the people who played a key role in your personal development;*
- *how you were able to move from one project to another thanks to these people and the networks you are involved with;*
- *the people and networks who might help you in your future development.*

Part 1: Mapping key people and networks
In the first part of the exercise the participants make a map of their key people, networks and activities.

Give each of them a piece of flip chart paper, a pen and post-it notes in three different colours. Ask them to put the flip chart in landscape format. Invite them to think about the men and women

87

who played a crucial role in their personal development and to write their names on separate post-it notes (one name per post-it note). They can also write down the names of any networks they are involved in. Then they stick the names onto the flip chart and cluster the names that belong together with the oldest influences on the left and the most recent on the right.

Ask if there are any questions and tell them they have got 15 minutes to do this mapping. Play some background music while they are working.

Part 2: Mapping projects and activities
In the second part of this exercise, they are told to think of the projects (pieces of work, assignments, previous jobs etc.) they have been involved in and write the names of these projects on different coloured post-it notes and link them to the people that are on the flip chart.

Give them 10 minutes to do this and play some background music while they are doing it.

Part 3: Mapping next steps
The final part of the exercise focuses on the next steps.

Acknowledge that some of them may already have concrete plans. Tell them to add the names of their projects and the people who will be involved onto a third colour post-it and to think of other people who could benefit from taking part in these activities.

Some may be satisfied with how things are going now. They too can think of other people who could benefit from taking part in their activities or who could profit in one way or another from what they are doing.

Others might have a strong urge to change but be unclear about their next steps. Tell them to think about networks of people organised around themes they are interested in and look for ways of engaging in these networks and to think about people who are doing stimulating or interesting things and see if there is something they could do with them.

Allow the participants 10 minutes for this exercise (again with background music playing).

Debrief
Useful questions for the debriefing of this exercise are:

- *What did you learn from listing the key people in your life during the first round?*
- *How do you look back on these people now?*
- *What did you learn about the connection between personal development and the people around you?*
- *What did you learn about the qualities you have developed during your career? How can other people help you to develop your competencies?*
- *What qualities do you have that made it possible for you to meet new people and to follow this path in your career?*
- *How did your own abilities and knowledge lead to networks?*
- *How could you expand these qualities and use them more in the future?*
- *How can you invite change by meeting new people?*

Allow 15 minutes for this debriefing.

What happens next

After this exercise you can move to an exercise in which the participants can discover their personal qualities and strengths. You can also explore their wishes for their professional future and let them interview one another about what would be different then. When you are working with human resources consultants, you can let them think about applications of what they have learnt in the field of competence development.

Comments

This activity resonates with several central thoughts in the solution focus approach. First, there is the appreciation of the progress the client has already made. This appreciative look helps your client to realise that he isn't starting from scratch and provides confidence to go one step further in his personal development. Second, making your client aware of his personal network helps him to realise that he can benefit from the support of other people. These people are part of his resources. Third, in solution focused work, we pay attention to what is happening in the interaction between people. The action is in the interaction, or as Prof. Dr. René Bouwen from the University of Leuven frames it: *Change happens between the noses, not between the ears.*

The exercise emerged out of a discussion with Prof. Dr. Bouwen, on competence management and relational learning. Competence management has lots of advantages: it involves a more dynamic view of organisations and provides opportunities for personal development. The pitfall however is that the development of the personnel is directed from the top, based on the organisation's strategic planning and it doesn't come from the capacities and wishes of the employees. Through this exercise, we come to realise that we acquire our competences through the things we do, and that we become involved in these activities thanks to some people we know and the networks they introduce us to.

The reference of the spirit of Ubuntu emerged from discussions with Josaphat Misaguzo Balegamire on African networks. Central to the idea of Ubuntu is that you experience the joy of being linked up with other people. It is about the gratitude you feel when you recognise that other people (each in their own way) have helped you to be who you are now. Even if some people thwarted your plans, you can still be grateful because of the other things that became possible. The joy of Ubuntu can also be felt when you share your knowledge, skills, resources and time with others and you discover that by working together you can achieve miracles which go far beyond your personal capacities.

It is highly probable that some participants will say that some people have played an important role in their life, not because they offered possibilities, but because they blocked certain plans. You can acknowledge this and ask how they look back at these people now and how this past difficulty has eventually helped them to arrive where they are now. Sometimes this can help them to look at these people with more compassion.

In the debriefing, people often express their wonder about the coincidences in their personal development. This is an excellent opportunity to talk about the difference between the neatly structured story we sometimes tell about our lives and the way in which it actually happened. This discussion also offers an opportunity to encourage the participants to think about how they could use this serendipity in their further development, for example by engaging in new networks or activities with no other reason than to find out what it will lead to.

An interesting theme to discuss with the participants during the debrief is to find out how they are (or could become) a key person in other people's lives. What would they do, to become such a person? Which aspects of the people that inspired them would they like to adopt?

You can extend this exercise if you ask the participants to add the competencies they have learnt in the different activities or projects in which they were involved. You can introduce this extra part after part three.

Acknowledgement

This exercise was developed by Liselotte Baeijaert and Anton Stellamans, based on conversations with Professor Dr René Bouwen on relational learning and with Josaphat Misaguzo Balegamire on Ubuntu.

About *Liselotte Baeijaert and Anton Stellamans*

– Ilfaro

Liselotte Baeijaert (MA in Germanic philology) took the master course in SF Management and coaching in Amsterdam (Fontys, Korzybski, Saxion and BFTC Milwaukee). She founded Ilfaro in 2007 with Anton Stellamans. Fond of using SF, they help people in organisations, schools and other settings to get in touch with their own resources, goals and solution strategies.

Address: Vlazendaallaan 22, 1701 Itterbeek, Belgium
Phone/Mobile: +32 2 5670980
e-mail: Liselotte.Baeijaert@ilfaro.be

Anton Stellamans (MA philosophy and history) was trained in Solution Focused Brief Therapy at the Korzybski Institute in Belgium. He applied SF to the field of peace building.

Address: Brieversweg 121, 8310 Bruges, Belgium
Phone/Mobile: +32 477 695693
e-mail: Anton.Stellamans@ilfaro.be
www.ilfaro.be

Anchors and buoys in the competence sea

Liselotte Baeijaert and Anton Stellamans, Belgium

This is an energising personal and team assessment tool, focusing on strengths and goals. It explores the group's tacit knowledge of resources and learning goals, allows for appreciation and recognition and stimulates exchange on best practices for workplace learning. It releases energy and is a good foundation for buddy coaching.

Setting

- Allow 60 to 90 minutes for the whole activity.
- Suitable for 5 to 20 people.
- Chairs in a circle. If there is a green and suitable outdoor environment, make use of it!
- Preparation
  - ✔ Make a poster with what you know already about the group's competences, using the participants' own words.
  - ✔ Provide post-its (two different colours, one for the buoys and one for the anchors).
  - ✔ Prepare enough cards with the buoys and anchor questions – one set for each pair of participants.

Context and purpose

The activity can be used in a team building event, in a self-development workshop or in a workshop on coaching. It focuses on the resources and learning goals of the group and gives a visual image of the group's diversity. It stimulates co-operation between people with complementary or similar learning goals, lets them get to know and appreciate each other better and builds confidence.

Personal development is more likely to happen when people feel they are not starting from scratch and when there is an attainable and desirable goal to focus on. That is why we ask for MANY buoys and only ONE anchor. In addition, the participants are invited to explore their personal learning preferences and to make use of these for their next learning goal. Knowing that there are other people in the group with similar learning goals or people who have useful resources to help you can be very stimulating.

Detailed description

Before the event
Interview the team leader and/or some participants of the group. Find out which competences are important in their professional activity. Make a poster showing the sea with small islands and give the islands the names of the crucial competences. Hang the poster in the room.

Exercise
1) The participants sit in a circle. The facilitator invites them to relax, to close their eyes if they want to and then to go on a boat ride and explore their sea of competences in the workplace ... In this deep and vast ocean, there are known and unknown territories ... The facilitator names some of the competences that are on the list and relevant to some or most of the participants. He might ask the participants to add more competences that are relevant to their context to the poster. (10 minutes.)

2) *Think in silence about the most important competences you have acquired during your working life. This is known territory for you; these are the places where you put your buoys. You feel quite comfortable there. What can you say about these places, these competences? How did you get there? What helped you to develop these competences? What challenges, random events, activities, people ... have stimulated you to grow?* (5 minutes.)
   If time and the environment permit, the facilitator may also invite people to take a short walk outside and reflect on these questions. Give a precise time when you expect everyone to come back. (15 minutes maximum.)

3) *Write your name on post-its and stick these on the islands where your competences are. You may also add new competences onto*

the map and stick your name there. These are your buoys. (5 minutes.)

4) *In pairs, talk about your buoys, asking each other helpful questions like those in the worksheet at Figure 2 below. (10 minutes each way.)*

Figure 2: worksheet – questions about existing competences

 Tell me more about your buoys

✔ What have you learned in your professional life that you are proud of?
✔ What do you really like doing and what are you good at?
✔ How did you manage to become ... (e.g. so well organised)?
✔ How did you learn to ... (e.g. influence people)?
✔ How did you become a ... (e.g. good people manager)?
✔ What helped you to ... (e.g. change from an expert to a leader)?
✔ Who inspired you? Who are you grateful to?
✔ What are the benefits of this competence for you? And for others?

✔ Give a compliment about what you have noticed about your colleague's buoys.

5) The facilitator invites the participants to take a seat again, relax and concentrate on their next step. *Think about the next place you want to visit. The one competence you want to add to all the things you already know. Which competence do you need in order to do your job even better or what challenge do you have right now?*

This is where you would like to throw out your anchor. Think about what it would be like if you were able to add this competence to your collection of competences ... what would be the benefits for you? And for the team? (5 minutes.)

Here again, if time and the environment permit, you may also

invite the people to take a short walk outside and reflect on these questions). (10 minutes maximum.)
6) *Write your name on post-its and stick them on the map of competences where you want to throw your anchor.* (5 minutes)
7) The facilitator invites the participants to make pairs again (these may be different from the first time) and ask each other about their anchors. The questions are written on a card that he gives to the participants. (10 minutes.)

Figure 3: worksheet – questions about competences to be developed

---

 Talk about your anchors

✔ Describe what the competence you would like to develop (your anchor) means to you.
✔ What do you already know about it?
✔ Who in this room could be helpful to develop this competence? (Take a look at the map of competences at where the buoys of your colleagues are.)
✔ Give each other good advice about possible ways to develop this competence.

What happens next

After this activity, the facilitator asks the participants the following debriefing questions:

• *What worked well in the exercise?*
• *What did you learn?*
• *How was this useful for you?*
• *What is one idea you want to bring into practice?*
• *What else will you take away with you?*

After the workshop, people can decide to start buddy coaching, they can meet again in the team and talk about the progress made or they can find other ways of sharing useful resources and activities to further their learning goals.

Comments

This exercise was developed during a project on learning in the workplace for experienced workers, in collaboration with our colleagues Sven De Weerdt, Mark Claus and René Bouwen. In this project we wanted to explore what keeps people over 50 years old motivated at work. We discovered that they liked talking about their rich experiences in an appreciative manner. Talking about learning goals and next steps was energising as well: you are never too old to learn. There is no age limit to growth and development. As long as people can learn, they are more likely to feel passionate and driven in their work.

The activity is solution focused because

1) Participants are treated as the experts in their own learning and learning goals.
2) They focus on their strengths and resources.
3) They are invited to make a first step toward a desired goal.
4) They can show mutual appreciation and encourage the others in the group.
5) The group reveals their tacit knowledge about how to develop certain competences.

Acknowledgement of sources

The ideas for this exercise emerged in collaboration with our colleagues Sven de Weerdt and Prof. René Bouwen (University of Leuven) and Mark Claus during the project 'Keep the fire burning' that was part of an overall project called 'Indicators for learning in the workplace' with the financial support of European Social Funding, 2005–2007.

About **Liselotte Baeijaert and Anton Stellamans**

– Ilfaro

Liselotte Baeijaert (MA in Germanic philology) took the master course in SF Management and coaching in Amsterdam (Fontys, Korzybski, Saxion and BFTC Milwaukee). She founded Ilfaro in 2007 with Anton Stellamans. Fond of using SF, they help people in organisations, schools and other settings to get in touch with their proper resources, goals and solution strategies.

Address: Vlazendaallaan 22, 1701 Itterbeek, Belgium
Phone/Mobile: +32 2 5670980
e-mail: Liselotte.Baeijaert@ilfaro.be

Anton Stellamans (MA philosophy and history) was trained in Solution Focused Brief Therapy at the Korzybski Institute in Belgium. He applied SF to the field of peace building.

Address: Brieversweg 121, 8310 Bruges, Belgium
Phone/Mobile: +32 477 695693
e-mail: Anton.Stellamans@ilfaro.be
www.ilfaro.be

The triple

– learning the art of celebrating success

Ben Furman, Finland

This activity can be used to teach workshop participants one of the most central principles of solution focused therapy and coaching: that is, how to discuss success in a way that elicits pride and ensures continuing support from other people.

Setting

- It will take you some 10 minutes to outline the instructions, then another 10 minutes for the participants to carry out the task. Allow 15–30 minutes for debriefing.
- Participants will be working in pairs or groups of three.
- Make sure there is room for the participants to sit comfortably together to talk.
- Participants will need to see the instructions in order to follow the steps of the procedure. Have a handout or instructions projected onto a screen. Alternatively you can ask them to write the instructions in their notebooks.

Context and purpose

This exercise can be used at lectures, parent evenings, workshops or in fact at any gathering where you want participants to have a personal, first hand experience of the solution focused way of meeting the world.

It will provide a learning experience for the participants. They will know that in many cultures talking about one's successes is considered bragging and is not approved of. They will realise that it is, in fact, important for all of us to learn to share our successes with other people. They will also get insight into the psychology of success; the importance of creating a context conducive to talking about successes, the significance of the way we respond to other people's success stories and in particular how to talk about success in a way that has a positive effect on the environment.

Detailed description

This exercise can be conducted in pairs or in groups of three. The following instructions are written for pairs. First A is the interviewer and B is the one who tells about something he or she has succeeded with. Then the roles are reversed. If done in groups of three, A, B and C all tell their success stories in turn.

A: Ask your partner to tell you about some recent success. If the word success seems too big, you can ask him or her to tell about something that worked well, something he or she feels somewhat proud of. The success does not have to be work related. It can just as well be related to hobbies or family.

B: Tell A a story about something you have recently succeeded with. Don't make it a long story, just a short story of something that worked well, something that you are a bit proud of.

A: Respond to B with a Triple, with what we call the Triple praise response. It consists of three parts. They are:

1. Exclamation of wonder. Show that you are impressed. Use your face and gestures and say something like *Wow! Great story!* or *I'm impressed!*

2. Declaration of difficulty: Make sure B knows that what he or she did was not easy. You might say something like: *That's not easy; Not everyone can do that; Many have tried and many have failed; I don't think I could have come up with such a brilliant idea.*

3. Request for an explanation. End the Triple with a sincere question. Keep eye contact and show that you are genuinely interested in how B managed to do it. Where he or she got the idea, how did he or she come to think of something like that or how he or she was

able to accomplish such a demanding job. You might say something like: *How did you do that? I'd be curious to understand how you were able to do it.*

B: Respond to A's question by acknowledging someone else, by becoming a bit modest and giving credit to someone else, that is, acknowledging someone who assisted you or made it possible for you to accomplish your success. You might say something like: *Well, to be honest, it wasn't my idea originally, I got the idea from so and so* or *Well, to be honest, I could never have done it alone. I got a lot of help from so and so.*

A: Return the credit: B is being modest and is giving the credit to someone else. Help B feel proud of his or her achievement by handing back the credit to B, where it rightfully belongs. You could say something like: *Come on, don't be so modest. It was you who did it!* or *OK, OK, but it would never have happened without you!*

B: Smile, appear delighted and feel proud.

The pairs or groups will need some 10 minutes to complete the exercise both ways. When they have finished, bring everyone together and give them the additional task of answering the question: What can you learn from this exercise?

What we hope that people learn from this exercise is:
- People don't usually talk about their successes unless asked to.
- It pays to talk about one's successes and there are many reasons why it is important that people share their successes with others.
- Nobody likes to talk about their successes unless they are confident that they can expect that others will respond positively.
- It is worth thinking about what constitutes a positive response. What is a positive response to some may be a negative response to someone else.
- Failing to remember to acknowledge others who have contributed to success may have dire consequences.
- It is important for all of us to feel proud of our accomplishments.

What happens next

After participants have completed the exercise and enough time has been spent talking about what they learned from the exercise, you should move on to teach whatever it is that you are teaching. The experience will have the effect of making the participants become more receptive to the idea of applying solution focused philosophy in various settings including schools and work places.

Comments

The solution focus concept is actually a misnomer. The approach is actually not focused on solutions at all. It is rather an approach where the focus is on progress; the focus is on finding out what progress clients have already made and what progress they expect to make. The miracle question is one of many ways in which information is elicited about what will constitute progress to clients. Searching for exceptions (better times or periods) and pre-workshop change (signs of recent positive development) are ways of gathering data of progress that has already been made.

To look for progress is often synonymous with looking for success. It is talking about times when things went well, when people succeeded in overcoming their problem or dealt with it successfully. Talking about minor and major successes is so central a theme in solution focused work that it certainly would not be misleading to call this approach success focused rather than solution focused.

Having said that, it is worth adding that talking about success is easier said than done. In many cultures talking about success is taboo. It is considered embarrassing or even improper. Many languages have the expression 'boasting stinks' which is used to discourage people from bragging and talking about their successes. However, talking about successes is the bread and butter of the solution focused approach. Therefore it is pivotal to help people to become comfortable with the idea of talking about successes and to understand the basic principles of how this can be done in socially acceptable manner without any overtones of boasting. The Triple activity will help participants become comfortable with talking about their own success, learn about how to respond to the successes of others and about how to give the person who has succeeded with something an opportunity to feel proud of his or her achievement.

You will find that the exercise inspires humour. For example, people often find it fun to think about what kind of exclamation of wonder would fit their culture, and you may also become inspired to joke about the subject. The exercise often stimulates a lot of laughter and lifts the mood of the participants.

We have conducted the exercise in many countries all over the word and in our experience the ideas conveyed in it are intercultural, applicable everywhere. The need to feel proud of one's successes and to have someone to share one's successes with is universal. This exercise seems to suggest that the rules of making it possible and pleasurable for people to share their success with each other are also universal.

Acknowledgement

I developed this exercise with my colleague Tapani Ahola. The idea of the Triple has been inspired by the way that Insoo Kim Berg often used to respond to clients when they told her about what they had done to make things better.

About *Ben Furman, M.D.*

Ben Furman is a psychiatrist and internationally renowned trainer of solution focused therapy and psychology. Together with his colleague Tapani Ahola he has written several books on the subject and developed a number of methods for working with different target groups. Reteaming (www.reteaming.com) is a solution focused method for coaching individuals, teams and organisations to carry out development and change processes; the Twin Star (www.twinstar.fi) is a teaching tool and an e-learning programme for teaching solution focused communication to managers and staff in companies and organisations; and Kids' Skills

(www.kidsskills.org) is a solution focused method for helping children overcome social and psychological problems.

Address: Haapalahdenkatu 1, 00300 Helsinki, Finland
Phone/Mobile: + 358 40 548 20 47
e-mail: ben@benfurman.com
www.benfurman.com

The walk shop

Developing new things and discovering resources whilst out walking

Gesa Niggemann, Germany

The Walk Shop is a workshop that takes place outdoors whilst walking in the fresh air and is particularly suitable for work in change projects. In change processes, people can often only let go of old ways, such as habits or behaviour patterns, if they discover skills and resources that enable them to see and think new things. To this end, the participants literally receive a physical and mental 'work-out': on a walk in the countryside (lake, park, in the surroundings of the company premises/hotel, city centre, botanical garden …), resources and answers are found through dialogue with different partners, using reflection questions. Sharing and integration rounds take place in the whole group in prominent meeting places (bench, boat landing stage, shelter). Fixed thought patterns are stirred up during the walk and are transformed as a result of the resources found. At the end, each of the participants can hold a resources speech at a natural Speaker's Corner (rose bed, pavilion, hill …). The Walk Shop is refreshing, invigorating and stimulating and is a genuine alternative to long reflection periods in the seminar room.

Setting

- Time required: about 2.5 to 3 hours.
- This activity is ideal for groups of 6 to 20 or so. At least 6 people are needed to get the benefit of changing partners during the activity and with more than 20, it is too difficult for the facilitator to talk to everyone with an extended area outdoors.
- If you haven't got an even number of participants, have one

group of three each time the pairs are re-formed.

- Of course, it is best to go for a walk when the sun is shining. However, the activity also works in the rain if people are wearing weatherproof clothing and carrying umbrellas.
- Each participant needs a clipboard and pen with worksheets containing the reflection questions.
- The route should be of 3–5 kilometres.
- You should have timed the route beforehand and should bear in mind that participants will walk more slowly when thinking than you did when planning the route. Make a note of paths and noticeable features along the route for breaks, meeting points and the Speaker's Corner. These might be places to sit, pedestrian footbridges, natural inclines, walls, etc.
- You will find it helpful to have a wheeled suitcase to pull along with materials and surprise drinks and snacks.

Context and purpose

The Walk Shop is a useful tool for achieving in-depth work and reflection, following an initial warm-up phase to allow the participants to get to know one another and to introduce the subject. It works well during change from old to new, from problem to solution. It is also useful for taking a fresh look at an old or unpopular topic. Even usually sceptical participants respond well once an explanation has been given.

The participants discuss their topic in great depth without being tied to their seats. Physical movement also helps people to go down new mental paths. Thanks to the changing pairs, there are frequent new suggestions and viewpoints which can bring about solutions. At the end, the participants feel refreshed on many levels by the walk and the many resources they have met on the way.

Detailed description

Following an introduction, the Walk Shop is divided into walk phases, in which the participants walk and work with one another in pairs, and talk phases, in which the whole group meets to share experiences and reflections and to take on new questions as an assignment for the next walk. You can have any number of walks and talks, although, in our experience, after four to five rounds a certain amount of habituation and tiredness sets in. A maximum of five rounds should therefore suffice!

Each walk phase lasts 8 to 15 minutes and the talk phases take 10 to 15 minutes. You therefore need about a kilometre for each walk to give participants enough time for conversation en route.

Preparation by the facilitator

The facilitator writes the questions on worksheets which are distributed to the participants before each round. If the facilitator wants to present something himself (figures, data, facts and the like), an A3 folder with perforations can be used in which large transparencies can be attached and folded back for display purposes. These can also be laminated for protection beforehand. Alternatively, gummed labels can be used on this base for outdoor facilitation.

Introduction by the facilitator

The facilitator and participants meet at the first meeting point, the Walk Shop departure point. This should be a natural meeting place in the chosen environment: a group of trees, a hill, a group of benches, etc. If the participants are meeting here for the first time and have not worked together already on the same day, you should hold a brief introduction round and give out name badges if people do not know each other.

The facilitator introduces the topic to be handled and explains the procedure

We have about 2½ hours to think about topic X with one another and to devise solutions for Y. The starting point for your consider-ations is XX / the results of XX / the problem XX / your desire for change in XX. In order to achieve this, we have a long path ahead of us, as we do in real life …

If necessary, at this point initial findings or figures, data and facts from the company can be provided as information.

The facilitator explains the approach

Our Walk Shop is divided into walk and talk phases. In the walk phases, you will have around 10 to 15 minutes to consider an issue in pairs or in groups of three and to share information with one another. I will give you reflection questions for each round on a piece of paper. Please write down your answers and ideas on this piece of paper. We will decide on a meeting place where we will share our ideas in the whole group – the talk phase.

... and the 'rules' for the Walk Shop

It is particularly stimulating to change partners after each sharing session (talk phase) so that you are constantly coming up against new ideas. And you will also get to know other participants from this group better. Please make sure that you observe the walking times. I know that everyone walks at a different pace. If you are faster, you can wait at the meeting place or do an extra lap. Enjoy the conversation!

The first walk phase

The participants start their first walk and discuss the questions.

Relevant questions for the first walk might be: *What might occur on this walk that will move you forwards in dealing with your questions?* or *If you think back to one of your last change processes, what was the best thing that you/managers/ colleagues/employees did to contribute to its success?*

In the quest for answers, they can take it in turns to speak, in a normal conversation pattern, or one person can give their views first and then the other. They can note down their initial ideas and answers on the reflection sheet while they are walking; a clipboard is therefore useful. They should summarise the main points of their discussion ahead of the next talk meeting place so that they can communicate the content more easily to the other participants.

The facilitator can either walk ahead of the group and wait at the agreed meeting point for the group or bring up the rear and make sure no one gets lost or left behind.

The first talk phase

The participants gradually turn up at the agreed meeting point. The facilitator starts with a question to prompt sharing in the group:

What answers and results have you come up with together?

He facilitates the discussion amongst the participants, acknowledges common ground and differences and leads into the second walk phase.

Continuation
Find a new partner for the next walk phase. Your next questions are as follows ... We will meet again at the next location ...

Relevant questions for the second walk round might be: *What do you regard as the first useful steps towards something new at the start of this change process?* or *How exactly will you notice that something is changing? What behaviour displayed by you/your colleagues/your employees will lead in the desired direction?*

Walk and talk sessions alternate. As the facilitator, you could surprise the participants with drinks and muesli bars from your roller suitcase. A break midway does no harm!

Resources speech
The resources speech is a nice opportunity to summarise thoughts from the conversations and to bring them close to implementation: each participant thinks up a two-minute speech during one of the final walks. Questions in preparation for the speech might be:

- *What have I heard during the conversations in this Walk Shop that was new for me with regard to the way my organisation deals with changes? What aspects of this do I want to retain at all costs?*
- *What were the most important ideas that we came up with?*
- *What are my next steps?*
- *Who will support me in this?*

These speeches will be held at a particularly attractive talk meeting place in a kind of natural Speaker's Corner (rose bed, pavilion, standing on a wall), and will be followed, of course, by appreciative applause from the other participants. This talk will therefore naturally last somewhat longer than the previous ones.

Conclusion
The participants come together for the final talk session. The conclusion may be a brief overall reflection concerning the Walk Shop. The following questions might be of use: *On a scale of 0 to 10, how helpful and beneficial in terms of fostering resources have you found today's Walk Shop?* The facilitator can set up this scale, for example, on a flight of steps or a section of lawn with trees or flower beds and briefly interview the participants about their position.

What did you find especially helpful in today's Walk Shop? How come you are at point X and not lower? How could this ranking be maintained or improved?

Next steps

The results of the Walk Shop reflections can of course be worked on further in the traditional workshop setting. The following options may be appropriate:

1. Participants who did not work with one another at all during the Walk Shop come together in a small group and share their most important findings.
2. All results are collated on pin boards and consequently presented to everyone again in visual form to ensure that the participants retain them.
3. Different viewpoints can be discussed in for/against groups.

Comments

The idea of the Walk Shop was prompted by William Bridges' book *Leading Transition*. The book describes how people in change processes have to move through three zones of transition: letting go, the neutral zone and the new beginning. We simply took this movement literally and from it created the Walk Shop. You can also apply it to topics other than transition. It is almost impossible to think in a problem oriented way while walking, since problem talk often causes us to stand still, and get stuck in the literal sense. As a facilitator, it is possible to put this visible signal to good use in order to support participants in the process of moving towards thinking in solutions. The facilitator can then invite them to acknowledge the difficult situation and ask the participants a coping question about they can continue to put up with the current situation. Or simply ask the participants to go on in silence for a while, making sure that they keep moving, and to observe what their first thoughts and ideas are as they imagine the desired goal.

For facilitators who themselves enjoy being out and about in the fresh air and often regret being cooped up in an air-conditioned seminar room when the weather is nice, it is a welcome change to be able to go outside – and of course, the same is also true for the participants.

The Walk Shop was particularly well received and enjoyed at the Frankfurt Palmengarten. We found ourselves in the prickly cactus garden, in the impenetrable jungle house or between the blooming rose beds. The scenery around us became an ideal metaphor for the contents under discussion.

Points worth noting and surprises

- The health of all the participants should be checked in advance to check whether they can walk the route without any difficulties.
- One surprise was that the routes selected often proved to be too short once the participants got a taste for walking and thinking. This meant that we had to think up additional routes on the spot which was not ideal. In the centre of Cologne we walked over the Rhine Bridges and sometimes it was too loud on the roadside for us to communicate and listen to one another. Therefore, it is essential to walk the routes in detail beforehand and not just carry out a rough assessment or work them out on a street map. Important locations and quiet spots should be pinpointed as talk meeting points.
- Another possible surprise may be that new issues as well as the ones the facilitator considered while he was preparing arise out of the talk sessions for the next walk. It is then a good idea to go with the flow and head in this direction with the question task for the next walk.

Acknowledgements/further reading

The development of the WalkShop was prompted by the study of the book by William Bridges *Leading Transition* (1995, ISBN 1–85788–341–1).

About **Gesa Niggemann**

– Neuland & Partner

Born in 1966, newspaper editor and graduate in social education, further training in solution-oriented brief therapy, including with Steve de Shazer at NIK/Bremen. Work focuses on the field of (creative) consulting in change and innovation processes. Mother of 2 children and singer in a cappella sextet 'Die Loreleyas'. Passionate about walking, gardening and lively training techniques.

Address: Von-Schildeck-Str. 12, PLZ/Ort: 36043 Fulda, Germany
Phone/Mobile: +49 661 93414–19
e-mail: gesa.niggemann@neuland-partner.de
www.neuland-partner.de

Quality mirror

Mirror, mirror on the wall – what resources can we find in the team?

Dr. Peter Röhrig – Germany

The Quality Mirror is a simple and smart method to make workshop participants' resources directly visible. It activates all participants and offers opportunities for appreciative feedback to others.

Setting

- Time frame: Individual work 10 minutes, then 15–20 minutes (according to group size) for walking around, completion and a short reflection round: overall 30 to 40 minutes.
- Optimal group size: 6 to 16.
- With more than 16 participants, the exercise becomes difficult as it is nearly impossible to gather all the different posters and comment on them.
- Some preparation is necessary. There should be half of a flip chart page ready for every participant as well as a thick pen and some adhesive tape to fix the posters to the wall. A flip chart and/or handout with the instructions and questions to be answered is also helpful.
- Desks and tables have to be moved away from the walls so that participants can freely walk around, and get close enough to read and comment on the posters.
- Comments and add-ons should be written in different colours.

Context and purpose

The aim of this activity is primarily to focus participants' perceptions of resources and competences: their own, those of their organisation and those of other participants. For many teams and organisations, this may be an unfamiliar perspective to start with if it is not (yet) part of the organisational culture. It offers a simple way of developing a joint understanding of qualities and resources in the organisation or team. Participants are encouraged to describe the most important resources and think about how to strengthen them.

The exercise also works in groups who do not yet know each other. It creates a platform for further trustful co-operation.

Practical benefits include a distinct gain in competence and self esteem, in a stronger feeling of affiliation and a better overview.

Detailed description

The facilitator starts the activity with a short introduction, preferably supported by written instructions on a flip chart or a handout.

Look at yourself and your organisation in the quality mirror: Write your name on the poster and describe the three most important aspects of quality

- *For you (in your job and/or leisure time)*
- *For your organisation (and its staff)*

Write down concise answers the following questions: What do you do especially well? What are you excellent in? What are you really proud of?

Leave some space on the poster for comments. You have 10 minutes for that. You'll find posters and pens over here.

The facilitator may walk around while participants are working and answer questions and offer encouragement. When they have finished their posters, ask them to stick them on a wall.

As soon as all posters are fixed, the facilitator says:

Walk around and read everyone's posters. Look for common and different understandings of quality. Think about how all these resources might be useful for our further work. If you know the person or organisation, add more of their features you want to appreciate. If you don't know them, just guess: what additional quality could the person or organisation have – and write it down. Please use a different colour for your comments.

What happens next

Reflection in the full group with questions like these:

- *What are essential qualities for our team or organisation?*
- *What can we do to strengthen these qualities in the future?*
- *What interesting similarities and differences did we find?*

Comments

The activity emerged from my concern about how best to introduce the awkward topic of quality development smoothly and simply in organisations. In many cases organisations begins by asking questions like *What does not work? What do we have to improve (to achieve better quality)?* My experience has been that those who focus on deficits and mistakes will at the best reach average quality and not excellence. In addition motivation decreases if you concentrate your efforts on the elimination of weaknesses, problems and faults.

I found out that it is much more promising to start by looking at resources. In workshops about organisational or quality development, the view of resources and successes is sharpened and participants consider consciously how these resources can be strengthened.

The activity helps participants to remember their own strengths. For many participants it is a real challenge to concentrate on the three most important resources. Everybody is curious to see what the others have written. For most of them, similarities and differences are equally exciting. Both perspectives offer starting points for learning from each other.

When the group knows each other, there is a great buzz as people comment on the posters and add all the things that appear to be remarkable. This is like giving presents to each other. The bright faces speak for themselves. On rare occasions there are questions about the meaning of some comments.

Acknowledgement of sources

This exercise is a favourite from my treasure chest. I led it for the first time in English at the first SOLWorld conference in Bristol 2002.

About **Dr. Peter Röhrig**

– ConsultContor · Consulting and Coaching

Peter is an SF organisational consultant, facilitator and executive coach, born 1948, with two children.

- *Formal education as an economist and social psychologist*
- *Advanced training in epidemiology, organisational development, total quality management (EFQM) and solution focused consulting*
- *11 years as general manager of service companies*
- *Many publications, mainly about self-management, leadership and quality development*
- *Partner of ConsultContor, consulting and coaching, in Cologne, Germany*

Renate Kerbst, one of his co-partners at ConsultContor, says about Peter:
Zeal for solutions is the name of an SF training series initiated by Peter, and this is a strong impulse for his professional functioning. His focus on practical resources and his attentiveness for simplicity are a solid foundation for his consulting and facilitating work. With subtle persistence he helps his clients to find surprising and furthering solutions.

As a recovering former manager he supports whole-heartedly people in challenging leadership positions – and people who want to create effective teamwork. One of his main working areas is quality development, with a special emphasis on the health and social sector.

Peter is committed to the international SOLWorld network and faculty member of the SOLWorld Summer University. He offers advanced training in SF consulting and workshop design.

Mark McKergow says about Peter:
The biggest quiet style – a giant with velvet hands.

Address: Balthasarstsse 81, D 50670 Cologne, Germany
Phone: + 49 (0)228–34 66 14 Mobile: + 49 (0)179-523 46 86
e-mail: : peter.roehrig@consultcontor.de
www.ConsultContor.de

Messages in boxes

Annette Lentze and Gabriele Röttgen-Wallrath, Germany

This activity is particularly suitable for personal development and for making a group aware of their own resources.

Setting

- Time: about 90 minutes.
- Suitable for up to 10 people.
- You need 3 large matchboxes for each participant. Paste a picture or symbol on to each matchbox.
- Small pieces of paper, pins, flip chart.
- A flip chart or slides with the questions for steps 3, 4 and 5.

Context and purpose

This is especially good when the participants have worked with each other in teams or in groups for some time. By focusing on resources, the activity supports the mutual acknowledgment of each other's abilities and promotes a culture of appreciation. Individual perception is confirmed and reinforced by feedback from other people. Many resources developed in the group process will be named which in itself can contribute to the improvement of working processes, teamwork and co-operation. It offers a good basis for further solution oriented processes.

Detailed description

Warming up
We have worked together for some time and you have achieved a lot. I would like to invite you to an experiment to reflect on our time together and to consider how you can use your resources to achieve your goals in future. And so I have brought with me some matchboxes with different pictures on them and small pieces of paper.

Step 1 (approx. 10 minutes)
Hand out the slips of paper to the participants. Ask everyone to write down three qualities they have observed in their colleagues or in themselves which have contributed to the group's success and brought new solutions to the group's work.

Step 2 (approx. 5 minutes)
Hand everyone a box, upside down so that they cannot see the pictures on them, and ask them to put their piece of paper into the box. Each box contains one resource note.

Step 3 (approx. 20 minutes)
Tell everyone to turn over the boxes so that they can see the pictures. Each participant chooses one in the light of the earlier work in the workshop. After everybody has selected a box, the group discusses the following question: *What drew me to the box I chose, in the light of our work together?*

Ask the participants to listen to each other without comment during this step.

Step 4 (approx. 30 minutes)
Ask the participants to open the boxes in turn and read aloud the resources noted on the slips of paper.

Ask them to comment, guided by the following questions:

- *What comes to mind about the group when you hear this?*
- *When have you noticed this resource being used by the group?*
- *What else occurs to you? What else?*
- *How can this resource support the group in future?*

Step 5 (approx. 10 minutes)
Finally, ask the participants:

- *You have received a treasure chest of ideas today. Which of all these ideas can you turn into a first small step and use tomorrow?*

What happens next

This activity brings to mind the group's resources allowing the workshop to proceed with energy and purpose. It allows participants to see what they are already doing well and where they need support.

Comments

This exercise was developed while working with a resigned, demoralised team who couldn't see a way forward.

- The pictures energise the discussions; people are interested in the pictures colleagues choose and the connections they make.
- The experience encourages them to acknowledge the group's resources back in the workplace.
- You can give the boxes to the participants as a gift – a visual reminder of what they have achieved.

Variations

- You can connect the pictures or symbols on the boxes the topic of the workshop – for example doors, means of movement, pictograms.
- In smaller groups (up to 5), the focus can be shifted from group development to personal development. Everyone selects one picture and one resource for each of the others in the group for personal feedback.
- We were surprised when two participants who didn't get on well together selected the same picture. This gave them a more positive impression of each other.

Acknowledgement

We learnt the idea of pasting pictures onto matchboxes from Heinrich Fallner, Bielefeld, and developed this exercise from this idea.

About *Annette Lentze*

As well as working as a trainer and personal consultant for executives, I am in charge of quality and projects at the Deutsche Gesellschaft für Supervision.

Address: Hillerstr. 37, 50931 Cologne, Germany
Phone/Mobile: + 49 221 7886176
e-mail: a.lentze@netcologne.de

About *Gabriele Röttgen-Wallrath*

Having been involved in family counselling for many years, my main field of expertise is systemic consultancy in youth and social organisations. As a trainer and consultant for executives, I work mainly with large industrial or service companies.

Address: Remigiusstr. 32, 50937 Cologne, Germany
Phone/Mobile: + 49 221 444883
e-mail: roettgen-wallrath@gmx.de

Love letters

Frank Taschner, Germany

Love letters is a written feedback method in which those involved give only positive feedback. The focus on positive feedback creates a framework for appreciation and counteracts the widespread tendency in many groups and organisations to provide feedback primarily in relation to behaviour that is seen as negative.

Setting

- Time required for the whole group variant: 15 minutes to present and explain the method plus approximately 3 minutes per participant. So, in a group with 12 participants, 15 + 12x3 = approx. 50 minutes for instruction and implementation.
- Time required for parallel variant: just 15 minutes to present and explain; the participants use breaks or reflection times to write the love letters.
- Love letters are particularly interesting for groups of about 6 or more, because the likelihood of each person giving everyone else feedback without the help of love letters declines sharply. An upper limit cannot be defined in general terms. It depends on the extent to which participants have worked with each other and thus be able to give any feedback. For example, 30 employees from one company who have been working together for 10 years will probably be able to write detailed love letters to one another. This will prove difficult for 30 participants in a workshop who have not previously met and who work in different teams during the event.
- Material: one A4 envelope for each participant, adhesive tape, (green) facilitator cards, possibly picture postcards for writing on.
- Flip chart or slide explaining the task.
- Preparation: 10 minutes to write the task onto a flip chart.

Context and purpose

Love letters are particularly suitable when the aim is to strengthen group cohesion, either for direct team building and team development measures or for events in which the focus is on the subject at hand and a high degree of mutual solidarity is necessary or desirable. For example, the new manager of a ten-strong team at a bank hired me to facilitate a two-day workshop which involved reviewing the work performed and planning future tasks. Using love letters in the whole group variant acted as a signal: As I am a new manager, this is a good time to express mutual appreciation and praise in the group.

With this method, the participants receive explicit encouragement to express mutual appreciation. The aim is to foster a culture of praise and break the fixation on the negative. The often unspoken maxim 'No news is good news!' is disproved in practice, since everyone simultaneously becomes the recipient of positive feedback and experiences the motivational impact for themselves.

Detailed description

Whole group variant
Sample situation: we are in the final stage of a 2-day team workshop, whose aim is to look back over work performed and improve certain work procedures. The facilitator introduces the method, making some comments on the significance of a well-functioning and positive feedback culture. He can pick up on comments already made by the group or clients which could be regarded as poor communication or a lack of feedback. He presents the love letters as a way of making a conscious statement of appreciation to others and giving them positive feedback.

It is of crucial significance that the method is not introduced in deadly serious way as an order: *Thou shalt praise one another!* but rather in a light-hearted way and as an opportunity. *Here you will have the time and space to do something that is easily lost sight of in everyday life.*

The facilitator then gives the instructions, which, in our 2-day team workshop example, could be something like this:
Please take an envelope, write your name on it and attach it as a kind of mailbox on the wall of the conference room. You will then

have 30 minutes to write love letters to the others and put them in the corresponding mailboxes. To do so, use the green facilitator cards or picture postcards of your choice. Please give your colleagues feedback on actual behaviour that you have personally experienced as positive. For example:

- *I appreciate ... in you, it has a positive effect on me ...*
- *This is something positive that struck me about you at this event ...*
- *... is your valuable contribution to this group/organisation ...*
- *Please continue to do the following ...*

Important: you do not have to write a message to everyone else, but you can if you want to. At the end of the event, take home a mailbox full of beneficial and motivational feedback. Enjoy!

Parallel variant

Sample situation: we are at the start of a 3-day event with approximately 30 field sales staff with open space elements. Participants work together in a variety of situations and settings. There is a high degree of focus on the subject and a certain amount of time pressure. The introduction is the same as in the whole group variant. The assignment is modified such that the participants have the chance to write love letters to one another throughout the 3-day event.

Next steps

The appeal of the method is not least down to the fact that it changes the situation for good. Everyone takes their mailboxes with the love letters home with them. The effect of the feedback emerges later. I have heard instances of participants who have celebrated opening their mailbox at home with a glass of wine on the sofa. Those who cannot wait to find out brighten up their journey home by taking a look at the love letters.

Comment

I have used this method successfully in train-the-trainer seminars and now also use it in facilitated workshops. The effects are very similar: the value of appreciation becomes tangible and something that people are conscious of. There is a significant chance that some participants will incorporate the love letters into their everyday routines.

I have experienced two typical critical situations:

*   Occasionally, participants express the fear that in the midst of all the praise, problems and criticism will be overlooked. This needs to be acknowledged and allayed, albeit using different methods. The following plea can be helpful here: *It is a question of doing one thing, but without overlooking the other!*
*   Very rarely, participants feel a sense of deep embarrassment about expressing, or writing down, direct praise. Tip: emphasise that it is voluntary and recommend that they start with small things.

About *Dr. Frank Taschner*

Born in 1970, education graduate, doctorate in education, trained as systemic consultant, many years in seminar and facilitation work in companies as well as in political and social organisations, academic work at the University of Würzburg, focus of work: facilitation, conducting discussions and negotiations, train-the-trainer.

Address: Von-Schildeck-Strasse 12, PLZ/Ort: 36043 Fulda, Germany
Phone: +49 661 9341434
e-mail: frank.taschner@neuland-partner.de
www.neuland-partner.de

The resource market

Discover unknown resources

Stephanie von Bidder, Switzerland

Reframing unwelcome traits in a fun way: the participants try to sell each other their less attractive characteristics by making them really desirable. This opens up surprisingly different perspectives.

Setting

- 30–45 minutes.
- 4–8 participants.
- Cards or paper (one colour); pens; enough room to walk around; a container for the folded cards; a bell or gong to mark the end of each phase; flip chart.

Context and purpose

One of the core competences in solution focused work is to notice resources in clients and participants. This exercise lets participants practise this in a fun way by looking at traits from different perspectives.

It can be used

- To enhance team work, team development and team coaching.
- To reframe traits and characteristics which may be seen as problematic.
- To help stuck teams get new ideas to get them off the old beaten track.
- As a starter exercise in the morning or after lunch.

Detailed description

The facilitator hands out cards (all in the same colour) and pens.

Sometimes team members draw attention to unwelcome attributes of their colleagues. For example, they may say 'x is always so impatient'. However, another possible way of drawing attention to the same behaviour might be to say 'x is very good at doing whatever that needs to be done right away – he's very efficient'.

Please think of one or more unwelcome tendencies of your own that you would like to change. (Give them some time to do that ...)

Now write down each of the tendencies you have identified on one of the cards. To make sure nobody can read what you have written, please fold the card in half and place it in this container at centre of the room. (Wait till everybody has done this.)

The facilitator mixes the cards well.

Please take one card each and silently read what's written on it.

Now it's time to go to market! In pairs, take it in turns to try to sell each other the attribute on the cards you have picked up. There is only one rule: it is absolutely forbidden to name the skill you're selling. Listen to your partner, what does she want to sell you? Who knows she might have the very skill you're looking for!

After about 5 minutes, ring the bell for the end of the round.

If your partner has convinced you of their offer, take their card, move to another partner and try to sell it to him. You can either use the same description as the one that convinced you or you can come up with a new definition. If you were not convinced, you may pick up another card from the container.

Repeat for a total of 3 or 4 rounds.

Debrief
What did you discover? What was unexpected? What worked? What was a challenge? How did you manage? What was your favourite reframing?

Collect the answers on a flip chart.

Comment

We are often very quick to give negative labels to traits that we don't like. This exercise offers participants an opportunity to formulate new meanings or new perspectives in a fun, easy and safe setting.

Acknowledgement

My thanks go to Gudrun Sickinger (NIK Bremen) who lent me this exercise which has since become one of my favourites. I developed it further by collecting the cards and putting them in a container so that participants do not have sell their own. This reduces pressure and increases the fun.

About **Stephanie von Bidder**

Stephanie von Bidder works as an independent coach and trainer in Basel. Together with Katalin Hankovszky she designs and holds solution focused workshops for companies and institutions. She is a co-trainer at Weiterbildungsforum Basel, Switzerland.

Address: Unt. Batterieweg 73, CH-4059 Basel, Switzerland
Phone/Mobile: + 41 78 809 24 36
e-mail: st.vonbidder@bluewin.ch
www.loesbar.org

CHAPTER 6

The future perfect: developing visions and strategies

This is the focus of SF work: what does the client want? What will life be like when the problem has vanished?

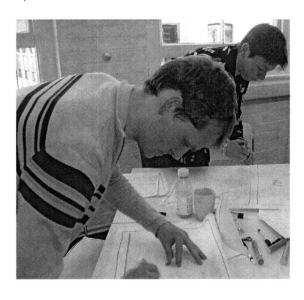

Dream theatre 20XX

Acting out the future perfect

Yasuteru Aoki, Japan

I use this activity in corporate workshops where people want to visualise how change can occur in their job situation. It is a lot of fun and energising. Doing the change when in the acting role and seeing the change when in the audience role can leave strong impressions of possible changes.

Setting

- Preparation 60–90 minutes; scenario presentations 30 minutes; debriefing 5–10 minutes.
- Usually done in groups of 4 in a total group size of 16–24, but can be flexible.
- Each group should have space to prepare in private, so they can conceal the content until the presentation.
- You may decide to give prizes or awards (to everyone!). These may be fake trophies or boxes of chocolates or anything that is suitable for the occasion in the local culture.

Context and Purpose

One of the key elements in SF work is seeing the solution first rather than investigating the current situation. Dream theatre 20XX is a way to humorously bypass the present and physically experience a positive future. It is a good bridge connecting SF knowledge and skills with real life situations. It is an amazing experience, allowing people to act and show their wisdom. Sharing the future happiness is the key and it generates hope and positive energy towards preferred actions.

I use this activity towards the end of a two day solution focused communication workshop when participants are already familiar with SF ideas. This is a good way to let people think about what kind of changes in their communication at work are possible. It also has the effect of generating team spirit among the participants.

Detailed description

Announce the activity in a humorous way:

Welcome to the dream theatre presented by XXX [company name]. Today we are going to enjoy our superb future acted out by our wonderful actors and actresses, yes, you!

The facilitator might also explain how doing this theatre work is helpful for the organisation using the future perfect concept.

Ask participants to form groups of 4 and give themselves a name. It can be something like a real theatre group name for fun.

In their groups, participants discuss communication scenes in their company they want to see improved. No real names should be mentioned. In management training, they often come up with scenes such as giving unclear orders to sub-ordinates, non-collabo-rative conversation with other managers, non-constructive communication in meetings, etc. (5 minutes)

Then they are asked to pick one of the topics and to work on two sketch scenarios: one before and one after SF. *Before SF was intro-duced our managers used to do ...* and *After SF was introduced our way of communicating improved so much that in the year 20XX it looks like this ...* All four people should take a role. One of them could take a narrator's role. (30–45minutes)

When they have prepared their scenarios, the groups are encour-aged to rehearse among themselves. (30minutes)

The theatre: participants sit in theatre styled seating. The facilitator takes the role of 'master of ceremonies' and introduces each group briefly. Each group is given 5 minutes maximum for the performance.

After each group's sketch, while the group is still on the stage, the facilitator comes back and asks the audience to give compliments to them

(Optional) At the end of all the performances, the facilitator can give awards. This can be done very briefly by giving appreciative comments and applause or it can be staged like the Academy Awards in Hollywood.

Now the groups get back together again and reflect on the process of this production and ask questions to themselves like *What did we learn from the development and performance of the sketch and the audience reaction? How could we notice that some of the things in the 'after SF' skit have come true?*

What happens next

The facilitator can ask the participants further future perfect questions like:

- *What other scenes can you imagine in the after SF mode?*
- *If all these scenarios came true, what effect would that have?*

Comments

- I usually set up the preparation for this over the lunch break. I form groups of 4 and let them discuss and develop the scenario over lunch. When they come back from lunch they can immediately go into rehearsals, with no time for an after lunch nap.
- I used to do role plays in corporate communication trainings in a flaw detection and correction mode. I asked a volunteer to come up to the front and do a certain communication sequence with another volunteer. I stopped them whenever I found a serious mistake and asked him to do it again correctly. I used to get comments like *Mr. Aoki, now I know what's wrong with me. Thank you.* I used to think that was a good effect until I realised knowing what is wrong does not necessarily mean knowing how to put it right. For the trainees it is more important to have a direct and concrete image of what is right.
- The quality of acting is not important at all. Usually it is good enough and there is always humour in the room. In the before

SF sketch, a problematic communication is often dealt within a light hearted way like a TV comedy so that people can laugh together. And when they see the after SF sketch, they see heroes and sometimes it can be very moving.

- Usually the contrast between the before and after sketches makes it easy for the audience to get the point. However, this activity can also be done without the before SF skit if you think that would be eliciting too much criticism.
- The points they make may not reflect solution focused ideas perfectly. Be generous in accepting any positive element in the after SF sketch. The important thing is to have a good image of the future at the workplace.

Acknowledgement of sources

I did not read any particular book when developing this exercise, but my earlier experience with Dr. Zerka Moreno in psychodrama helped a lot.

About *Yasuteru Aoki*

– Solution Focus Consulting Inc.

I am a solutionist based in Tokyo. I offer open SF seminars and in-house SF trainings. Individual SF coaching is also available. I was trained as a trainer for self-growth trainings. After being certified as Master-practitioner of NLP in 1991, I established NLP Japan Ltd. As my experience in incorporating SF into my work grew, I became convinced that SF suited my nature well and was full of potential to contribute to organisational situations and started Solution Focus Consulting Inc. in 2005.

Address: 3–21–CN201 Kanda-Nishiki-cho, Chiyoda-ku, Tokyo 101–0054, Japan
Phone/Mobile: +81 (0) 3 5259 8011
e-mail: aoki@solutionfocus.jp
www.solutionfocus.jp

133

The reflecting telescope

Annie Bordeleau M.A, Germany

A reflecting telescope is an optical telescope, which uses a combination of curved or plane mirrors to reflect light and form an image. It has higher magnifying power than the lenses telescope and helps astronomers detect invisible light. This exercise also enables the participants to look into mirrors to detect and form images of their future. Each question asked magnifies and focuses on little changes that will occur after the workshop.

Setting

- Allow 20 to 30 minutes for this exercise.
- Ideal for groups of 6–16 participants.
- You need a large enough area to move about easily.
- SF questions on cards (see template).
- A bell or other signal.

Context and purpose

The aim of this activity is to enable each participant to begin with the end in sight by exploring what will be different after the desired change has occurred. It also challenges the group or team members to think in a more solution focused way.

There are many uses for the Reflecting Telescope:

- It is an excellent ice-breaker encouraging a lot of interaction between the group members.
- It can prepare the group for a goal setting session.
- It is ideal after a team has defined the future perfect, so that each individual can see how their own behaviour will change.
- It can also be used as a closing activity to facilitate the transfer of learning to the workplace.

134

Detailed description

1. Create a large enough space in the room to make a circle with all of the participants.
2. Next, ask half the group to form a circle in the middle, facing outwards. These are the mirrors.
3. The mirrors receive a solution focused question (see template) written on a small card.
4. The other half of the participants are asked to stand in front of a mirror, in other words in front of a person holding a card.

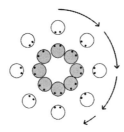

5. The facilitator explains the activity with the following 3 points:
   - *You now have the opportunity to look through the reflecting telescope and see your future in focus. What do you see?*
   - *The mirrors will ask you a question when the starting signal is given. The answers to these questions allow you to see more clearly. The mirrors listen attentively and can ask further questions or What else? to help you focus even more on the little details that make a difference.*
   - *After one and a half minutes, a rotation signal will be given. The outer circle will move clockwise to the next mirror and answer their question.*
6. Before starting the exercise, the facilitator can give an example and ask the group to practise one rotation.
7. Once the outside circle has rotated completely around the inside circle, the mirrors switch places with the outer circle.
8. The activity stops after two full rotations.

Suggested Questions (Template)

These are a few examples of questions the mirrors could ask to help the participants focus on the desired change and the impact of this change on their environment.

Suppose you stopped doing what isn't working, what would you be doing instead?
What's the first sign you will notice, that tells you that things are changing?
What will be the advantages of these little changes for you?
Who will be the first person to notice that something has changed?
How will others react if this change occurs?
How will you know that coming here was useful for you?
If I were a spider living on your wall, what little differences would I notice?
Suppose you were doing things differently, what would you want others to notice?

What happens next

If this exercise is used at the beginning of a workshop, as an ice-breaker, the next step could be to ask the participants to write down on cards one or two specific actions they would like to do after this workshop and present them to the group: *This workshop will have been useful for me, if at the end I can ...*

If it is used in the middle of a workshop or team coaching, the next step could be a scaling exercise.

If it is used as a closing exercise, it might be a good idea to give the participants time to write some personal notes and reflect on their answers before they leave.

Comments

- If the group is a team, they will be able to support each other later when implementing the change, as they will have heard what to look out for.
- Each participant could focus on a personal concern or problem during this exercise. In a short period of time, they might detect a little light they hadn't seen before.

- This exercise is also energising because everyone is active and interacting at the same time.

About *Annie Bordeleau*

Annie Bordeleau is a Communication Skills Trainer and a Solution Focused Coach. She specialises in enhancing the efficiency of communication processes in international companies. Her current interests include team coaching international project teams which need to implement change and tailor-made and interactive communication skills seminars. She is Canadian and speaks English and French as well as fluent German and Spanish.

Address: Querstr. 10, 48155 Münster, Germany
Phone/Mobile: + 49 (0)177 235 32 56
e-mail: annie@bordeleau.de
www.bordeleau.de

Wish soup

A playful recipe for success

Dominik Godat, Switzerland

Wish soup is a playful activity, where the participants add the ingredients (goals and wishes) and cook the soup together. If desired the soup can be refined, flavoured or garnished (e.g. with resources, things that already work, change of perspectives and next steps). Thus the participants can creatively and playfully add their own ideas. The picture of the desired menu gives the participants an overview of their own goals, resources, and possible solutions.

Setting

- Time needed: 30 minutes to several hours, depending on the chosen version.
- Optimal number of participants: 4–6 people for groups with common goals, 4–15 people for groups with individual goals.
- Flip chart paper, pens, post-it notes or other white paper cards for every participant, adhesive tape, flip chart with work instructions.
- Plenty of space to write on the flip chart paper and post-it notes, to hang the flip charts on the wall and to walk around and have a look at the results.
- Flip charts, one with the instructions and another with drawings of the plate, the silverware, the glass and the dessert bowl.
- A big pot and stirring spoon.

Context and purpose

This method can be used to explore the wishes and goals of the participants or, in an extended version, as the main part of a workshop. It can be applied with teams with common goals or with groups with individual objectives.

138

The aim is to explore the wishes and goals (and in extended versions the resources, things that already work well and possible solutions) playfully and to illustrate them in a way that is figurative and easy to remember. The chosen metaphor of cooking is very useful, because there are lots of things that cooking and solution focused work have in common (e.g. questions like *What do I want …? What resources do I have to reach this goal? What should it look and taste like at the end to make it worthwhile?*) as well as the fun of trying it out and refining it.

In addition, the picture helps the participants to remember the results of the workshop in their everyday life.

Detailed description

The activity starts with a short introduction. For this the facilitator needs two flip charts. On the first he draws a plate from an aerial view, with a fork on the left side of the plate and a spoon, a glass and a dessert bowl on the right side. The step by step procedure is written out on the second flip chart. In addition he hands out some post-it notes or white paper cards and pens.

Procedure with teams with a common goal
The facilitator needs a big cooking pot and a stirring spoon on a table. The facilitator now plays the role of a cook and could wear a chef's cap and uniform.

First we need the ingredients of the soup: the goals and wishes of the team.

The facilitator starts with questions like:
What should happen today in this workshop to make it useful and worthwhile for you? What's your goal? What would you like to reach? What will you tell me in a year's time about your successes? What will make you especially proud? etc.

The participants write their answers on the post-it notes and throw them into the cooking pot. The facilitator stirs, takes out the post-it notes, reads them aloud, and sticks them on the plate on the flip chart. It is useful to ask the group how to arrange them in clusters.

If this activity is used just to explore the wishes and goals of the participants, the cooking is now finished and the facilitator can go on with additional solution focused processes.

However, the soup can be developed with resources and things that already work well by asking the following questions:

What resources helpful in reaching the goal has the team already got? What resources do the individual members of the team have? What resources make your team special? What could you do to help the team succeed? What have you already done that was useful? What works already well? etc.

As before, the participants write the answers on post-it notes and throw them into the cooking pot. The facilitator stirs, reads the post-its and sticks them on the silverware.

Now you could add some change of perspective to your soup (the answers could be stuck on the picture of the glass) with the following questions:

How will your clients realise that you have reached your goal? How will your employees realise it? How will the members of the team or yourself realise it? etc.

To enrich your soup with next steps, you could ask question like *What would be a next useful step on your way to your goal? What will your next step after this workshop be? What would be an action that your clients would realise for sure? etc.*

The answers to these questions could be stuck on the picture of the dessert bowl.

Procedure with groups with individual goals

If the members of the workshop group have their own individual goals, every participant cooks his own soup. For this he needs a flip chart of his own where he can draw his plate, silverware, glass and dessert bowl. Because the participants are their own cooks, the facilitator is more like a choirmaster who moderates the exercise with questions. After the cooking, it is nice to hang up the flip chart papers on the wall, so that the participants can have a look at the other results, comment on them or if desired complement them.

Step by step overview

1. Introduction and preparation of the kitchen (cooking pot, stirring spoon, flip chart with the picture of a plate, silverware, glass and dessert bowl).
2. Questions exploring wishes and goals.
3. The participants answer the questions.

4. Reading the answers and sticking them on the plate.
5. Questions exploring resources and things that work well.
6. The participants answer the questions.
7. Reading the answers and sticking them on the silverware.
8. Questions exploring change of perspectives.
9. The participants answer the questions.
10. Reading the answers and sticking them on the glass.
11. Questions exploring the next steps.
12. The participants answer the questions.
13. Reading the answers and sticking them on the dessert bowl.
14. If desired more questions.

What happens next

If the soup is only used to explore the goals and wishes, the facilitator can go on with additional solution focused processes. When it is the main part of the workshop, I recommend focusing next on the participants' confidence in reaching their goals, next steps, etc. This way you can build a bridge from the workshop into their normal everyday life.

Comments

• The similarities between cooking and solution focused work have amazed me for quite a while and therefore I came up with the idea to find a way to illustrate the results of a workshop metaphorically. This way it is easier for the facilitator to focus on goals, wishes, resources, things that already work well, different perspectives and next steps. It also seems to be easier for the participants to get involved with a solution focus and cook their future playfully.
• The facilitator can compliment and expand the wish soup as he likes (e.g. with questions to increase the confidence of the participants, to explore positive exceptions in the past, miracles, etc.).
• Thanks to the figurative and playful approach, the illustration of their desired future is very memorable and if they take the picture away it helps to remind them.
• With teams with common goals, the activity works best when every member of the group is open to the whole variety of

possible goals, wishes and next steps and when there is little or no hierarchy within the group. If there is a strong hierarchy or much disagreement on possible goals, this intervention is not the right one.

Acknowledgement of sources

I developed this method, inspired by several playful workshops, e.g. at the SOLWorld Conference in Interlaken and the discovery of the similarities between cooking and solution focused work.

About **Dominik Godat**

As an economist, HR specialist and founder of Godat Coaching, Dominik Godat invented Random Coaching in 2006. He works mainly in Switzerland as a coach with profit and non-profit organisations helping them to implement solution focused management ideas. He also trains and coaches individuals, managers and teams who are looking for success in their private and business lives.

Address: Hechtliacker 44, 4053 Basel, Switzerland
Phone/Mobile: +41 76 420 19 18
e-mail: coaching@godat.ch
www.godat.ch

Once upon a solution

Solution focused story spine

Michael Goran, Canada.

The story spine is a fast, collaborative and equal-opportunity mechanism to quickly bring any team or group into close alignment around a topic. Sometimes, before the solution focused work can begin, it is necessary to obtain a common frame of reference or starting point. The story spine, a group story construction exercise, is a fun and creative method for eliciting commonality and preparing a team to achieve their desired solution more quickly.

Setting

- Setup: 5–10 minutes; Practice Round: 5 minutes; Execution Round: 10 minutes; Debrief: 30 minutes max. (you may choose to debrief for less time).
- Suitable for small to medium sized groups, from 4–15 people. Larger groups can be accommodated by breaking up the large story (i.e. a more complex problem) into 'chapters'.
- One chair for each participant.
- At least two flip charts, with the Story Spine Structure written on it.

Context and purpose

Story spine is excellent where there are factions with differing agendas (for example management and line workers, marketing and sales). It can accelerate solution focused work by helping participants paint a richer picture of their group's future perfect. It can be used as an alternative or adjunct to the Miracle Question.

For team building, story spine promotes a very democratic atmosphere, allowing each participant to make an individual contribution to the overall story. This can be especially useful for those whose voices are not often heard, or even dismissed outright in group settings. In this way, it supports the notion of interactional behaviour, since no one person can influence the story unduly, thus making everyone responsible for the solution. It can also be used to crystallise the vision of what the starting point for the solution is to be, therefore also fulfilling the need to uncover who is the customer and for what? Story spine can be used by a senior management team as a quick thumbnail of a company's vision or mission, using as many iterations as required (or tolerable) to arrive at the final draft.

Detailed description

The story spine is best deployed by presenting the structure first, plugging in an example from literature, and then using an example from current events (for example the day's news). Introduction and exemplification twice make it faster for the group to incorporate the structure and work within it.

Setup:
I'm going to introduce you to a very quick way to get everyone on the same page, and perhaps even reach a solution. I have a curious question first: What does a fairy tale have in common with a business case? ... They both follow a story structure. Every story ever told follows a structure called the story spine.

THE FOLLOWING IS WRITTEN VERBATIM, IN ADVANCE, ON A FLIP CHART

STORY SPINE
ONCE UPON A TIME ...
AND EVERY DAY ...
UNTIL ONE DAY ...
BECAUSE OF THAT ...
BECAUSE OF THAT ...
BECAUSE OF THAT ...
UNTIL FINALLY ...
AND EVER SINCE ...

Facilitator's briefing to the group

Tell the group
We are going to tell a story, your story, using this structure.
We will go in order, around the group, so that each person gets their turn.
When your turn comes, use the next appropriate phrase in the sequence to begin your sentence.

Example: the facilitator can use this story, or make up one of their own. The story can be written down in advance, or made up on the spot, if the facilitator has good improvisation skills.

Person 1 might say: Once upon a time, there was a small company named Apple Computer.

Person 2 might say: And every day, while everyone in the world was using computers with long, complicated text instructions, the Apple people were busy trying to simplify the way people used their computers.

Person 3 might say: Until one day, the Apple people borrowed an idea for a computer interface that used a mouse, and pull-down menus instead of typing long, cryptic command lines to get the computer to do things.

Person 4 might say: Because of that, the Apple people started selling the Macintosh computer, which revolutionised the personal computer industry.

Person 5 might say: Because of that, they started to outsell IBM, a big established company.

Person 6 might say: Because of that, this sales activity caught the attention of Microsoft, who was frightened of the new, visual, window-based computer interface.

Person 7 might say: Because of that, Microsoft developed Windows as their new operating system.

Person 8 might say: Until finally, Windows started outselling Macintosh all around the world.
Return to Person 1, who might say: And ever since, the Macintosh has been far behind Windows in computer sales.

Additional ground rules

A participant may pass when their turn comes, but only once. Encourage them not to put pressure on themselves to be clever or funny when their turn comes, but simply to add the next logical piece of the story, especially if it sounds or feels boring. Boring is perfectly OK in this context. Trying to be too creative will actually grind the story and the exercise to a halt.

Debrief

Here are some suggested debriefing questions. This is by no means an exhaustive list; feel free to add your own, as long as they support a collaborative conclusion.

* *How did you feel when your turn came?*
* *When this worked well, what was happening?*
* *How did you make it work, even just a little?*
* *Did you feel obliged to make a 'big' contribution or were you okay with a 'small' contribution when your turn came?*
* *How does it feel to tell a collective story in this way?*

Add some questions about the story: what does it say about where we are going?

What happens next

Afterwards, participants can be encouraged to write their own individual stories describing their future perfect for the team, presenting them back to the group.

Comments

* This team storytelling activity emphasises the solution focus principles of Go slow (small steps ultimately lead to big results) and the Action (ie: the story) arises out of the interaction of story elements.

146

- This activity is a non-threatening way to make sure everyone gets a voice in creating the story, and levels the playing field, since each person is limited to one sentence at a time. The quiet people will get a chance to speak without being judged and the more dominant personalities can be reined in by the structure.
- What is often surprising during this activity is how quickly people realise that no single contribution is more important than another, and that in order to have any success at all, people have to build on each other's ideas to make the story come out sensibly.
- It takes several rounds to get people to the point of creative solutions to their team issues, but the rounds pass quickly, and the more iterations of the story, the quicker progress is made.
- Teams can keep the parts that work from each round and agree on what needs to happen in each successive round to sharpen their focus on the solution.

Acknowledgements

Several years ago, Jim Duvall of Brief Therapy Training Centre in Toronto, realised that solution focus and improvisation are near mirror images of each other in form and function, in that the training principles follow very close paths. He said improvisation is an excellent, isomorphic training mechanism for teaching and training solutions focused practitioners.

I first saw this used in a team setting over 10 years ago, by Kat Koppet, an improv teacher from the USA. Its exact origin is unknown, but it is lifted from improvisational performer training, where it is used to teach or reinforce story structure so that improvisers can collaboratively tell a story that has an unknown or uncertain outcome (which is the point of all improvisation).

Further Reading

Impro (Keith Johnstone); *Impro for Storytellers* (Johnstone); *The Artist's Way* (Julia Cameron)

About *Michael Goran – CorpJesters*

CorpJesters® invigorates your communications & creative problem solving abilities by focusing on solutions – not problems. We train individuals, teams and organisations to think on their feet and implement solutions that they know work well. Coupling this with coaching in empathic listening skills results in a team that understands the issues, composes their own answers and gets the job done.

Address: 41 Seymour Avenue, Toronto, Ontario M4J 3T3, Canada
Phone/Mobile: +1 416 712 9196
e-mail: mike@corpjesters.com
http://www.corpjesters.com

A round trip to the future

Packing your resource suitcase

Michael Hjerth, Sweden

The round trip ticket helps people travel to a preferred future, find resources and experiences there, and then travel back with all the resources and experiences packed in an imaginary suitcase.

Setting

The round trip takes about 30 minutes. No debriefing is necessary, but it can be a good idea to take a break or a stretch afterwards.

There is no limit to the number of people who can be involved in the activity. For maximum effect, the group should be 12 people or more, seated at round tables with 5–10 people at each table. If there's room, it can easily be done with a thousand people. No equipment is needed, but evocative PowerPoint slides can be used to set a mood of travelling.

Context and purpose

The activity is fantastic towards the end of large group meetings, such as conferences, but works equally well in situations where we are interested in inspiring, motivating and creating a resource focused atmosphere with many people at the same time. I have used it mainly towards the end of an event, but I can easily imagine it used at many other times in an event such as a planning meeting, team building or training, or anywhere where your work involves building resources of all kinds.

The round trip to the future creates a sense of possibility for individuals as well as a sense of common achievement. It helps people experience what resources and experiences a preferred future will bring them. In general, people who have done this activity feel pumped up with possibility, relaxed and ready to go. If done at the end, it helps bring about an open closure, that is, an end which is felt as a new beginning

Detailed description

Preparation
Set up the room with round tables, or, if no tables are available, in circles of chairs. If you like using PowerPoint slides, good evocative images can be used to enhance the sense of traveling. Images of trains, stations, suitcases etc. are particularly useful.

Step by step procedure and suggested instructions
1. Tell the group that you are inviting them to take a trip to the future and back. They will take a suitcase with them on the journey. Ask them to imagine what their suitcase looks like. Is it big, small? What colour? What material?
2. Ask participants to stand up.
3. Say *We are going to have a guided trip to the future. In a while I will ask you to turn to your left and take twelve steps, one at a time, one for each month. And when you have taken 12 steps you will be back at your chair, one year in the future, and sit down there.*
4. Guide the people to move around the table, one full circle, one step at the time:
   So let's take the first step, now we have gone from 12th of October to the 12th of November. The autumn is arriving, some of the trees have already beautiful colours, the air is fresh like only early autumns can be.
   Take another step: the 12th of December. Christmas is approaching, a lot to do, but the anticipation of the holidays make it worth it, soon a new year with new possibilities, Christmas: parties, children laughing, presents, good food, a lot of food. Don't forget to buy champagne and cigars for New Year's Eve.
   Take another step [and while they are taking it say: *Happy New Year we just passed New Year's Eve: cheers*] *... and 12th of January. Wintertime, it might be snow, beautiful white, glistening snow ...*

[Continue to guide people, a step/month at a time until we are back at today's date, one year ahead]

We are now at 12th of October next year. Please sit down.

5. Welcome people to the future
   Welcome back! Good to see you here again. Take a good stretch, and a few deep breaths after the long journey ... make yourself comfortable and look around the room ...
   It has been a while, it was one year ago that we were sitting in this very room, having such a good and creative time, thinking about our futures. And now we are back here, how time flies! I heard rumours that things have been going well for you ... that there have been a lot of developments, you've had lots of success ... have achieved many things ... successfully met many challenges ... developed new skills, made new contacts, built new networks. I'm sure you wonder what the others have been up to, too. Why don't we catch up by talking to each other at the tables: what good experiences do you have now that you didn't have a year ago? What resources do you have now? What have you developed? What new networks have you developed? New contacts and collaborators? New skills? New ways of working? Talk to each other about this for a few minutes [The groups can be smaller, 2–3, persons or the whole table, whichever you prefer] *Oh, and by the way, do you have your suitcase with you? I just wanted to make sure. Please catch up now!*
6. Invite people to silently gather their new experiences, skills and contacts and pack them in the suitcase.
   Now please bring out your suitcase. You can close your eyes if you want to see it more clearly ... In the suitcase pack all your new experiences, skills, achievements, new contacts, resources. Pack them carefully since you will be taking them on a trip. [Continue talking to help people pack. Use a slow, clear voice with lots of pauses, to help imagery.] *Now that your suitcase is packed, close it carefully ... now store your suitcase somewhere in your body where it can be kept safe and easily accessed. It can be anywhere that feels right, the belly, the left hand, the heart, a finger, the back of the head, even the knee or a toe, anywhere that feels right to you ... Remember it should be safely stored and easily accessible in this part of your body.*

7. Take the trip back to now.
   Now, that the suitcase is safely stored, please stand up, we are going to travel back. Now, I'm going to guide you back a year in time. Turn to the right please. This time, we are taking twelve steps in the opposite direction by going backwards. [Guide them month by month, but more briefly this time, just a phrase or even just the date is enough]
   Now we are back at the 12th October this year, please sit down. Take a stretch and a few deep breaths ... Welcome back! Wow, what a journey! Would you please check that the suitcase is still there? Can you find it?

8. Suggest that the suitcase of resources can be available anytime people need it, in times of challenge, confusion, or whenever a boost of resources and possibilities is needed.
   I'm glad you have the suitcase safe and accessible. That suitcase will always be there for you anytime you need it – in times of challenge or confusion, when you need a boost of resources, when you need to remember what is possible or simply when you want to feel good for a moment.

9. End and transition. It is a good idea to have a stretch or coffee-break after this activity.
   After a lovely journey like this, some refreshments cannot be wrong! So, there is coffee and fruit available outside. And we meet here again in 15 minutes.

What happens next

It is usually a good idea to take a stretch or a coffee-break after this activity to let the conversations continue informally. This activity works best towards the end of an event, and might be followed by activities designed to make concrete plans or to develop next steps or by activities that deepen commitment to change, such as the scaling party described in Chapter 9.

Comments

I developed this technique together with Christer Eliésersson as a part of the closing process for a conference on solution focused work with unemployment in 2006. We were looking for something that could be done with about 200 people sitting at round tables, something that would flow from and utilise the natural round table converstion, but from a future perfect perspective. I had been working for a while on different concepts of time/space shifts, wanting to fit the miracle question concept to a variety of contexts. From my experience using the scaling-party I knew that moving your body can assist in time/space shifting. But how to make this happen with 200 people at the same time was a problem, unless we re-arranged the room. After some brainstorming, the solution was obvious: we let people move in a circle, like a spiral, and back again. This made it possible for people to spiral walk to the same spot, in a different possible future state. From the actual to the possible and back again, all without leaving the table.

The next step was to figure out a metaphor to help people remember their learning. And since the general metaphor was travelling, a suitcase was the obvious choice. I got the idea of storing the suitcase somewhere in the body from hypnotic techniques.

The round trip exercise has quite a lot in common with the miracle question in SF therapy. It utilises trance-like techniques but without any real trance-work. Central to my way of viewing solution focused work is the concept of the actual and the possible. I suggest there are two domains of human reality: the actual (the real) and the possible (what *could* be real). Problems are always real: they are there, they are facts. The miracle question invites people to consider an alternative possible reality: this is a possibility and not just imagined. The miracle in the miracle questions is something that could happen. To illustrate: when children play, they seem to pretend to be a prince or a princess, but they are not really a pretend prince. They are a possible prince: they know they are not a real prince, but neither are they just a boy pretending to be a prince. The child is, in a very real sense, a possible prince. They are both a child *and* a prince. In brief: we are talking about two domains of reality: the actual (the real) and the possible (what *could* be real). Growing up, we lose much of our ability to think and be in possibility states. Education is partly to blame for this: children are taught that there are right and wrong ways of doing things. They are taught how things are, not necessarily how they *could* be. Thus, a lot of our creativity is blunted. Fortunately many schools are now starting to teach creativity, inspired by accelerated learning and people like Edward de Bono.

One thing that is really attractive to me in SF is how we use a variety of tools to invite people to think in terms of possibility, to rekindle the child's natural way of exploring what could be. All questions starting with *suppose* do this. For example *Suppose this is a successful meeting, what would be different when we leave the meeting?* or *Suppose you were one step up the scale, what would you be doing then that you are not doing now?* Questions like these invite people to leave the actual for the possible for a moment, and then let the possible influence the actual. To me, the miracle question, as stunningly elegant and efficient as it is, might just be the beginning of a range of time/space shifting techniques. Theatre techniques where people act out a possible reality and the solution focused constellations techniques of Matthias Varga and Insa Sparrer are really interesting new developments in this area.

Acknowledgements

I thank Christer Eliésersson for co-developing this technique with me and for being such a wonderful co-host for the conference where we used it for the first time.

About *Michael Hjerth*

– SolutionWork

Michael Hjerth was born in Stockholm 1960. After a career as a musician and music teacher he studied psychology and philosophy at the University of Lund Sweden and graduated in 1991. Michael developed the PLUS-model of solution focus and Micro-tools: techniques to integrate SF-practice in the fast-paced work life. He has been influenced not only by philosophy and language, but also by research evolutionary theory, neuroscience and cognitive science.

In Sweden, Michael is highly sought after and well known for his combination of clear philosophy, scientific grounding and minimalistic practicality.

He is active internationally and has appeared in conferences in many European countries. He was the secretary of the European Brief Therapy Association and is on the steering group of Solutions in Organisations Linkup.

Address: Segelflygsgatan 39, 128 33 Skarpnäck, Sweden
Phone/Mobile: +46-703258837
e-mail: michael@solutionwork.se
www.solutionwork.se (Swedish)
www.openchanges.com (English)

Future perfect: documentary

Paul Z Jackson, United Kingdom

This is a lively and memorable way for a team to think about, articulate and capture their collective Future Perfect.

Setting

- Allow 30–40 minutes for the drawing phase, and up to 30 for the presentations and discussion.
- This is suitable for a group of 4 or multiple groups each with up to 6 members.
- Paper and pens for the storyboard.
- Tables for making the drawings.
- Wall space to display the results.

Context and purpose

Setting a direction is an important part of solutions focused work. I use this activity when a team or group is ready to contemplate and articulate their joint Future Perfect. Put another way, they get to describe 10 on their scale or to picture their answer to the miracle question.

The team does not need to know anything about or have any interest in SF.

Detailed description

Form the teams, creating groups of between 4–6 people. Hand out the briefing note to each group. Make sure that everyone has the materials that they need. It can help to read the briefing aloud, to find out if anyone has any questions. You might also show an example of a storyboard or a frame. Tell them to make twice as many frames as the number of people in their group – so 5 people make 10 frames.

The date of the documentary can be either Tomorrow (that is to say the day after the miracle), three months from now or some other specified time in the future that is appropriate for the team.

Briefing
You are a member of a documentary production team. We are in the early stages of the research phase for a new documentary about an amazingly successful team – you!

We last visited them in – insert current date – , and found out a lot about them. Since then we have heard that they have gone from strength to strength.

Our first task is to find out what this teamwork means in terms that we can show to our viewers? We want to gather a storyboard for the documentary.

Everything must be visible or audible, tangible evidence to illustrate our themes. You can caption pictures, or use speech bubbles for dialogue.

Choose frames which will reveal to the audience:

- *who these people are and what they are here for*
- *cameos of the key processes with which they are involved, and why are they the important ones. (We won't have time to cover everything, so some prioritisation here please.)*
- *things that are unique to this team, that you wouldn't necessarily see in other industries, on other sites or in other teams*

The result will be a storyboard – a series of pictures with captions – which forms the basis for the documentary about this team illustrating its excellence in working as a team to achieve its objectives in the style they want.

Example of a storyboard created by a previous client:

When the storyboards are complete, invite the groups to display their storyboards in the room and then describe the outputs to the other teams (or to the facilitator if there is only one group).

What happens next

The activity can either stand alone, or can lead on to further discussion of the future perfect and the small actions that might be taken towards it.

Comments

- This activity developed as a very collaborative way to get groups to articulate a future perfect. The energy is highly creative, and seems to take people away from the arguments that can develop if there is a verbal description of a future perfect. It also creates a tangible and visible record of the work which can be referred to later during a workshop, or even revisited after several months.
- Sometimes I invite the group to present the storyboard as a 'Day in the life'. I have also used a variation where they create a newspaper page, with pictures and headlines illustrating the future perfect achievements of the group.
- You can ensure a fuller equality in the activity by inviting each participant to be the star of one of the picture frames.

Acknowledgement of sources

Original activity designed by Paul Z Jackson, The Solutions Focus

Book reference:

Paul Z Jackson and Mark McKergow, *The Solutions Focus: Making Coaching and Change SIMPLE*, Nicholas Brealey, 2007

About **Paul Z Jackson**

– The Solutions Focus

PAUL Z JACKSON is an inspirational consultant, coach and facilitator, who devises and runs training courses and development programmes in strategy, leadership, teamwork, creativity and innovation. His expertise in improvisation, accelerated learning and the solutions focus approach has attracted corporate public clients worldwide. Paul is a co-founder of both SOLWORLD and the Applied Improvisation Network.

Address: 34a Clarence Road, St Albans, AL1 4NG, UK
Phone/Mobile: + 44 7973 953586
e-mail: paul@thesolutionsfocus.co.uk
www.thesolutionsfocus.co.uk

Metaphor magic

Working with metaphors as representations of present and future situations

Loraine Kennedy, UK and Lina Skantze, Sweden

Metaphor magic is a fantastic activity early on in a workshop, specifically during change processes. The application and contexts can be wide reaching. Participants' energy and the imagery they evoke can be harnessed and developed throughout the rest of the workshop. Taken back into the workplace, the results of this activity provide common ground, a platform for future discussions as the metaphors become code words for the group – one word gives access to the whole concept. Explanations rarely give the same clarity as quickly and as easily. The image or perception evoked by a metaphor is explicit and concrete.

Setting

This exercise works with any number so long as there is enough space for quiet work in groups of 2 or 3. It typically takes between 30 minutes and an hour. For larger groups it can take longer, with a break suggested between parts 3 and 4. Time for feedback and discussion in the main group varies from 10 to 30 minutes depending on the number of groups, the topic and the link to the workshop and its main purpose. Usually there is enough material to keep going for longer if one wishes.

You will need sheets of paper, ideally pages from a flip chart (especially if the visual representations are to be displayed) and coloured pens/pencils.

160

Context and purpose

Working with metaphors can be an excellent way to introduce a change process into an organisation or team and to involve team members in designing and engaging in a different future. Participants often find metaphors to be useful as they are easy to adapt, they communicate ideas that are easily grasped and they complement reason and cognition. Early on in a change process the Metaphor magic activity can free participants to explore and express their conceptions of the present and of a future scenario. The activity offers an opportunity to discover what is currently working well and should continue, as well as identifying what needs to be different. A metaphoric symbol for the future scenario can help to construct hope, give direction and create effective change.

A fundamental principle of SF work is leaving the problem in the past and creating a successful future. This activity, in which participants create a metaphor of their perfect future, enables them to explore and play with creative ideas at an imaginative level. Freed from the constraints of reality, they discover new insights and perspectives and open up new ways of dealing with issues. Participants typically experience a powerful emotional attachment to their metaphor which propels them to the future.

It is recognised that giving something up, or loss, is part of change. Focus during change processes is often on the losses and their effects. By shifting the focus of attention to the future with freedom to create their own positive attributes and outcomes, participants share a sense of ownership in the new world and hence work towards this. At the same time they discover ways to take the valuable resources and things that currently work well into the new future as they shape it. Working with metaphors – which operate at a different level to reality – removes inhibiting or constraining factors and can be a fun, enlightening, empowering and also deeply meaningful experience.

This activity can be used early on in a workshop in order to stimulate creativity and help participants to share perspectives about the present and the future. The language, images and symbols that are created and generated during this activity are useful in any processes or activities that follow.

161

Detailed description

Part 1 (5 minutes)
Introduce the idea of metaphors, explaining how people can think by storing information in the form of images and pictures in our minds. By creating and exploring metaphors we can discover new insights and are challenged to think and perceive things differently. This leads to a more compelling experience than using words which are less powerful. You can explain that using metaphors is a light-hearted way to look at things differently.

Describe how the participants will work: in pairs, small groups or larger teams.

Part 2 (10 to 15 minutes)
Give the instructions and explain that the responses can be in words, drawings or other visual representations. We suggest this to be written on a flip chart or in a handout:

Select an image or metaphor that represents the current situation (for example how the team currently delivers a service or how the organisation is perceived by the participants). What are its characteristics?

Give 10 to 15 minutes to find an appropriate metaphor for the present situation and to discuss what it suggests. Encourage participants to draw or represent their metaphor.

Stop the groups when they all seem to have found a metaphor and had some discussion about its characteristics.

Part 3 (15 to 20 minutes)
Instruct the participants to make a new metaphor for the future scenario. They could also choose to use the same metaphor and develop or alter it.

From the example above *How might your customers want to experience the service 12 months from now?* or *What will our organisation look like when we have managed this change?*

Tell participants you want to discover what has stayed the same and what will have changed.

Solution focused questions can be written on a flip chart or provided in handouts as a framework for the discussion. Examples:

• *Describe the metaphor and its characteristics*

- *What is happening around it?*
- *What does it make you think and feel?*
- *What is important about the metaphor?*
- *What is working well currently with this metaphor?*
- *What else is working well with it?*
- *Who has helped with current successes?*
- *What does the metaphor need to work well?*
- *Which are the things you would like to see changed?*
- *What are the positive benefits of this?*
- *Who will benefit from those changes?*
- *What difference will the changes make?*
- *What else is there about that metaphor that will help you create a positive future?*

Part 4 (10 to 20 minutes)

After 15 to 20 minutes ask the groups to reconvene into the larger gathering and if appropriate, post visuals of the metaphors onto a wall and allow a few moments for viewing.

Ask some of the groups to present and explain their first and second metaphors and to describe the changes that took place as they projected into the future.

Ask clarifying questions and facilitate discussion on the issues raised by each image.

Follow this by extracting common elements and differences from each group.

Conclude with individual comment on what participants have experienced and what positive learning they will take with them into the future as it unfolds.

Finally, in order to determine concrete steps forward in the change process, we suggest a scaling exercise (preferably walking – see for example the Scaling Walk by Paul Z Jackson in Chapter 7 of this book) where participants indicate on a scale from 1 to 10 how close they are to the future metaphor. What is already happening that brings them up to the point they have chosen on the scale, and what would a next step be? Encourage them to visit point 10 on the scale and experience what it is like being there.

What happens next

The power of metaphors remain vivid and can be invoked quickly long after words and discussions have been forgotten. The images can be a reference point and a valuable resource back at the work place. Images can be placed on walls or work-stations or referred to in team meetings. They can become shorthand for reminding people of how they expect things to be.

The metaphors can be used as a platform or starting point for follow-on discussions or workshops. By reviewing where are we now with another scaling exercise, participants are able to assess progress towards change.

Comments

Working with metaphors is common, for instance in Milton Erickson's work (Rosen, 1982). We have found working with metaphors with individuals who wish to change a highly useful process. Our work with individuals is the root of this activity. We put our heads together and designed an activity that could involve whole groups, allowing the participants to be creative and realistic at the same time.

Metaphors give wings to creativity when forming images of the future and become code words for the group – one word gives access to the whole concept. Explanations rarely give the same clarity as quickly and as easily – the image or perception is explicit and direct. The solution focused questions contribute to making the exercise resource oriented and hopeful.

We have noticed that people often use metaphors when they describe something. Neuropsychology shows that people do not only think in words but also in pictures and symbols. Metaphors are a simple and powerful way of summarising and interpreting a situation in its context. We have noticed that people are filled with enthusiasm and enjoy working in this way: forming and talking about metaphors. Metaphors naturally inspire an explorative approach to forming and expressing solutions which enhances the chance of finding useful solutions.

Acknowledgement of sources

Rosen, S. My voice will go with you. The teachings and tales of Milton H. Erickson. New York: Norton (1982)

For scaling exercises, see for instance Jackson, P.Z. & McKergow, M. *The Solutions Focus, the Simple Way to Positive Change.* London and Maine: Nicholas Brealey Publishing (2002)

About **Loraine Kennedy**

– LK Developing People

Loraine provides coaching, training, workshops, and facilitates learning and events primarily in the UK public sector and with small businesses. Her experience as a senior operational manager and, latterly, HR consultant, means she brings a wealth of practical expertise to her activities. Regarded as an energising trainer, she is seen as both compassionate and pragmatic when working with clients towards solutions in both their life and business contexts.

Address: 18 Claremont Road, Marlow, SL7 1BW, UK
Phone/Mobile: + 44 7967 353 638
e-mail: loraine@lkdevelopingpeople.co.uk
www.lkdevelopingpeople.co.uk

& Lina Skantze, MBA

– ManAge AB

Lina is a senior executive with a broad range of international experience, focused on leadership and organisation, marketing and business evaluations. Her experience has brought a strong understanding of company management and board activities. Presently, she is working as a presenter and independent consultant, running workshops on leadership and change, as well as management coaching and training.

Address: Jungfrugatan 22, 114 44 Stockholm, Sweden
Phone/Mobile: + 46 704 337071
e-mail: Lina.skantze@man-age.se
www.man-age.se

Looking back to the future

Hans-Peter Korn, Switzerland

Looking back to the future serves to discover ideas for solutions, ways towards solutions and new points of view. The activity can be used in any kind of workshop, especially those held to create visions, to find ideas for new products and services and to process plans for complex projects. The scenic simulation methods foster engagement, spontaneity and creativity in the participants.

Setting

- 20 to 90 minutes depending on the number of roles and which version you are using.
- Suitable for groups from 4 to 25 people. Larger groups should be split and asked to deal with different sub-topics or to take different roles.
- You need some pinboards for the notes and a room with enough space.

Context and purpose

This process is helpful when teams have to come up with ideas to help their clients. It produces a lot of ideas from different points of view which serve as a basis for more detailed conceptual work to follow.

By looking back from the position of mastering the task, participants focus on the solution and on how they successfuly coped with the challenges they faced.

Detailed description

1. Start
The facilitator shows statements of the workshop's goal in terms of visible results – for a project, an idea for a new product or service,

167

changes to a work process, a new organisational structure. Examples include:

- *The help desk for XYZ is fully available in Bucharest.*
- *Our branch offers a choice of unrivalled products and services.*
- *The time taken for goods inwards inspection is cut by 30 per cent.*
- *The R&D co-operation unit is split into separate R&D branches in the different departments.*

2. Invitation

The facilitator invites the participants to experience how things will be when they have achieved the goal, in specific, concrete terms. That means standing at the peak of success and enjoying the view. Often it is easier to see the path to the peak from the top than it is from the valley below.

He tells the participants that everything they do in this step will serve as raw material for the detailed work later.

3. Prepare the space

Put two or three pinboards along one wall. Move the tables and spare chairs to one side and arrange the chairs (one for each participant) in a semicircle. Ask everyone to stand up anywhere in the room.

4. The Time Machine

The facilitator says

Now I invite you to an experiment – to a time jump! To jump to the time when you have successfully done what you set out to do. The result [... he mentions the visible result ...] has been achieved. Are you ready for this time jump?

The participants show they are ready by small gestures or words like OK.

Take a seat please ... I am turning on the time machine NOW ... plus 6 months ... plus 12 months: now we are in [he says the month and year] *... plus 2 years ... plus 3 years* [the facilitator lets the time machine run for the appropriate time] *... and now we are in* [he says the month and year] *... and I'm switching it off NOW!*

5. The Video

Now we are in [month and year]. *Our plans have been sucessful. The result* [... *he mentions the visible results* ...] *has happened. Yes, it was a hard work for everyone involved. Of course, some challenging situations must have been mastered – you worked out how to do this. And now you are very happy about this big success ... and maybe a bit proud ...*

And so the organisation wants to produce a small video to document the successful conclusion to this process. They want to do this by interviewing some of the people who made it happen – project managers, experts, developers, pilot clients [as appropriate]. *The interviewers will be some of the important stakeholders (for example journalists from the trade press, public contributorities, customers' organisations ...)*

6. Assigning roles

The facilitator asks the participants to propose some typical roles of doers and interviewers. In total the number of roles should be about half of the number of participants, but not more than 5 roles of doers and 5 roles of interviewers. The participants (not the facilitator) decide who takes what role.

For the interviews, it is very important to talk about the way the project was successfully mastered. If you must talk about difficulties, please talk about how they were resolved. To strengthen the solution talk, I need two people to act as solution monitors. Their task is to stop the interviews if they run into problem talk (describing the problem and its causes in detail) and to lead the interview back on the solution trail. Who is willing to act as a solution monitor? Will the rest of you please act as observers and write down what you hear from the doers when answering the questions of the interviewers. Summarise what they say in key phrases on post-it notes. Those notes will serve later as source material for the detailed work.

The interviewers' questions should focus on

– *What have we achieved?*
– *What has changed since the beginning of the project?*
– *What have you noticed, specifically?*
– *How did we overcome some difficulties?*

169

7. Interviews for the simulated video
(It would be counterproductive to record this for real. It might lead to exaggerated acting out and reduce the spontaneity.)

The interviews are conducted in front of the semi-circle of chairs. On the stage there are chairs for the doers and interviewers.

7.1 Version for small groups
(In this example the doers are called A and B and the interviewers X, Y and Z.)

As a warm up, the facilitator asks the doer to say something about his own role: *I am ... I have been in this job since ... my specific role in the project was ...*

After this warm up, the doers are interviewed using the questions above.

The facilitator and the solution monitors pay great attention, to make sure that the doers are talking in the present tense and are specific about everything that is different now that the plans have been completed.

The observers take notes and put them on the pinboards after each interview.

You can either draw the order of the interviews by lot or sequence the interviews so that A interviews X, then Y then Z, and then B interviews X, then Y, then Z.

7.2 Version for larger groups where there are many roles
The stage is set as if for a live discussion on TV. All the doers and interviewers are on stage. The interviewers can ask the doers questions in any sequence. The facilitator starts by asking each doer and interviewer to say something about their own role *I am ... I have been in this job since ... my specific concern for that intention is ...* This serves as warm up of the roles.

The facilitator and the solution monitors pay great attention, to make sure that the doers are talking in the present tense and are specific about everything that is different now that the plans have been completed.

The observers take notes and put them on the pinboards.

8. Coming out of role

The facilitator thanks all the actors for their work and asks them to come out of their roles with a movement of the hand and to sit on their chairs in the semi-circle.

9. Time machine backwards and short break

Sorry, we cannot stay in [month and year] *any longer ... we have to return back to the present time. Attention please: sit quietly in your chairs ... I'll activate the reverse gear of the time machine NOW ...* [The facilitator calls out each month and year as time reverses to the present day] *... OK ... we are back today again ... I'll turn the time machine off NOW ... Please get up and leave the time machine! Now we'll have a short break of about 10 minutes.*

10. Sharing

After the break, the facilitator asks everyone to sit in a circle and to share what they learned about this future. *What surprised them? What was interesting? What was better than expected?* [The wording *better than expected* is important to reinforce the positive results – in contrast to for example, what worked well? or how was it?]

What happens next

The participants might collect the post-it notes and cluster them as they think appropriate.

This activity results in a large collection of ideas from different perspectives to be used later in the workshop – for example structuring, assessment, making it more specific, prioritising etc.

Comments

This activity is one example out of many for solution focused scenic improvisations. It uses the psychodramatic methods' surplus reality, role play and role reversal which I find especially effective.

The activity avoids focusing on things that might lead to failure. Such risks are not ignored: instead they are treated as difficulties and challenges which – looking back – were resolved. This allows a positive mood to be created without negating difficulties and risks.

Acknowledgements and references

The method was developed by the author of this contribution.

Korn Hans-Peter, Staging of Strategic Solutions for the Future Business, in: Lueger/Korn: Solution-Focused Management, Rainer Hampp Verlag, München 2006

Korn Hans-Peter, Creating Management-Solutions by Sociodrama, in: KAPS (Korean Association for Psychodrama and Sociodrama) bi-annual journal, Jan. 2007

About *Dr. Hans-Peter Korn*

– KORN AG

Starting as scientist (PhD) in nuclear physics he worked for many years as line and project manager. Today, as Chief Manager of KORN AG, he works as an OD and PD consultant, coach/mentor and lecturer in universities focused on change, co-operation & communication processes in enterprises and complex projects. Further training in systemic management, solution focused work, systemic constellations, group psychotherapy, soziometry, sociodrama & psychodrama.

Address: Turnweg 13, CH 5507 Mellingen, Switzerland
Phone/Mobile: +41 79 461 33 79
e-mail: contact@korn.ch
www.korn.ch and www.SolutionStage.com

Strategy hike

– even for people who don't like hiking!

Christine Kuch, Germany

The strategy hike enables a group to formulate strategies to (re)start a desired change process in an active, fast and playful way. It's possible either to find preset solution focused strategies or to come to new ways during the hike. Finally, concrete actions are agreed upon.

Setting

- Time needed: 30 to 90 minutes, including preparation and post-processing. The strategy hike itself takes between 10 and 30 minutes.
- Number of participants: 5 to 30 people (possibly more).
- A room with enough space to arrange the chairs in a circle.
- Ideally another room in which to lay out the twelve strategies on the floor, each printed on A4 cardboard.
- Postcards and pens for the participants.
- Pin board(s) and flip chart.

Context and purpose

One of the principles of the solution focused approach is that the affected people themselves are responsible for designing the changes they want. The strategy hike follows this principle in a playful manner. It offers a reassuring frame for the process design and thus a way to ensure that concrete changes can be implemented. This intervention can bring lightness into difficult change processes.

The strategy hike is especially helpful in (re)starting change processes at team, departmental and organisational levels and in

173

clarifying the next steps, for example, when operational procedures are to be improved or replaced, a project must be started or a problem needs to be solved.

Detailed description

Preparation – What's the focus?

Before using this exercise, you should make sure that the group or the team you're working with wants to participate actively in the change process and feels itself able to do so. Additionally, you should establish a trusting relationship, so that the participants are ready to be involved in the process you propose. There are several tools which help to achieve this elsewhere in this book.

Then, ask the group about their shared goal: *What goal do you want to reach? What do you want to be different after the change has taken place?*

It's also possible to do this with a group of people with different sub-goals. Then the questions could be *Please think of a project you want to start. What's your goal? What's different after the project?*

You write the shared goal, for example *We are number one in our field* or *We offer the best consulting service to our clients* on a big sheet of paper (try to keep it short).

When the focus is clarified, you direct the group to another part of the room (or to another room), where the twelve strategies of the strategy hike, each displayed on A4 cardboard, are set in a circle on the floor. Each strategy is displayed with a figure and example sentences. Put the shared goal in the centre of the circle.

Strategy hike

Ask the participants to form a circle around the strategies on the floor. Then explain the process, best displayed on a flip chart:

1. Hiking (1 minute)
2. Rest and write postcards (2.5 minutes)
3. Chat – exchange and get support (3 minutes)

And again from the start: hiking, rest and chat (one to two repetitions)

> ***Typical strategies***
> [you can replace these with whatever seems appropriate]
>
> ➤ Start with a pilot
> ➤ Define clear goals
> ➤ Go slowly – take small steps
> ➤ Start with the motivated people
> ➤ Define clear responsibilities
> ➤ What's in it for me? – recognise benefits
>   to the individual
> ➤ Get support from the leadership
> ➤ Get support from other stakeholders
> ➤ Build on what works here
> ➤ Expand the network of support
> ➤ Be open to new participants
> ➤ Treat it as an experiment

You can facilitate this process like this (or similar):

I will ask you in a moment to go on a hike for one minute. Look at the strategies and search for those you like, perhaps because you have had good experiences with them or because you think that they could work in this situation. After one minute I will interrupt the hike and you will go to the strategy you like most so far.

After one minute ring a bell, a small gong or you make yourself noticeable in some other way.

Now take a rest at the strategy you liked most during your hike. Consider what you could do next with regard to this strategy. Write your ideas down on postcards and place them next to the strategy. You have two and a half minutes to do this. Please go now to the strategy that appealed to you most.

After two and a half minutes, give a signal again.

If others are at the same resting place, please form little groups of 2 or 3. I will ask you in a moment to have a three minute chat with

*your neighbours. You will show your cards to them. And they will
tell you what they like about you and your ideas. Then they show
you their cards and you will tell them what you like about them
and their ideas. You now have three minutes for this.*

After three minutes give a signal again and ask the group to set off
on a new hike, which you facilitate as before. You can also ask the
participants to add a new strategy if one they like is missing. The
hike can be repeated a third time, if it seems to be useful.

Finally, you ask the participants to take a seat again and thank
them for their active participation.

The next steps

The strategies chosen during the hike are now pinned on a pin
board together with the participants' postcards. After you have
appreciated the result, you ask the group if it's necessary for all
participants to agree on a process to reach the goal(s) or if every
participant can follow his own individual strategy.

If the participants decide that an agreed process is necessary, a
group discussion can be facilitated using the results on the pin
board. Questions like *Is something missing?, What should be done
first?* help to structure the discussion and to develop a concrete
action plan. In this way, small concrete actions for the relevant
strategies will be developed and agreed upon and then implemented
within the next days and weeks.

If the participants decide that every participant can follow his
own individual strategy, everyone is asked to think about a tiny
little step with regard to his chosen strategy, which he can make to
move in the direction of the goal he's set himself. He decides what
concrete action he will pursue. If the group isn't too big, every
participant can say what he or she is going to do and when. This
can help to support commitment and, additionally, it becomes clear
how many things will be done to reach the shared goal.

Finally, there should be space for mutual appreciation –
supporting tools can be found elsewhere in this book.

In addition, it is helpful to arrange a second meeting to review
the process and appreciate everyone's efforts and small successes.
(What went well?, What should we do again?, What should we do

differently in the future?, etc). Within complex projects, the next steps can also be agreed.

Comments

The strategies used here were developed on the basis of an interview study I conducted with people who were engaged in solution focused and systemic organisational development. The strategies were also evaluated by leaders and employees of organisations in the health care system and other service industries. The idea behind the activity is to get the participation of as many affected people as possible in deciding how to design a change process. In addition, the activity should give practical experience of co-operation, which is necessary for change processes.

This becomes obvious when participants say things like *I'd never have thought that such a short process would be so effective. And can be so relaxed. To be honest, what became most clear for me is that I have to change something about myself. I would not have thought of this before. And it is much easier than I thought.* [In this team, the hike lasted 10 minutes.]

But what should you do if someone doesn't like any of the given strategies? I ask the person to describe what they see as necessary for a successful change process and to add this as a new strategy. The activity allows the formulation of new strategies and, therefore, is open to change itself. Sometimes the participants say that it is very satisfying to participate in decision making where the boss doesn't have the only say. Therefore, it is important to clarify with the leaders of the team how much freedom the employees have in designing the change process.

Reference

Kuch, Christine (2006) Initiating Organisational Development. In: Lueger/Korn: Solution Focused Management, Rainer Hampp Verlag, Munich, pp. 249-57

About *Dr. Christine Kuch*

– medcoaching

Psychologist, quality manager in health care system, solution focused consultant/trainer. Since 1994 solution focused consulting for service and health care organisations, from strategic development to practical implementation. Main topics as trainer and coach: quality and organisational development, project management, leadership and communication. Research in organisational development and interaction.

Address: Karolingerring 24, 50678 Cologne, Germany
Phone/Mobile: + 49 (0) 221 3489300
e-mail: kuch@medcoaching.de
www.medcoaching.de

Dream team

Armin Rohm, Germany

At the end of a workshop, the participants project themselves into the future and imagine that the goals that have been worked out together have been achieved in a very impressive way. They then take on the role of journalists of well-known magazines and describe from their point of view and in the typical style of each particular magazine the unique success story.

Setting

- You need approximately 10 minutes for introduction and setting up small groups, about 40 to 60 minutes to write the articles in the small groups, and about 5 minutes for the presentation of the articles. Total time for the activity presented here – subject to the number of small groups – 60 to 90 minutes.
- In general, this activity can be carried out with small or large groups. The number of the small groups will depend upon the size of the whole group. It is well suited to 8 to 25 participants.
- You need enough copies of the task description, a pen and A4 paper for each small group.
- The plenary room must be big enough for everyone to hear the instructions and the presentations, preferably with a circle of chairs without tables.
- A break out room for each small group.

Context and purpose

After agreeing ambitious goals during a workshop, groups often face reality together at the end of the workshop. Concerns and doubts suddenly crop up. *Have we taken on too much? Will we be able to achieve all this alongside our daily routine?*

Dream team is designed to channel the energies of the participants at the end of the workshop toward the intended common goal. Success – and not possible failure – is the focal point of attention. Compelling images of a desirable future emerge and it becomes obvious to everyone that their combined efforts are worthwhile. Possible problems, fears and opposition are not denied. On the contrary, they are elegantly embedded into the view of the future: participants raise the issue of successfully overcoming barriers and identify necessary resources.

Dream team leads to practical application in a creative way and seeks to create an exciting and usually amusing conclusion to the workshop.

The activity lends itself particularly to workshops where attractive common visions of the future should be established and strengthened. As well as team building workshops, other examples include workshops dealing with visions, goals and strategy, the development of models or kick-off events of complex change projects. Dream team is suitable for work with individual teams as well as for workshops with representatives from various corporate divisions.

Detailed description

The following example of a Vision Workshop at XY Corporation will clearly demonstrate how the sequence of events may look. The workshop is attended by 25 people from various levels in the hierarchy and from all departments.

The facilitator gives the following instructions to the participants:
To conclude I would like to invite you to take part in a exciting exercise. So please form four small groups of about the same size.

After the groups have been arranged, the facilitator continues:
Let's assume it is three years hence. Everything that has been jointly resolved by the executive board and the employees during the Vision Workshop in [this year] – and even more – has been perfectly implemented. Actually the XY Corporation has just been selected as Company of the Year by a top-notch international jury. The media reports enthusiastically.
The participants of your small group are journalists of a well-known magazine. Write a press report together telling the success story of XY Corporation.

- *Come up with a striking headline*
- *Report the unique success story of XY Corporation.*
  - ➤ *What has been achieved by the executive board and employees during the last 3 years?*
  - ➤ *How was this possible?*
  - ➤ *What obstacles had to be overcome?*
  - ➤ *What do customers, suppliers and competitors say about the XY Corporation today?*
  - ➤ *What exactly is the secret of their success?*

Look for somewhere where your group can work without being disturbed. You have got 45 minutes to write your story. Before starting, please agree on which magazine you are writing for. Be sure to compose your article using the typical style of this magazine. Also, please agree on one or two people who will read this article out loud when we get together again afterwards.

Additionally, the facilitator hands out a copy of the instructions. Then the editorial staffs adjourn, agree on the magazine they are writing for and develop a text together.

During this phase, the facilitator takes a back seat. He should, however, check the progress every now and then and give time checks from time to time. Near the end it might be necessary to play down perfectionist tendencies and say that it's OK to leave some parts in the form of key words. The facilitator says nothing about the content.

At the end all participants assemble together again. The facilitator briefly reminds everyone where they are (three years later than today, and the XY Corporation has been chosen as Company of the Year) and asks the first group to present their press article. The group decides who takes part in the presentation.

After each presentation the presenters receive their deserved applause. After all groups have made their presentations, the workshop ends with a few words from the initiator of the event expressing his gratitude. Analysis of the contributions is consciously avoided.

Comments

- This is about the future, so speculation is allowed, and indeed is necessary. Desires, dreams and fantasies are in the spotlight, not objective facts. Dream team elegantly directs the energy of the participants to the emotional aspects of the transformation and their common desired aim.

- Because the participants are not reporting from their professional perspectives, but rather from that of a journalist, the reports can be much more daring. This way, it is much easier to integrate, overcome or ignore taboos of an organisation in the stories in a humorous way.

Here are some more tips:

- Sometimes it makes sense for the facilitator to form the small groups, for example to ensure maximum diversity representing all divisions and levels in the hierarchy or if it is suspected that the presence of the executive board in a small group may inhibit creativity. In this case, it makes sense to define the executive board as a separate group.
- During step 2 (writing the articles), the facilitator should ask the names of the selected magazines and decide on the sequence of the presentations. It is best to begin with serious legitimate journals and build up to the more sensational, provocative and flippant ones.

There are various other versions of Dream team. A few examples:

- The names of the magazine also can be set in advance. The facilitator defines small groups, puts them in different places and gives them worksheets with the logos of well-known magazines. The spectrum can run from legitimate business journals to tabloids. The groups aren't told which magazine the others are writing for. During the final presentation, they may guess what magazine is involved.
- Instead of writing a press article, the challenge could also be to create a report on the success story for a newscast. The participants can shoot video clips with fictitious interviews for the purpose of integrating them into newscast.
- If time is short, the instructions for the small groups may be to take just 10 minutes to compose three to five sentences in telegram style for a 'news ticker". The groups then stay together in the main room. Using this version, tempo and creative chaos are more important than eloquence and intellectual style.

What happens next

Usually, it makes sense to end the workshop straight after the presentations so that the optimistic mood of the participants isn't destroyed by a rational *Yes, but ...* analysis. The activity remains effective long after the workshop. These stories of success are usually highly memorable and entertaining. Many companies publish the texts as a 'Memory of the future' on their bulletin boards or in their in-house magazines. In this way, Dream team light-heartedly and humorously intensifies and activates the positive common mood.

Moreover, the texts provide useful information for the facilitator both in regard to the resources as well as in reference to the organisation's hidden agenda items. He may pick out these aspects as a central theme when preparing the feedback for the client and/or to keep in mind for successive workshops.

Acknowledgement of sources

In the German speaking countries, the basic idea for this intervention emerged primarily through the title *'Rückblick aus der Zukunft'* by Roswita Königswieser and Alexander Exner. Today, there are many versions of the tool with the name Dream team primarily used in the Reteaming approach. However, the Reteaming method uses it as an intervention at the beginning of the workshop, not the end.

About *Armin Rohm*

*Self-employed process consultant, coach and
trainer since 1994. Additional qualifications:
systemic process manager (main emphasis on
change management); systemic coach; licensed
consultant for MBTI, Power Potential Profile®
(PPP), Reteaming; training in NLP,
Transactional Analysis, solution focused
consulting and hypnotherapy. Armin Rohm
offers a two-year training course leading to a qualification as a
systemic coach and process consultant.*

Address: Haselnussweg 9, 88436 Eberhardzell-Mühlhausen, Germany
Phone: + 49 (0) 7355 9340 44
e-mail: info@armin-rohm.de
www.armin-rohm.de

Focus five

Critical success factors at a glance

Klaus Schenck, Germany

All critical success factors for the completion of a task or project can be collected and aligned along a timeline: goals, sense and purpose are located in the future, resources and boundary conditions are based on decisions in the past, input and process describe the proceeding in the present. Focus five folds this timeline into a concise one-page-format enabling the clear collection and thorough consistency check of all ingredients of a solution.

Setting

- In newly founded teams and in larger groups, Focus five may well take one hour. As an interim check or as a brief self-inquiry, five minutes may be sufficient.
- Useful for oneself as well as for large groups; optimal for groups of 3 to 30 people.
- The basic version of Focus five needs one piece of flip chart paper divided into five areas, plus small format paper cards for the participants to write on. Using felt tip pens ensures better readability of the entries in any photo documentation. Using post-it notes makes it easier to move the entries later during clustering or similar process.
- With larger groups the format can be projected in readable size with PC and beamer.
- When used for self-inquiry, an A4 sheet of paper and a pencil may be enough.

Context and purpose

Focus five can be usefully applied whenever the next big step in a project, work task or meeting has to be assessed, aligned and checked for consistency and completeness. It is especially useful for keeping a project's or meeting's focus on the desired outcomes and their intended consequences.

Focus five is useful whenever clarification and alignment of purposes, goals, resources, rules and proceeding merit a check up.

It can be applied in groups or alone, on a piece of paper, a flip chart, an overhead transparency or in larger formats (depending on the sizes of task and group involved).

Just as the meaning of a message can only be deduced from text *and* context together, the sense of a project or a meeting can only be judged sensibly after including their context and their boundary conditions. Hence, time to reflect these boundary conditions and to agree upon the goals early on is well invested time. What is the intended outcome? What will that be good for? What's the required input? Do we have all the resources we need? Who is involved? For whom do the results matter? In what way? Which rules or code of conduct do we want to apply? Focus five summarises the answers to these questions on one single page, with a good balance between detail and overview. This way it creates clarity right from the beginning, and later on at intermediate time points whenever needed.

Detailed description

In addition to the title and date (indicated on top of the page), the basic format consists of five fields outlined in three layers, with the middle layer itself divided into three areas as shown opposite.

Keywords for all essential aspects of the topic are written down in the relevant fields, either by the facilitator or, better still, by the participants themselves. In paper versions, it is best to use post-it notes to keep the entries mobile as the work progresses. (Tip: when participants themselves stick their notes on to the chart they literally get going and gather momentum – and so does their thinking . . .)

Usually the first two fields to be filled in – with contributions from everyone present – are Outcomes (Field 1) and Larger Context (Field 2). Outcomes means: what we'll have at the end of our meeting, ready to take it out of the room (A report? A model? An action plan? . . .). Larger context means: relevant components of a desirable future towards which today's output will itself be a useful input.

These two fields are carefully checked for plausibility: can we

186

---

②

LARGER CONTEXT
Systemic embedding of the outcomes:
– What do today's outcomes make sense for?
– What will they contribute to? Who will they benefit? In what way(s)?
– What will be the next larger task or project?
– ...

③	⑤	①
Starting materials: **INPUT**	Desired proceeding: **AGENDA**	Desired (concrete) **OUTCOMES**
Description(s) of current situation	Agenda	What result (milestone) will we reach here?
Materials and documents present	Project plan	– qualitatively: what exactly will we have achieved?
Special talents of people present	Process of transformation: – how much? – of what? with what? – in what sequence?	– quantitatively: how much of it/to what extent?
...	...	...

④

Basement: Rules, Restrictions, further Resources
Important values (possibly not as self-evident as assumed)
Presuppositions (so far maybe only implicit)
Rules & code of conduct (so far maybe unwritten)
Restrictions and boundary conditions (so far maybe overlooked)
Any further relevant resources

---

reach these outcomes, realistically, today? Do they contribute to the larger whole? Could we define better goals and outcomes which contribute to the larger project as well or better? Are the elements of the larger context attractive and worth pursuing? Who benefits from them? Etc. etc. . . . Any inconsistencies will trigger appropriate changes or amendments.

Next, the two fields Input (Field 3) and the Basement (Field 4) are filled in. Input means: all materials and resources (documents, output from former sessions, models, special talents of people ...) that are present in the room and relevant for the defined outcome. Basement is the place to note all additional resources which might be helpful as well as all restrictions and rules to be agreed upon by the participants, that are not routinely applied or self-evident by culture. (Sometimes code of conduct presupposed self-evident turns out not to be so – then it is a good time to explicitly write it down here! ...)

This is the time for an enlarged plausibility check: Do we have all input required for the desired outcomes? Do we have to change, remove or add rules for a successful code of conduct? Have we noticed participants' special skills and additional talents (as resources!)? Are there any other restrictions to be taken into account? etc. ...

Whenever aspects don't fit, where do we have to make changes? Do we have to cut goals or increase resources? Do we have to post-pone outcomes because relevant input needs to be obtained first? Do the rules make sense?

The last section to agree upon is the Agenda (Field 5). When the other four areas have been carefully prepared and well checked for compatibility and complementarity, the agenda should fall into place almost automatically. Once the group (or, during self-inquiry, one's own inner team) agrees with the completeness and aptness of the focus chart's descriptions, work can start full steam.

Whenever changes (including progress) occur, the focus chart may be readjusted and updated by all involved. (Using post-it stickers keeps the entries mobile and re-arrangable according to needs and progress.)

What happens next

After having compiled a Focus five in a joint effort, the work may start according to the agreed agenda. Whenever doubts about the direction of the work in progress arise this may be checked, and corrected as needed, using the Focus five. Depending on progress it is periodically updated.

Comments

Focus five is derived from the Flow Flower, as described in Flow Team, a special methodology for effective team work. It combines several aspects especially useful for solution focused team co-operation:

- Focus five creates a meta-level to provide orientation before work itself begins. It helps to avoid the otherwise frequently observable hectic start in the wrong direction.
- Already during this orientation phase everyone is active and involved, which also signals that initiative and participation are welcome.
- Right from the start, work is directed towards concrete and meaningful goals and benefits for customers.
- There is co-operation right from the start.
- Something concrete is being produced immediately.
- Goals and their context are visualised for everybody, so the risk of misunderstandings is minimised.
- When accepted goals and agenda are compiled in a joint effort, commitment rises.
- The common focus can be adapted easily to any changes of the situation.
- Focus five is easily scaleable, not only with respect to group size but as well with respect to the scope of work under scrutiny. It works equally well for a large project or for a single step within it. Clarity about the overall context, about the critical success factors and about the first steps can be achieved at the same time.
- The desired outcomes and their sense-making have top priority! That's because when a piece of work doesn't have a goal or doesn't make sense at all, there's no point in discussing rules for conducting it.

Acknowledgement

The basic format of Focus five refers back to Michael Brower of the consulting firm GOAL/QPC. Under the name Flow-Blume (Flow Flower) it is well described in Martin Gerber & Heinz Gruner: FlowTeams – Selbstorganisation in Arbeitsgruppen (Self organisation in work groups), Credit Suisse, Goldach (CH) 1999; pg. 37ff. (accessible online in German via www.flowteam.com). A similar chart of the Swiss Institute for Excellence directly derived from this was called Fokus Chart. (www.ife-web.com)

A comparable concept, the Context Model by Consensa (www.consensa.com) is described in: Mayrshofer, Daniela; Kröger, Hubertus A.: Prozsskompetenz in der Projektarbeit (Process competence in project work), Windmühle, Hamburg 2001 (2. Auflage); S. 190ff.

About *Dr. Klaus Schenck*

Klaus Schenck is engaged wholeheartedly in helping organisations and the people working there to remember their strength, skills, successes and potentials, and to utilise them intentionally and interactively: to design and implement a future they find attractive and desirable, and to contribute to attractive futures for others. He is dad of two adult sons and works internationally as a solution focused coach, process consultant, management trainer, and academic teacher.

Address: Eichendorffstr. 19, D-69493 Hirschberg, Germany
Phone/Mobile: + 49-1736696562
e-mail: doc.ks@web.de
http://klaus.schenck.googlepages.com

CHAPTER **7**

Spotting progress

The scaling walk   *Paul Z Jackson, United Kingdom*

Error management   *Susanne Keck, Germany*

Coaching time out   *Thomas Lenz, Austria*

Reflection break   *Daniel Meier, Switzerland*

SF facilitators are interested in asking for signs of progress: when are things better, even a little bit? By exploring what's different when things are better, ideas for further steps emerge.

The scaling walk

Paul Z Jackson, United Kingdom

Here is an opportunity to introduce or reinforce the concept of scaling by getting the group to physically experience different points on the scale. The Scaling Walk enables each participant in a working session to address an issue of importance – such as raising their performance in an aspect of work.

Setting

- Allow 15 minutes, and 10 minutes to debrief.
- This works for any number of people, limited only by the space available. Make sure there's enough space for people to walk beside each other in a single line.

Context and Purpose

Scaling is a fundamental tool in the SF kitbag. This activity is used to introduce scaling in detail, by considering it in the context of a participant's issue at work or in any activity they pursue. I usually use it after introducing the Future perfect, but it can stand alone if necessary.

The activity gives participants a powerful insight into how they can raise their own performance. It also combines both the experience and a discussion of scaling in an active and memorable few minutes.

Detailed description

➤ Either create a big enough space in the room or take the participants outside.
➤ Ask everyone to think of an issue at work in which improvement is necessary or desirable. Check that everyone has something to work with. If you prefer, you can use a sport or hobby that they

currently engage in and would like to be better at.

➤ Then say something like
Ten represents you performing consistently at your personal peak, in your chosen activity – the best you can be. One is you stuck at the worst you can imagine it could be for you. Where on that scale are you now?
So we can work together, let's call that number (whatever it is) n.
Ask them to keep the number to themselves.

➤ Then let them know that that there is now a scale in the room, show them which end is 1 and which is 10. Ask the participants to join you, standing up at a point about half way along the scale (the middle of the room), that you designate as n.

➤ When they are standing on the line, ask them if they would rather face 1 or 10 ... most participants prefer to face 10.

➤ Ask them all to face 10 and then ask them what is appealing about facing this way as opposed to 1. Get a few answers. These might range from fantastic to scary. You can point out that different people view 10 differently.

➤ Now ask them *What does being on a scale imply?* Tease out the answer that being on a scale implies the possibility of movement to a different point on that scale – that it implies the possibility of progress (or regress, for that matter). The idea of movement is built into the idea of a scale. Scales presuppose movement. Simply by placing yourself on a scale, you have the implication of potential movement – and therefore possible progress.

➤ Ask what comes to mind when they turn to look at 1. They may say *failure, depression, hard work*. Listen for someone saying *learning, resources etc* or introduce the idea by saying something like *I'm guessing that to get to where you are on the scale now, you've done some impressive things, learned a lot, overcome obstacles and had some successes. Maybe this space between 'n' and 1 represents that learning ... or a sea of know-how and counters that have got you to where you are.*

➤ Explain that we are not going to visit 1 on the scale and ask the group why that might be. *What's significant about 1? What do we need to know about 1? How much detail do we need to have of what 1 looks or feels like?*. The answer is that 1 represents problem talk and that as solution focused practitioners, we generally find it a lot less useful to focus on problem talk than solution talk.

➢ Ask them to take a moment to appreciate all the skills, know-ledge, successes etc, that make up that sea of know-how, maybe even to give themselves a pat on the back.

➢ Now walk the entire group along to 10 on the scale, the other end of the room. Ask them to visualise 10, closing their eyes if they find it easier. *What is it like? What are they doing that tells them they are at 10? What do others notice? What can they see? What is being said? How does it feel? What is happening?*

➢ Ask *Who has been at 10, for real, for a period, a moment, one swing of a golf club ... (That's the source of useful know-how too.)*

➢ Give them a few moments to visualise 10, then ask them to open their eyes and ask for two or three volunteers to share their experiences of 10. Again here it is useful to notice, if relevant, people's different experiences and expectations of 10.

➢ Ask *What does 10 represent? How much detail do we want about 10? What's the point of mentally visiting 10 on the scale?*

➢ Invite participants to now come back to n ... and ask them what's different now about looking to 10. (Often people say they feel inspired, motivated, they know something they didn't know before.)

➢ Ask if they can go straight to 10 from where they are now. If they could, then as a coach you would invite them to do so. If not, what might they be able to do now. The answer is to make a small step – just one point up the scale to n + 1. And we can do this by looking at the know-how we've used to get to n, including what we've learned about 10.

➢ Then ask them to close their eyes, for them to notice what would be the first sign that would tell them that they have moved up the scale say half a point or one point. What would they be doing, seeing etc? Then invite them to think of a small step they could take in the following days/weeks that would move them up the scale, and when they have thought of the step to physically take a step forward ... then to open their eyes ... and notice that 10 is nearer.

➢ Invite them to turn around again, and ask what is in the space between 'n' and where they are now. The answer is fresh know-how and recent momentum that might help them make further progress.

➤ Ask the group to return to their seats, ask any questions they have about scaling and make any notes that will be useful.

What happens next

A more detailed discussion of how and when to use scaling. For example, scaling alone is not always solution focused. Asking people how come they are not at 10 leads to a gap analysis.

Comments

- I like to make learning concrete and experiential. Walking the scale seemed the way to achieve this with the concept of scaling. I introduced it at an EBTA conference workshop, and have developed it since then.
- People generally say they like the physicality of the activity and many say they experience a profound visualisation – especially at 10.
- It was surprising when some participants said they now realised they didn't want to be at 10. You can ask them then what number they would like to be at.

Acknowledgement of sources

Original activity.

Book reference:

Paul Z Jackson and Mark McKergow, *The Solutions Focus – Making Coaching and Change SIMPLE*, Nicholas Brealey, 2nd edition, 2007

About **Paul Z Jackson**

– The Solutions Focus

PAUL Z JACKSON *is an inspirational consultant, coach and facilitator, who devises and runs training courses and development programmes in strategy, leadership, teamwork, creativity and innovation. His expertise in improvisation, accelerated learning and the solutions focus* 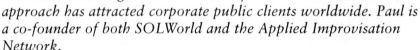 *approach has attracted corporate public clients worldwide. Paul is a co-founder of both SOLWorld and the Applied Improvisation Network.*

Address: 34a Clarence Road, St Albans, AL1 4NG, UK
Phone/Mobile: + 44 7973 953586
e-mail: paul@thesolutionsfocus.co.uk
www.thesolutionsfocus.co.uk

Error management

Susanne Keck, Germany

Error management is an activity that helps participants to focus on what is going to happen instead of concentrating on something that has gone wrong. This happens using a timeline set up on the floor and a sequence of solution focused questions. It is especially applicable for teams that work together but can also be applied to groups of independent individuals.

Setting

- Time: a minimum of 75 minutes, depending on the number of participants.
- Number of participants: 2–10 (With larger groups it takes too long to give everyone the chance of participating actively; therefore it makes sense to split the group up and bring it back together at the end.)
- Somewhere to collect the results and make them visible for the participants, e.g. flip charts or cards with a pin board.
- A roll of adhesive tape or a long rope and some cards of different colours.
- Flip chart, Powerpoint or overhead projector to display the questions.
- It is very useful to take pictures of the results to give to the participants as a record.

Context and purpose

Many people react to errors and mistakes with detailed analysis to avoid doing the same again. While this is a very good method in the case of technical problems, it often fails in the interpersonal arena. The reasons for unwelcome results are almost infinite and everybody has his own (legitimate) opinion on the question of guilt. This makes discussions long-winded and unproductive. The goal of this activity is to view the error from a different perspective and thereby extend the room for manoeuvre and reassure the participants. In addition, it develops concrete steps that can improve the situation in the near future and makes working on a solution possible.

It is useful for teams but it is also possible to do it with a group of individuals, for example in executive development workshops, so that everybody can concentrate on their own errors and share the experience with the others.

Detailed description

In the beginning it is usually necessary to listen to your participants' problem talk, that is talk about the problem, its causes and its dire consequences. We show respect when we listen to their experiences and worries. After a while (when you realise that that it is getting frustrating), you can ask the participants whether they want to join in a special exercise with unusual questions. You can introduce the activity as follows: *We want to make the sequence of incidents visible on a timeline together.*

Timeline
Mark a timeline at least 2.5 m long on the floor with adhesive foil or a long rope (the more participants the longer the timeline).

Cards
Give 3 different coloured cards to the participants: one represents the incident (the error), one the present and one a time in the future when the problem will be solved or the incident successfully dealt with. Ask them to arrange the cards on the timeline as seems appropriate. Allow discussion in the group and only intervene if the instruction is misunderstood or conflict arises. If the latter case, the rule is that everybody is right with his appraisal and that the task is to come to a compromise.

Future
Ask the participants to stand on the timeline in the future when they are coping well with the situation. Of course, they cannot all stand on one point, but let them cluster around it.

198

Ask
- *How do you become aware that you have successfully coped with the error/incident?*
- *How do others (managers, teams, competitors, customers) notice?*

Put the questions on a flip chart or slide where they can refer to them if necessary.

You can assist the participants by instructing them to imagine that the time of coping has miraculously arrived. They have met you by coincidence, and of course you ask how things have gone since you last met and how they coped. They tell you that (despite the serious situation) everything turned out well. Their task is to describe – in the present tense and in as much detail possible – how things are today and how they managed to cope with the incident so well.

Here you can continue with the thought experiment: *How did the participants manage to cope so well? What did the group and every individual contribute to make this possible? What do the participants know now (in the fictional future) that they did not know before the process of coping? What did they learn?*

Collect the responses on a flip chart and display it so that everybody can see it. Show interest and appreciation for each constructive contribution that shows resources. All the other contributions (e.g. pessimistic ones etc.) are also welcome and displayed in the same way.

Past
Ask your participants to move to the past point on the time-line and ask the following question:
- *What were we doing right which prevented the error/incident from happening earlier?*

Present
Move to the present and ask
- *What have we done well since it happened, e.g. coping strategies etc.?*

Collect the resources on cards or flip chart like you did before – possibly some distance from the results of the previous question period.

It might be hard at first for the participants to find something positive because the error might dominate everything else. Give them some time to tune in to the drastic change of perspective. If they can't think of anything they have done right (which is not often the case), you can end this question round and give compliments to the participants for showing such stamina in a difficult situation.

Future Steps

Focus the participants' attention to the future again when the error/incident has been coped with. Ask them to take one step towards this point. Everyone is free to make the step as small or big as he likes. Let the participants describe the situation one step on:

- *What exactly is different and how do I notice this?*
- *What do others notice?*

Collect the statements in the usual way.

Meta level

Ask your participants to leave the timeline and have a look on the events from the outside. Give them the chance to reflect on the exercise thus far and ask about possible changes.

Ask the next question after they are finished:

- *What will we do next?*

Collect the ideas in your usual way. Dig deeper if some statements are too abstract or noncommittal. One question could be: *What concrete ideas do you have about moving one step further?*

You can assist the participants by asking them to imagine filming their future actions with a video camera. What exactly would we see them doing successfully on the film?

At the end you can give the participants a photo of the results captured on the flip charts.

What happens next

Later, it can be useful to go into more detail about the concrete measures to improve coping and to discuss how to transfer the learning back to the workplace.

Comments

I got my most important insight concerning errors through the solution focused approach: the best way of dealing with errors is to talk about them less and instead talk about the things that work. The focus is less on avoiding errors and more on doing the best you can. I hope this activity will provide a slightly different way of thinking about the error and give participants the creativity to deal with their situation.

Acknowledgement

The topics of error culture and error management have featured in management literature for some time and they are strongly influenced by a problem focused approach. Only a few writers have approached the subject from a resource oriented perspective that values errors and mistakes – under certain circumstances – as something useful or at least normal. The work of T. Werner and Prof. Frese from University of Göttingen inspired me

About **Susanne Keck**

– Solutionspace

I want to offer psychology as a service that creates lasting solutions. This requires an extremely good fit between the solution and the customer's goals, abilities and attitudes. Otherwise the solution will soon fall prey to the routines of everyday life. Systemic and solution focused approaches provide me with a tool to reach this aim.

Address: Schachnerstrasse 5, 81379 Munich,
Germany
Phone/Mobile: + 49 89 38102661, +49 173 6911767
e-mail: sk@solutionspace.biz
www.solutionspace.biz

Coaching time out

Thomas Lenz, Austria

What can we do when a training or simulation session becomes difficult and any learning seems to be fading away? Coaching time out is an activity that makes time for real development: the facilitator interrupts the exercise and with some distinguished solution focused questions he puts the work back on track so that the development of learning structures is sustainable.

Setting

Coaching time out takes about 10–20 minutes depending on the size of the group and the need for discussion. The workshop should not be interrupted for any longer than this.

The activity can be done with just one person or the whole group.

It works best in the open air where people can stand or sit together and talk. But it has worked well for me indoors as well. The important thing is that people should be able to get together somewhere where they can hear each other well.

Context and purpose

This is best used during long workshops or outdoor simulations. Topics may include leadership, process development, project management, organisational development, teamwork, co-operation or other corporate challenges.

Long and complex outdoor exercises can easily become tiring and long-winded and sap the learning effects. Many positive effects can get lost. The coaching time out activity underlines the laboratory character of outdoor exercises where participants can make experiments and try out new behaviours. Participants enjoy success in challenging tasks and anchor abilities that brought them there. They learn from fun and success instead of failure and analysis.

Detailed description

The example described here is about leadership and process quality. For example, the team is working at an exercise in which a cable car has to be built by a group of about 20 people. Therefore the team has to work out a plan, make calculations, supply material, describe roles and structures, delegate tasks and execute them. Group dynamic processes, the natural surroundings and maybe the facilitator's interventions have generated problems for the participants. Crisis and conflicts follow. In such difficult situations, people normally fall back on survival strategies. And normally it is too long until the next reflecting loop – so that participants find it hard to structure their experiences as measures of their development.

This is the time for facilitators to recognise the need for a time out. The people concerned – this may be one or more individuals or the whole group – are called together and to a neutral place, still outside.

This could be a possible dialogue between the facilitator and the participants:

Facilitator: *I see and appreciate the amount of enthusiasm you are investing in this exercise. I thank you for that. It proves to me that you are taking this game very seriously.*

Before we decide on how to go on I'd like to put an important question to you. What has gone well so far?

Participants respond.

Facilitator: *Now that I have seen your enthusiasm, I am sure that there are some things that are likely to make a difference to this difficult situation. Now what was it that you saw here that you really liked – with others and with yourself?*

Participants start to talk about for example working as a team, the delight of physical movement, the pleasure of finding the right place in the forest, the joint development of a great communication system, clear roles, creativity, initiatives ...

Facilitator: *This is quite a lot. To make it simple let's call these things information resources. Which of these resources can help you as we continue the exercise? And who in your group should do that?*

Participants start to think and structure their learning. For example they discuss further rules how to stick closer to roles, have better communication, to make better decisions ...

Facilitator: *This sounds promising. Now, I would like to see how you continue the exercise applying the resources you have described. This could pay off for all of us.*

In this situation the facilitator should be generous and fair in the handling of the game rules without changing the character of the simulation. Then the exercise continues.

The facilitator can even increase the effect of the coaching time out when it happens more than once. Possible questions here:

Facilitator: *How did the changes improve things? What differences have you seen? How could you improve your situation even more?*

Debrief
While debriefing the exercise, the facilitator mainly focuses on the differences. Thus the participants are focused on their potential of developing themselves, instead of – as usual – their deficits.

Possible questions while reflecting:
Which new situations and behaviours did you see here? What ideas does this give you? How can you utilise these insights in your daily business?

Comments

Once some participants in one of my outdoor seminars complained – and deservedly so – about not doing much in a longer outdoor sequence. I could see only two possibilities then: either to increase the challenges or to support the learning within the group. The second choice was more exciting for me. It was about asking: *When did the exercise work well? When were the sequences really thrilling?* Their answer was: *When participants had the chance to express their light bulb moments and the secrets of their success.*

The first time I used the coaching time out was when a training group really lost the plot in a difficult exercise in a high mountain region. The whole thing was about to be cancelled. In order to prevent that, I took the first opportunity to talk to the group leader off the record. I recommended him to show leadership and I asked him how he might do this.

He called a crisis meeting. In a very articulate and emotional speech, he motivated the group to try for a last time (they had to build a bridge). This eventually led to success. And the 5 minutes of his speech were a thrilling role model for good and careful leadership. Years later that he told me how important those 5 minutes had been for the development of his management life. He had consciously taken responsibility for his own actions.

This gave me the impulse to implement solution focused ideas in my trainings. And there are mainly two aspects that I try to elaborate:

- Resource orientation instead of failure diagnosis. The outdoor trainer always has a certain authority. Participants accept praise and criticism from him. I prefer to focus on positive experiences.
- To boost potential by perception of differences: there are always ups and downs in outdoor games. I ask about perceived differences.

What happens next

Reflection on an outdoor exercise is usually held the following day. New structures, rules and agreements for the group's own organisation are agreed here. It sometimes makes sense to provide follow-up coaching and some companies decide to have a follow-up outdoor event.

Acknowledgements

Insoo Kim Berg and Harry Korman provided me valuable tips during the BFTC course.

About *Thomas Lenz, MBA*

– Lenz & Partner Consulting

I have been a trainer, consultant and coach since 1993, specialising in leadership and organisation of work. I prefer to work outdoors. In addition, I – and my customers – like alternative formats like music, clown-work, theatre, rhythm, storytelling, physical work, social and cultural projects – all of them enriching forms for developing solutions. I like to do all of it on my 14 hectares land in the mountainous region of Lilienfeld where I run a development centre.

Address: Platzl 1, A – 3180 Lilienfeld, Austria
Phone/Mobile: + 43 2762 52310
e-mail: thomas.lenz@raumpuls.at
www.raumpuls.at

Reflection break

Daniel Meier, Switzerland

Stopping for reflection is a simple and efficient opportunity to note the progress that has been reached so far in the workshop, to replenish the energy and to determine the next useful steps of the process together in a very goal-oriented fashion. It is an exercise that offers the participants the opportunity to plan their next steps together with confidence and a sense of security.

Setting

- 10 to 30 minutes maximum.
- Suitable for any number of participants.
- You need post-it notes, board, flip chart, markers.

Context and purpose

This tool is very useful for workshops lasting more than one day. It can be deployed flexibly. I use the reflection break primarily

- to make sure that the activities so far have been useful;
- to receive hints about what could be a useful next activity;
- so that the group can see and maybe even celebrate signs of progress which has already happened during the workshop.

The benefit of the reflection break can be seen in two areas:

Recognising first signs of progress
Team workshops are often held in order to change things or to develop something. In solution focused work, we assume that change happens continually and cannot be avoided. It is often useful for the group to become aware of the first small changes that take place even after only a few hours together. This helps the team to generate energy and confidence – especially in situations which seem hopeless at first.

Planning next steps
As a facilitator, I lead the team through a process with the help of various activities. On a hiking trip, it is useful to spend some time occasionally looking at the map: are we on the right track giving us the greatest chance of reaching the goal in time? In the same way, the facilitator receives direct and helpful information for the further development of the process, what adjustments might be necessary and what a next step might look like.

Detailed description

The reflection break is structured in three phases:

Phase 1: Usefulness scale
Define a scale in the room:
Please stand up and think for a moment about how useful what we have done together has been so far for you. 10 over here means that it was totally useful and 1 means the opposite – a complete waste of time. Please place yourself at the point on the scale that corresponds to your assessment. Form a pair with the colleague who happens to be standing next to you. Please share the three or four things that have made the workshop useful to you so far. What tells you that you are already at an X and not at 1? (3–5 minutes conversations in pairs)

Phase 2
Would each pair please grab a few cards or post-it notes and a marker and sit down together. I am aware of the fact that we are just starting to determine the next steps in the direction of your goals and that we haven't got very far yet. However, I think that you have identified some small signs of progress in the last couple of hours which point in the right direction. I would like you to take a few minutes to note these first small signs of progress on the cards (or post-it notes). These first small, maybe even hardly noticeable, signs of progress can be signs that you noticed in yourself or signs that you noticed with other people. Please pin the cards onto this board (or stick the post-it notes onto this flipchart). (2–7 minutes)

Phase 3
Then ask the participants to position themselves back on the usefulness scale at the same point they were at before.

How are you going to notice that you have moved one step up this usefulness scale? What will you be doing differently? What will you notice others doing?

The results of this short phase are collected in the full group and noted on a flip chart (5–15 minutes).

What happens next

In my experience, it is useful to have a tea or coffee break after the reflection break. That gives the facilitator the chance to plan the next phases.

Comments

- What I find interesting with the reflection break is the fact that it does not take very long and that it can be used in many different ways. It enables me to adapt individual phases so that they fit the given topic, the team or the facilitator well.
- I came across another very nice variant of phase 2 (first signs of progress) when I did not let the participants write the signs of progress they had detected on cards or post-it notes but separated the existing pairs and asked them to form new pairs. The newly formed pairs exchanged the signs of progress they had found. I then mixed up the group again and called it creating rumours of progress. Rumours will always develop in teams and they often have great influence. So why not use this factor as a positive reinforcement?
- At first I was looking for something which would enable me as facilitator to choose really useful activities for the team development process. Too often had I found that participants spoke up only shortly before the end of the workshop or even in the final evaluation and mentioned that we had done a lot of very exciting things, but that they had expected something totally different or that some topic or other had not been mentioned or that all in all it had not been helpful. When you only have 15 minutes left of the workshop, there is not much time left to change that. The reflection break helps me to stay close to the needs of the team during our work together and to target the activities accordingly.
- After some experience with the reflection break, I became

convinced that such a break can also be used to support the learning process of the team. Evaluations should not only provide the facilitator or the customer with important information but also provide the participants themselves with some learning or purposefully support them in their progress.

Acknowledgement of sources

You can find further information about solution focused team processes in my book: *Team Coaching with the SolutionCircle*, SolutionsBooks, 2005

About *Daniel Meier*

– Solutionsurfers

Daniel is the co-founder and managing partner of the international Brief-Coach training institute Solutionsurfers®, based in Switzerland. He is the Director of the German speaking part of this association. Solutionsurfers® offer solution focused Coach Training in different countries and different languages leading the trainees to a certificate by the International Coach Federation. Daniel has been coaching managers and teams in a solution focused way since 2001. His latest book is Team Coaching with the SolutionCircle *(Solutionsbooks, 2005)"*

Address: Waldstätterstrasse 9, CH – 6003 Lucerne, Switzerland
Phone:+ 41 (0)41 210 3973
e-mail: daniel.meier@solutionsurfers.com
www.solutionsurfers.com
www.weiterbildungsforum.ch

CHAPTER **8**

Interaction in action

The UNO game   *Kirsten Dierolf, Germany*

Your team in flow!   *Bert Garssen, The Netherlands*

Mini-coaching with maxi-effect   *Daniel Meier, Switzerland*

Learning from good examples   *Peter Röhrig, Germany*

Solution focused interview with absent team members
Insa Sparrer, Germany

We live in an emergent world, where change is happening all the time. People act in response to the world – including other people.

The UNO game

Success factors for intercultural encounters

Kirsten Dierolf, Germany

UNO is one of the world's most popular family card games, with rules easy enough for anyone over the age of about 7. This UNO game is a great introduction to the topics of intercultural communication or management. The participants can gain first-hand experience of how they react when they are playing on an international playing field with partners with different expectations about the code of conduct. The debrief then helps participants to distil the most important factors for the success of the intercultural interaction. The exercise is a lot of fun and provides participants with many first-hand insights and Aha effects. The exercise can be used whenever you are dealing with people whose expectations about the rules or procedures of collaboration are different. For example, it can also be a good exercise in situations of mergers, acquisitions, integration of two teams or general restructuring measures.

Setting

- You need approximately 25–30 minutes for the exercise and at least 15 minutes for the debrief. Often there is enough energy and there are enough insights to warrant 30 minutes debrief.
- It is suitable for groups of 9 to 20 people.
- You need
  - ✓ Three UNO card games without special cards (but keep the +2 card)
  - ✓ three handouts with the rules (see below)
  - ✓ flip chart and pens for debrief

Context and purpose

The UNO game energises and is fun and insightful. Therefore, you can use it as an icebreaker or first introduction into the topic of intercultural communication or collaboration.

Participants are led into ambiguous and confusing situations in a very playful manner and can reflect afterwards on what helped them to deal positively with the ambiguity. This experience is usually remembered for a long time and therefore might help participants master real ambiguous situations a little better. The game itself is not threatening, but rather playful and fun. This positive anticipation of ambiguity is one of the main success factors of intercultural communication, or communication between different team cultures or national cultures.

Detailed description

Introduction

The UNO game works best if you do not say much by way of introduction and don't introduce the topic in much detail. You can joke a little bit about the real UNO (United Nations Organisation) and that they too have to deal with different cultures all the time and this is the reason why it is useful to start the workshop with a game of UNO. If someone is really curious about the rationale of the game you might say something like *I will be handing out new rules to the well-known game UNO, and I would like to test your capacity to learn new rules quickly.* Don't ruin the surprise for the participants!

The Game

Form 3 small groups and distribute one pack of UNO cards per group. Take out all special cards (recognized by the black background) apart from the +2 card. Then distribute one sheet of rules to each group. Each group receives a different set of rules. However, the participants do not know that they have been handed different rules – they should be seated far enough apart so that they do not overhear each other's discussion of the rules.

Learning the Rules
Tell the participants to play the game according to the (new) rules for 10 minutes. If you feel that every group is clear on the rules, you can also stop their game earlier.

Collecting the Rules
It is very important that you collect the sheets with the rules after this phase, so that the groups cannot refer to them in the next phase.

Mixing Groups
Now you mix the groups. Each new group should consist of members of all the original groups. Ask the groups to play again, but now they cannot speak to each other. You can even sell this instruction as a more difficult test of learning new rules quickly. Observe the groups while they are playing. It is always great to watch how a kind of absurd and very humorous game develops after initial bits of irritation and misunderstandings.

Debrief
The following questions have proven useful for the debrief:

- *How was it for you?*
- *What were you thinking about the others?*
- *What was interesting in this situation?*
- *What was fun for you?*
- *How did you manage to continue playing?*
- *What did you do to agree on rules?*
- *What was useful behaviour, what wasn't?*
- *Have you ever behaved similarly in intercultural situations?*
- *What did you notice when someone was doing something useful?*
- *What could you be better at?*
- *If this had anything to do with intercultural communication/our merger situation/our different team cultures, what could that be?*

UNO – an intercultural game

Objective: To get rid of your hand as quickly as possible. The winner of the game is whoever puts down his or her last card first.

Rules – Version 1:
- Every player gets 8 cards. The rest of the cards are put face down in a stack in the middle. One card is pulled from the stack and placed face up next to it.
- The players take turns counterclockwise.
- Each player must put down one card with either the same colour or the same number as the last open card on the stack. If he or she does not have such a card on his or her hand, the player must pick up two cards from the stack.
- When a +2 card is played, the next player must pull two cards from the stack and then continue to play the remainder of his or her turn (either put down a card or pull another card from the stack).
- When a player has only one card in his or her hand he or she must say "UNO". If he or she fails to do so before the next player finishes his or her turn, he or she must pick up two cards, if the other players notice it before it is their turn.
- The game ends when the first player has put down all his or her cards.

Rules – Version 2:
- Every player gets 6 cards. The rest of the cards are put face down in a stack in the middle. One card is pulled from the stack and placed face up next to it.
- The players take turns clockwise.
- Each player must put down one card with the same colour or the same number as the last open card on the stack. If he or she does not have such a card on his or her hand, the player must pick up two cards from the stack.
- When a +2 card is played, the next player must pull two cards from the stack and then continue to play the remainder of his or her turn (either put down a card or pull another card from the stack).
- When a player has only one card in his or her hand he or she must say "UNO". If he or she fails to do so before the next player finishes his or her turn, he or she must pick up two cards, if the other players notice it before it is their turn.
- The game ends when the first player has put down all his or her cards.

Rules – Version 3:

- Every player gets 8 cards. The rest of the cards are put face down in a stack in the middle. One card is pulled from the stack and placed face up next to it.
- The players take turns counterclockwise.
- Each player must put down one card with the same colour or the same number as the last open card on the stack. If it is the same colour, the number on the card must be higher than the one preceding it. If the player does not have such a card on his or her hand, the player must pick up two cards from the stack. When no-one in a given round can play a card that is higher than the card on the stack, any colour can be played .
- When a player plays a card identical to the one on the stack, he or she can take an additional turn.
- When a +2 card is played, the next player may play two cards from his or her hand (or pull another card from the stack if he or she cannot play).
- When a player has only one card in his or her hand he or she must say "UNO". If he or she fails to do so before the next player finishes his or her turn, he or she must pick up two cards, if the other players notice it before it is their turn.
- The game ends when the first player has put down all his or her cards.

What happens next

Later in the workshop you can continue to refer to different ways of working with different rules. For example, you can talk about the unspoken rules in team or national cultures right after the exercise. And in merger situations you can also follow up with group work on *What rules of collaboration have proven especially useful in our respective companies?* or *What rules and conventions proved so useful in our old team that we want to continue using them in the collaboration in the new team?*

Comments

- I developed the UNO game because it is very difficult to make intercultural situations tangible and observable within a seminar room. I wanted to create a light, fun and relevant game which automatically points out the most important success factors of intercultural communication. The participants experience the lightness and fun of the game and can realise the connection to the riches and benefits of intercultural situations immediately. What previously might have seemed necessarily threatening, possibly now even has an interesting and maybe amusing note.
- This exercise becomes solution focused mainly by focusing the debrief on the strengths and resources of the participants. It is very important to ask what went well in the exercise and connect it with the participants' skills in intercultural situations.

About *Kirsten Dierolf*

Kirsten Dierolf M.A. works as an executive coach and an organisational and human resource developer mainly for large corporations in global projects. She has developed several leadership development programmes, team trainings and human resource development programmes on intercultural communication, virtual teaming and communication. She regularly speaks at international conferences.

Address: Kalbacherstr. 7, 61352 Bad Homburg, Germany
Phone/Mobile: +49-6172–684905
e-mail: kirsten@kirsten-dierolf.de
www.solutionsacademy.com

Your team in flow!

Bert Garssen, The Netherlands

This exercise demonstrates how to establish and take participants into an experience of flow. Being in flow as a team will give an idea of swarming.

Setting

- The activity takes about 10–15 minutes. Time to debrief depends on the range of experience to be shared.
- 8–10 people are needed and the activity works for groups of up to 30.
- A large room with a chair for everyone and lots of space to move around.

Context and purpose

- Teambuilding and strengthening co-operation.
- Listening to each other.
- Practising this exercise will give people a real life experience of flow through being a particle in a swarm.

The activity may produce some confusion at first, and then empowerment when the exercise succeeds. It is a lot of fun, and it gives a lot of energy to the group.

In addition, it shows some solution focused principles:

1. The action is in the interaction.
2. If something works, do more of it.
3. If something isn't working, stop it and do something else.
4. If something works, share it and teach it to others.

Detailed description

Give a short introduction, describing briefly what the group is going to experience. Tell them there is just one general rule: they are not allowed to talk to each other.

1. First ask a person (A) to come on stage (I mostly work with groups in a circle) and ask another one (B) to precisely copy all the movements A makes when walking round the room. B walks behind A and copies him.
2. All the other group members carefully watch A and B.
3. When the audience is content with B's copying, they clap their hands in the rhythm of A and B's movements.
4. Ask a third person (C) to walk behind B and copy all his movements precisely.
5. The audience clap hands only when A, B and C succeed in moving completely simultaneously.
6. Ask a fourth person (D) to follow C. As soon as D starts to copy C, C is told to separate from A and B so that there are two pairs.
7. The group still clap their hands if all four people are moving simultaneously.
8. Ask the people in the audience to choose a moment to join the group on stage, one person at a time, so that everyone ends up walking behind another member of the group and copying him (all in pairs).
9. Ask them to pay attention to the other pairs and invite them to create a movement in the whole group, with everyone doing the same movements at the same speed, so that it looks like one person is moving.
10. Debrief: *How did you succeed? How could this experience be useful for your team? What else?*

Short break.

11. Arrange the chairs all over the room and ask everybody to sit down.
12. Ask one participant to stand up some distance from his chair, leaving that chair empty.
13. This person's task is to walk to an empty chair and to try to sit down on it. But ... the other members of the group try to

prevent that by changing chairs, so that someone else is sitting in the original empty chair.

14. However, there are some rules:
    - Everyone has to walk in a certain way – like a penguin!
    - When anyone has left his chair, he must move to another chair – he is not allowed to return to his original chair.
15. When the first person has found an empty chair and sat down, there will be someone else without a chair. This person is the next searcher for a chair, starting from a point far away from the empty chair.
16. You can repeat this until there is a wonderful flow in the group, where the movements have become smooth and all the mistakes in the beginning have vanished: a real swarm is happening.

Comments

I developed this exercise, joining separate exercises together, because I found elements of flow and swarming in them. They had great impact on the group and the individuals: people liked it, they had a lot of fun, they experienced step by step progress, they became aware of useful resources in their teams, they had many reasons to compliment the others in the group, and so on. So, many basic SF rules could be experienced and swarm intelligence became more than just a theory. The vivid bodily and emotional experiences make it an unforgettable activity.

Acknowledgement of sources

I learned these exercises from a clown Roelant de Vletter, (speel-wiejebent@hetnet.nl), who sometimes comes to my training groups.

About **Bert Garssen**

– Impuls

The founder of Impuls (1985). Broadly educated in the field of training & coaching, with the focus on solution focused work and a lot of experience. I like to work dynamically in groups, appreciate humour and am convinced about the resources of people. In my work I love my idealism in helping people to connect and use their resources in an effective way. My patience is then very helpful. Being a teacher I also like to teach people in the SF way of working.

Address: Kerkweg 6, 6974 AM Leuvenheim,The Netherlands
Phone/Mobile: +31.6.53.78.20.74
e-mail: bgarssen@impulsorganisatieadvies.nl
www.impulsorganisatieadvies.nl

Mini-coaching with maxi-effect

How short coaching interventions can create magic workshop situations

Daniel Meier, Switzerland

Solution focused mini-coaching sessions are goal oriented, short conversations which we can have with individual participants in front of the full group. They cannot be planned in workshop situations and they depend on the ability of the facilitator to deal with unpredictability and to recognise suitable situations. Mini-coaching is always possible when participants would like to clarify or question something or would like a 'how-to' answer for something.

Setting

- Mini-coaching can be used in groups of up to 15 people.
- The time needed varies. Some coaching conversations only take 2 minutes, others up to 10 minutes.

Context and purpose

One of the fundamental tenets of the solution focused approach is that the customers are the experts and have all the resources to solve their questions or challenges. We often forget that participants in our workshops bring a lot of knowledge and experience with the topic to the workshop. Mini-coaching offers the opportunity to activate these resources.

We also assume that questions (if they are not purely informational questions) are harbingers of the individual answers that fit the questioner. With these short coaching sequences you can help participants to find their own answers.

Mini-coaching is not really a classical workshop tool but it depends very much on the situation in the workshop. These conversations help the facilitator to work with ease and without any pressure to be the sole provider of content. They can be used to offer individual participants the opportunity to gain their own insights or to come up with decisions for themselves. Often they also help participants to solve a conceptual problem or get unstuck.

Detailed description

There are no step-by-step instructions for mini-coaching conversations, since every situation is different. A procedure which has often (but not always) proven useful is to work with scales:

1) Clarifying the goal:
   What exactly is the objective of your question?
2) Current position on the scale:
   Imagine a scale where 10 means that this question is totally clear and has been answered for you and 1 is the opposite. Where are you now in regard to your answer?
3) What is already clear?
   Ah, you are all already at X (for example 4). What is already clear for you that lets you say that you are at a 4 and no longer at a 1?
   (Often this is all you need to do – by telling you about what they already know in a structured way, the participants often become clear on the rest.)
4) Perspective:
   Suppose you moved up one step with regard to your answer during the next hour: what would be a clear sign for you that you are already a little bit further than X? Who could support you in this?

And here are two examples to illustrate how you can use mini-coaching in your workshop:

Scene 1: from a workshop on solution focused team leadership
The participants are just returning to the plenary session after working in small groups.

Participant: *Now I am confused. We just talked about the differences between team coaches and facilitators. What exactly is the difference?*

Facilitator: *Oh, I am not so sure myself. Can I ask a question first? How is it important to you to have an answer to this question about differences?*

Participant: *Hmm ... I think I have been mainly facilitating up to now. I am just realising that a coach somehow does something different. It is a bit similar but it seems easier because he doesn't take responsibility for the content. He leaves the responsibility with the team. It would probably be easier for me to facilitate if I were more of a coach.* (The other participants laugh in agreement.)

Facilitator: *Ah – OK — how would the participants in your workshop notice that you are more coach than facilitator?*

Participant: *Just that: that I leave the responsibility with them. And it may be that by doing that as a coach I give them more choices in their decisions than if I was pressing the team to finally come to a decision on how to proceed. I would simply be more open and accept different ideas – so that everyone could find solutions according to his or her resources, which all support the common goal. OK, now I am clear!*

Facilitator: *On an answer scale of 1 to 10, where are you now with regard to this question?*

Participant: *I am now at 8 and that is good enough. Now I simply have to implement this in my next workshop!*

Scene 2: an internal workshop on flexibility in dealing with customers

Felix: *The discussion seems very laborious. We are not really getting anywhere, nothing is happening. We didn't have to discuss these things before, things were running smoothly.*

Bea: *Felix is right. How about finally getting to the point?*

Coach: *OK, Felix, I see that you are getting impatient.*

Felix: *No not impatient. I simply want to move on!*

Facilitator: *How useful has what we have done been for you so far on a scale of 1 to 10?*

Felix: *A 2 max.*

Facilitator: *OK, what has been useful in our conversations so that you can rate it at a 2 and not at a 1?*

Felix: *Mio and Bea told us a little bit about their previous job. That was new and good. I think the question of what had been working in the first two months also helped.*

Facilitator: *Yes I think that was really helpful. Do you have an idea about what we will have to talk about here so that we can move two points up the scale within the next hour?*

Felix: *We keep talking about flexibility, and nobody knows what exactly is meant. What exactly are we doing when we are flexible? I want concrete examples and possibilities. And then it would be good if we had something like a description of our central processes. We could start with that afterwards.*

Bea: *Yes, a process description would also be very helpful for me because then we would have it on paper!*

Facilitator: *Yes, these seem to be really sensible suggestions. First I would like to finish with the topic that we were just talking about. This won't take longer than 10 minutes. And afterwards we will try to identify concrete examples of flexibility. In a third step we can start with a definition of the processes. Is that OK?*

What happens next

Continue with the programme and adapt it to the new situation.

Comments

- As a solution focused practitioner who had mainly worked with individuals, I became increasingly aware of the fact that I was working very differently in workshop settings: I took up every question with enthusiasm and tried to give my clever answers – usually with mediocre results. I took on responsibility for the group's results and always tried to steer the group in this direction. Most of the time the results in the implementation phase were not remarkable – and on top of that it was enormously arduous for me (and also for the participants). Then I started letting go of the idea that the facilitator in workshops and seminars is the expert. I started seeing myself as the provider of the framework: a frame which facilitates optimal learning and development and at the same time stays open to what develops. I began practising the art of not knowing and trusting that the participants actually did have enough resources to solve their challenges with their own custom-made solutions.
- The special appeal of these mini-coaching conversations is that deep insights develop in a very short time. The participants

provide their own answers and realise that they can trust them-selves and their own competences. These are exceptional moments – people usually experience the opposite: they are told what the matter is, how you have to do something, and what is right or wrong. Such moments don't always happen – but when I integrate these short coaching sequences, the chances of personal insight and learning improve, and thus change can happen. These moments are very impressive.

Acknowledgements

It is very difficult to identify a clear source. I think the mini-coaching was developed in our research team of Kati Hankovszky, Peter Szabó and myself.

About **Daniel Meier**

– Solutionsurfers

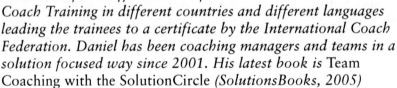

Daniel is the co-founder and managing partner of the international Brief-Coach training institute Solutionsurfers®, based in Switzerland. He is the Director of the German speaking part of this association. Solutionsurfers® offer solution focused Coach Training in different countries and different languages leading the trainees to a certificate by the International Coach Federation. Daniel has been coaching managers and teams in a solution focused way since 2001. His latest book is Team Coaching with the SolutionCircle *(SolutionsBooks, 2005)*

Address: Waldstätterstrasse 9, CH – 6003 Lucerne, Switzerland
Phone:+ 41 (0)41 210 3973
e-mail: daniel.meier@solutionsurfers.com
www.solutionsurfers.com
www.weiterbildungsforum.ch

Learning from good examples

Peter Röhrig, Germany

The exercise offers a simple clearly structured frame with which to organise a fair and useful experience swap.

Setting

Number of participants: 10–100.
Time: Briefing and assessment 15 minutes, and another 15 minutes for each round.

- This exercise requires some preparation. You will need a poster or flip chart with the rating criteria and at least two self-adhesive dots for each participant – one red and one green. In groups of less than 10, give everyone two dots of each colour.
- It is helpful to have the rules for exchange displayed on a flip chart or slide.
- You will need enough space in the room or outside for several groups to stand together in exchange rounds.
- The exercise can be done with large groups. I did it with 80 people from different professions and sectors at the annual meeting of the Bonn section of the German Society for Quality. The exercise was one of the major benefits the participants mentioned afterwards. I needed more preparation for this: I had the rating and exchange rules on worksheets and facilitated the exercise with a PowerPoint presentation.

Context and purpose

This exercise encourages exchange of good practice. When people from different sectors plan a project together, it provides a very good start, letting them experience facets of quality in their respective workplaces. In groups of people from different organisations, it helps to establish an atmosphere of confidence. And even in teams that have already worked together for a long time, it offers a

229

chance for a fresh view on routines and for mutual learning without great effort.

In introducing a quality management system, this exercise may help to enliven the apparently abstract and formal quality criteria and systems.

A special benefit of this exercise for knowledge management lies in its focus on interaction. Traditional knowledge management puts a lot of emphasis in extensively documenting the collected know-how. Many valuable ideas and tips are however more easily communicable orally than in a written form. The exercise offers suggestions about how knowledge can be communicated even more effectively and how it can be adapted more easily to different workplaces.

The goals are to:

- Encourage learning from good examples.
- Use the diversity of experience in groups.
- Let people talk about things and developments they are proud of.
- Show how a fair exchange of experience works.

Detailed description

Assessment system
As a starting point for the experience swap you will need a simple assessment or criteria system on a poster or flip-chart. I like to work with the Excellence model of the European Foundation for Quality Management (EFQM) which can be applied universally. It describes all the important facets of organisations by which quality may be assessed and developed in nine criteria.

You can also work with your own criteria developed in line with the workshop topics and the workplaces of participants. You will find examples in the comments paragraph below.

Excellence model of the European Foundation for Quality
Management (EFQM)

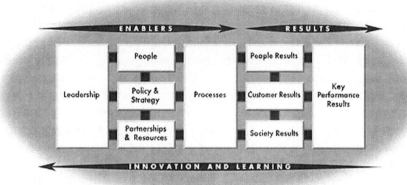

If the participants are not yet familiar with the chosen criteria, present them briefly and with simple examples. For the EFQM model you could say:

This system has been approved throughout Europe to support companies and organisations in the assessment and development of quality. The first 5 criteria are called Enablers and give answers to the question of how a company might proceed to achieve excellent results. The other 4 criteria show what comes out of these efforts. In the criterion People, for example, all the activities that contribute to helping people to do their jobs as well as possible are assessed. What is done in concrete terms to qualify, inform and support people in their workplace etc.? In the criterion People Results, all the measurable results, such as job satisfaction, identification with the company, absenteeism, labour turnover etc. are listed.

Assessment instruction
Use the EFQM model now to locate your strengths and areas for improvement. Stick a green dot in the box where you and/or your company have special strengths. This might be a criterion in which you could report on a good idea or a successful method that might be inspiring for others. Then stick a red dot in a box where you see a need for improvement. Please choose a criterion where you need urgent suggestions for quality development.

231

Now ask the participants to take a close look at the dot assessment and comment on the results. How are the dots scattered over the map of criteria? Are there any salient clusters or criteria without a dot? What is remarkable or even surprising to the participants?

Focus now on the criteria in which you find at least one red and one green dot. The criteria with many red dots and just a few green dots are the most interesting for the following experience swap. Ask who has pasted the green dots in these criteria. Write down keywords on a flip chart for the ideas or suggestions behind the green dots. The presenters of suggestions should only very briefly describe their idea and make other participants curious about it.

In this way you gather several topics on the flip chart. Then for each keyword, ask how many participants are interested to hear more about it and write the number beside that keyword. How many votes you allow each person depends on the size of the group, their curiosity and enthusiasm. Normally I allow as many as people want.

Now assign a rank order of interest and conduct the swap in that order. If you have 20 participants, call to the front the two or three presenters whose ideas found most interest (with smaller or larger groups, fewer or more presenters). Explain – with the help of a prepared flip chart or slide – the rules for the swap:

In a minute you will stand around the presenter from whom you want to know more. First decide who will be the time keeper and keep track of time for your group. The presenter will briefly outline the concrete benefit which came from implementing the idea at his or her workplace. This might for instance be more satisfaction with results or any other improvement. You have exactly one minute for this! As soon as the time keeper says that the minute is over, you may ask the presenter questions about how, what, who or when in order to find out what you really want to know about the idea or method. Avoid why questions as they tend to put the presenter into a defensive position. And this exercise is not about who is right or wrong but about learning from each other. The presenter does not have to answer all questions. If he or she thinks that a question goes too far, he or she can just skip the question and answer the next. For questions and answers, you have exactly 10 minutes. When the timer keeper says time is up, we'll meet again in the full group.

What happens next

If there are many topics of interest or if there are far more than 10 people interested in one topic you should organise more rounds with the same rules.

Helpful questions for the debriefing could be:
What were our highlights; what will give us most benefit?
What other suggestions or support do we want to implement these ideas successfully?
How can we use this kind of experience swap in our workaday life?

Comments

People like to talk about good ideas they have developed or implemented, especially in a trusting atmosphere which you can create by setting fair rules. It is helpful to presenters to know that they can skip questions – even if they rarely do so in my experience.

People with good ideas are inclined to talk with enthusiasm about all sorts of things, whatever they think might be useful for others. Here the presenters are instructed to speak very briefly about the personal benefit, focusing on everyday practical aspects and the listeners are then given the chance to ask whatever they want led by their own many and varied interests. Within a relatively short span of time – 10 minutes – even complex ideas and methods can be described so vividly that everybody learns a lot – including the presenters!

In smaller groups it can be useful to write down keywords for all the green dots, even if there are no red dots in the corresponding criteria boxes.

Examples of different criteria models

In experience swaps with people from doctors' practices, the chosen criteria might be processes that support patient care, such as patient information, patient security, qualification of people, practice organisation, quality development etc. Or you could list examples of particular aspects of patient care, like reception, diagnosis, treatment, documentation etc.

Sometimes it is even better to choose aspects of an overarching topic. For example, if people from social organisations want to exchange experience about fundraising, the criteria could be choice of target group, objectives, publicity etc.

The total number of criteria to be assessed should not exceed 10. That will enable a clear process of assessment and exchange.

Acknowledgements

I developed this exercise from different modules of experiential learning.

About *Dr. Peter Röhrig*

– ConsultContor · Consulting and Coaching

Peter is an SF organisational consultant, facilitator and executive coach, born 1948, with two children.

- *Formal education as an economist and social psychologist*
- *Advanced training in epidemiology, organisational development, total quality management (EFQM) and solution focused consulting*
- *11 years as general manager of service companies*
- *Many publications, mainly about self-management, leadership and quality development*
- *Partner of ConsultContor, consulting and coaching, in Cologne, Germany*

Renate Kerbst, one of his co-partners at ConsultContor says about Peter:
Zeal for solutions is the name of an SF training series initiated by Peter, and this is a strong impulse for his professional functioning. His focus on practical resources and his attentiveness for simplicity are a solid foundation for his consulting and facilitating work. With subtle persistence he helps his clients to find surprising and furthering solutions.

As a recovering former manager he supports whole-heartedly people in challenging leadership positions – and people who want to create effective teamwork. One of his main working areas is quality development, with a special emphasis on the health and social sector.

Peter is committed to the international SOLWorld network and faculty member of the SOLWorld Summer University. He offers advanced training in SF consulting and workshop design.

Mark McKergow says about Peter:
The biggest quiet style – a giant with velvet hands.

Address: Balthasarstsse 81, D 50670 Cologne, Germany
Phone: + 49 (0)228–34 66 14 Mobile: + 49 (0)179-523 46 86
e-mail: : peter.roehrig@consultcontor.de
www.ConsultContor.de

Solution focused interview with absent team members

Insa Sparrer, Germany

The solution focused interview with absent team members is suitable when not all the relevant people are present, perhaps because of illness or urgent business. This activity makes it possible to include the missing person(s) in the work symbolically, using representatives. It helps to generate ideas for shared solutions as if everyone in the group were present.

Setting

Normally the interview takes between 20 minutes to at most two hours, depending on how many people have to be interviewed. There should be at least two more people in the group than the number of team members who have to be interviewed. There is no obvious maximum number of group members. In small groups, it is possible to work with symbolic objects instead of people.

The large group should be sitting in a circle, where they can see all the members of the team. The constellation is done in the centre of the group.

Some flip charts and pin boards are useful.

Context and purpose

In this activity, it is possible to

- integrate absent people into the solution focused process,
- gain missing information (aspects, issues, values or people),
- visualise issues which are difficult to verbalise,
- generate specific new ideas.

It is well suited to large groups: for supervision, for individual teams and project groups, in conflict situations and to generate

236

ideas. It can also be used when all the members of a group are involved in an issue. In this case there are some additional aspects which have to be taken into account which I will mention at the end of the steps.

Detailed description

Step 1: Describe a common issue or theme
The facilitator (we prefer to speak of the host) asks for a sub-group or team with a common issue to explore, for example how to improve working relationships, work on a specific project or conflicts. This group is then asked to come up to the front and the different members of the group are asked to briefly outline how they view the issue and describe how they would later notice that the interview had been helpful for them.

Step 2: Choose the representatives
In a small team, every member can choose a representative for themselves from the large group. If the team has more than 8 or 9 people, parties can be built, e.g. for, against, neutral; or male, female; or plan A, plan B, plan C, plan D. Each party can also choose a code name for itself. Then each party chooses a representative for itself from the large group. The team chooses representatives for absent people or parties.

Step 3: Set up the first picture
The host asks the team members one at a time to stand behind their own representatives, put their hands on their shoulders and slowly lead them around the room until the position feels right to them. As they do this, the host says:

Notice your contact with the floor, breathe deeply and touch your representative lightly on the shoulder blades. Take a small step forward and let yourself notice where your feet lead you. Somewhere in the room feels right ... let your representative stand there.

This trance induction helps to shape the positioning process of setting up from bodily awareness rather than from conscious thought.

The representatives for absent people are then set up by someone chosen by the team. Representatives for parties can be set up by

237

more than one of the original team together. When all representatives have been set up, we have got the first constellation picture.

Step 4: Read the first picture
This first constellation of the representatives can show a lot: who can see whom; who is in contact with whom; who looks where; who is standing apart; who is in the centre.

Step 5: Ask and echo the representatives about their bodily sensations
When the representatives have all been constellated, they get *representative perception*, that is their bodily sensations, emotions and thoughts change in a way which normally makes sense for the person who has the issue. The host now asks each of the representatives what differences they feel in terms of bodily perceptions. We focus attention on concrete differences in bodily perception, because here there are fewer expectations and hence less interpretation.

The host in each case repeats most of what the representative said, so that everyone can hear it. If representatives said something in an unappreciative way, the host repeats the wish behind this or qualifies the statement by saying: *From X's perspective the perception is Y.* If representatives talk a lot, the host can summarise what they say. If representatives give interpretations, the host returns the focus to concrete difference in the bodily perception.

Step 6: Ask the actual team members
At this point it is important to ask the original people whether their representatives' statements are appropriate for them, whether they are on the right page. If this is not the case, the original can step into the place where the representative is standing and look at the constellation picture from there. Usually the picture makes sense. Throughout this activity, the host should watch whether the originals can follow what is happening. If this is not the case, a step can be repeated, or the original can step into the place of the representative and the step can be repeated with the original, or modified.

Step 7: Reposition representatives
As a preparation for the following solution focused interview, there are some minimal changes of the constellation. If representatives

are standing with their back to the rest of the team, turn them around through 180 degrees so that they can see each other. After these changes they can be asked again about differences in bodily sensations.

Step 8: Add more representatives
If there are suggestions that someone is missing, find another representative for that person or party.

Step 9: Conduct a solution focused interview with the representatives
Now give all the representatives chairs and ask them to sit down. The host also sits down. Begin the solution focused interview with the following words:

We are sitting here because there are some difficulties with ... There is a wish for ... There are different opinions in terms of ... I would like to begin our conversation with a question which may be difficult and a bit unusual. Each of you can sit comfortably and listen to this question. Maybe answers will come to you. If so, you can voice them afterwards. Till then let yourself be surprised what comes to your mind.

At this point, the group version of the miracle question follows (the dots indicate pauses):

When after this conversation you all go back to your work and do what still has to be done today ... and then it is evening and everyone goes home ... maybe you relax, maybe you took some work home, maybe you eat with your family or go out, maybe with friends ... at some point in the evening you get tired and go to bed and fall asleep ... and suppose ... during the night a miracle happens ... and the miracle was that what brought you here is solved ... just like that, that would be the miracle ... and if that happens so quickly, it would really be a miracle, wouldn't it? ... Now the next morning you wake up ... but no one tells you that the miracle has happened ... how would you notice it? ... What is different? What do you do differently? ... maybe you think differently ... maybe you feel differently ... What else is different? ... and maybe there is something else that is different ... or maybe you will not notice the miracle in the morning ... when would be the first moment when you do notice the miracle? ... How? ... Does anyone else except you notice the miracle? ... Who? ... How? ...

What does he or she notice? ... How does he or she react to this? ... And now that the miracle has happened, how do you react to this? ... Does anyone else notice the miracle? ... Who? ... How? ... How does she or he react to it? ... But now that the miracle has happened, how do you react to this? ... Are there any additional differences after the miracle? ... Who would like to speak first about her or his miracle? ... Who would like to begin?

Now the representatives can speak about their miracle in turn. If someone is unclear, the host asks: *And how do you notice that ...?* With regard to actions, changes and contradictions to other miracles that have been expressed, the host asks the representative how he imagines the other members of the team will react to his change and, when the miracle has happened, how he will react then to all this. As soon as a representative forgets about his miracle, the host reminds him of it.

Step 10: Identify actions
If actions are mentioned during the interview which can be carried out immediately, for example creating contact, dialogues, changing places, expressing wishes, needs, sorrows or emotions, these steps towards a solution can be sometimes symbolically achieved immediately with the representatives. (If not they should at least be brought to the attention of the members of the team present by mentioning them.)

Step 11: The original people take the places of the representatives
When all representatives have talked about their miracle and taken symbolic steps towards a solution, the original people are asked to stand where their representatives were and look at the picture from this perspective.

Step 12: Discuss ideas for solution steps
The original people sit down in the main group again and report what has changed for them and what new ideas they want to follow and how to do this. The host can note the most important steps on the flip chart.

Variant

It is useful to do this activity in a business organisation where everyone is involved because everybody gets to know each other's perspectives. In this case, note the following aspects:

– The representatives are chosen in such a way that nobody is as a representative for himself, so that representative perception is not impaired by personal knowledge.
– It is valuable to change the representatives before the miracle question and near the end of the interview, when everybody has answered the miracle question, so that everyone gets to see things from a number of different perspectives.
– The host should stress that everything that is said when someone functions as a representative should be taken as a metaphor and not understood literally. If statements of representatives are disrespectful, the host should restate these in a socially acceptable way. It is important that everyone saves face, because the group has to go on working together.
– If there aren't enough people for representatives, symbols like chairs can be used instead. People can take it in turns to sit on the chairs and answer the questions.

What happens next

After the interview, ideas for solutions can be written onto the flip chart, and the next steps can be worked out with the team members. The members of the large group can support this process with suggestions. Then you can have a discussion about what the members of the large group learned from this whole process and where they can use the ideas.

Comments

This tool was developed in a seminar on solution focused interviews, in which a team of three wanted to work on an issue. Unfortunately, one of the three was absent. Based on my experience in Systemic Structural Constellations, I suggested choosing a representative for this team member from among the participants. I asked the two members of the team who were present whether they also wanted to be represented during the interview. They found this idea interesting and chose three representatives whom they set up in the room. Before the constellation, the conflicts and problems within this team were not mentioned. During the solution focused group interview, the representatives talked about solutions which were convincing for the originals, and also about details which they couldn't have known about, e.g. that one team member wanted to leave and another was working on very specific computer graphics. The originals were surprised about this correspondence of the answers and also quite astonished, because they had not expected this.

Since then I have been using this format more and more for supervision questions and conflicts and for improving co-operation in teams. It is important to ensure that the representatives give their answers based on their representative bodily perception and not on thinking.

Acknowledgements

This activity stems from work of Steve de Shazer and Insoo Kim Berg. The solution focused interview with larger groups was developed further by Insoo Kim Berg. The work with representatives has its roots in the sculpture work of Virginia Satir and in the Systemic Structural Constellations which I developed with Matthias Varga von Kibéd.

References

Insa Sparrer (2006): *Systemische Strukturaufstellungen. Theorie und Praxis*, Heidelberg (Carl Auer)

Insa Sparrer (2007): *Einführung in Lösungsfokussierung und Systemische Strukturaufstellungen*. Heidelberg (Carl Auer)

Insa Sparrer (2007): *Miracle, Solution and System*, Cheltenham (Solutions Books)

About *Insa Sparrer*

– SySt-Institute Munich

Insa Sparrer, Dipl.Psych., psychotherapist with approbation, has worked in her own clinics in Munich since 1989. She founded the SySt-Institute in Munich in 1996 With Matthias Varga von Kibéd. They give seminars on Systemic Structural Constellations (SySt), a form which they have developed together. Insa Sparrer gives trainings in Systemic Structural Constellation work in Germany, Austria, Switzerland, Italy, Slovenia, the Netherlands, Greece, Hungary and England, as well as courses at universities in Austria and Germany.

Address: Neureutherstr. 1, D-80799 Munich, Germany
Phone/Mobile: 0049-(0)89-27275911/-
e-mail: info@syst.info
www.syst.info

CHAPTER 9

Taking the learning back to the workplace

Noticing your secret buddy   *Jane Adams, Canada*

How I see you – and how I think you see me   *Madeleine Duclos, Switzerland*

Footsteps   *Dominik Godat, Switzerland*

Team treasure chest   *Josef Grün, Germany*

Perspective X   *Josef Grün, Germany*

The scaling party   *Michael Hjerth, Sweden.*

My secret good resolution   *Peter Röhrig, Germany*

Taking it forward – from ideas to action   *Janine Waldman, United Kingdom*

How do we make sure that the learning, insights and good intentions which emerge during the workshop find their way back to the real world workplace?

Noticing your secret buddy

Jane Adams, Canada

This activity is very quick to set up. Participants are asked to pay attention to a specific person in the group – over a period of time – and to look for personal deeds or words which move the group in the direction it needs to go. It builds individual affirmation skills as well as friendship networks and teams.

Setting

This is a two-part activity: the set up and the wrap up. The set up takes 5 minutes. The wrap up can happen at the next meeting or at the end of an event such as a workshop or conference. Allow two minutes for each person to give their wrap up Affirmation.

It can be used with groups of up to 10. For larger groups, consider adapting the activity so that people form groups of 10.

Provide a piece of paper for everyone.

Context and purpose

Use this activity when you want to build the team over several meetings and to create a structure within which people notice what is working well in their context.

The purpose is to build bridges, overcome prejudice or indifference and to practise using the language of appreciation and positive regard. It also encourages people to behave in ways that contribute to the preferred future, by contributing to positive regard ... for themselves and others! Great teams are made up of exceptional one-to-one relationships within the team.

Detailed description

Everyone is given a small piece of paper on which they write their names. They crumple the paper up into a ball and toss it into the centre of the room. Everyone then picks up a crumpled piece of paper. Tell them that if they get their own name they have to toss it back and get another one. *Keep the name you have drawn a secret. Do not reveal it until we meet again as a group.*

Explain that the purpose of the activity is to give everyone an opportunity to notice the ways the person they are secretly admiring works well and what they contribute to the preferred future, as described by the group. Tell them to continue to do this until the wrap up (say when that will be).

At the wrap up, ask people to reveal whom they have been noticing, and what they have noticed. Ask one person to start, and then go around the room in a circle from that point, asking everyone to contribute. You can also give each and every person an affirmation for their observations!

What happens next

This is a stand alone activity which can fit easily into a variety of situations. Please change or adapt it to suit your own context.

Comments

People like to feel they are associating with people with lots of great qualities. They don't like to think they are associated with limited people. As facilitators we want to help them see each other in the most positive light. We want to see that everyone gets compliments throughout the team building process. This gives them the strength, courage and energy to continue. You could use this activity several times if you wish. It means that everyone gets to notice several other co-workers in a solution focused light!

Acknowledgement of sources

I believe versions of this activity are used worldwide. I first learned it from some people from the Philippines. It can be used in many different ways: at a group celebration; over the course of days, weeks or months in a workplace setting; conference; workshop; learning event or even a family get together.

247

About **Jane Adams**

– Jane Adams & Associates

Jane Adams M.Ed. contributes to public interest organisations' capacity to provide quality, strategic resources and to work harmoniously.

Address: 275 Major Street, Toronto, Ontario M5S 2L5 Canada
Phone/Mobile: + 01 416-921–3489
e-mail: janeadams@sympatico.ca
www.janeadams.ca

How I see you – and how I think you see me

A pat on the back

Madeleine Duclos, Switzerland

This is an interactive activity. You can use it at any time in a workshop or seminar, when you want to highlight individual resources, qualities and capabilities and how to communicate them in an appreciative way. The activity can also be used as a feedback exercise, especially for groups who have difficulties in expressing positive feedback. Moreover it is a very active exercise with energetic effect. It creates connections and therefore stimulates teamwork.

Setting

The whole activity takes about half an hour, depending on the size of the group: 5 minutes for briefing and fixing the paper on each other's back, about 15 minutes for writing on each other's back, about 5 minutes for writing down the qualities we hope to discover on our own back, about 10 minutes for reading the paper, asking questions, writing a credit card and reading out loud our qualities.

As a minimum I would suggest about 8 people for the activity. It can also be adapted for large groups (50 people and more) if you have enough room to move, but then not everybody can write on everybody else's back. Moreover, as you will discover further on, you will have to be creative in the last step of the activity (reading qualities out loud).

Make sure the room is big enough for people to move about easily.

For each person you need 1 small clothes peg, 1 sheet of heavy paper (you need heavy paper to keep their clothes clean), 1 sheet of A4 paper, 1 marker pen and one credit card size piece of card.

Context and purpose

The activity gives people the chance to review each other's resources – their positive qualities and capabilities. This is valuable in challenging times as it improves the relationships among team members and hence the working environment. It also strengthens coherence in the team, boosts self-esteem and mutual trust and helps people to evaluate the quality of their work and to become more aware of their impact on others.

Since this is one of my favourite activities, I use it a lot in workshops:

- For teambuilding, early on in the beginning of a workshop – to show the participants that you don't need to know each other well in order to perceive positive qualities and positive first impressions in each other
- Whenever a team lacks appreciation or when the team has difficulties in expressing positive feedback or appreciation
- At the beginning of a project in order to make an inventory of the existing resources in each person
- After a successful project, it is a nice way to give each other positive feedback
- If people in a team underestimate themselves

Detailed description

The participants fix a piece of thick paper on each other's backs with a clothes peg. The easiest place to fix it is on the collar. Then the facilitator asks them to pick up a pen and stand up and, without speaking, write clearly on everybody's back a positive quality of this person (in big groups on as many backs as possible).

Depending on the aims of the exercise, people are invited to write a resource, a quality, a talent, a first impression, a feedback on a given subject/project etc. – something positive and appreciative.

Afterwards everybody sits down again (the paper stays unread fixed on their back!) and writes on another piece of paper the qualities they think the others have written on their back. In other words, they note what they think that the others think about them. Then – and only then – can they take the paper off their back and compare the two sheets. They are allowed to ask questions for clarification – no explanations or justifications.

Then everybody underlines the three comments that touched them the most. Afterwards they write these on a small credit card size card, and finally everybody reads their three favourite qualities to the group: *I am ... and ... and ...* Make sure they use the word 'I'.

In very large groups (more than 15 people), you have to find other ways – for example building small groups – to make it possible for everybody to read their qualities out loud, while maintaining the attention of all the listeners.

After the activity, the cards can be put in a pocket, in a handbag, in a purse etc. to be taken back to work and fixed on a board above the desk or put close to the telephone etc.

What happens next

There are a lot of possible follow ups, for example:

- Johari-Window
- Rules of feedback
- Self-evaluation
- Appraisal interviews
- Appreciative solution focused talk
- Self-esteem
- My impact on others
- What else

Comments

It is very important to formulate the task so that people write only positive qualities. Some will be embarrassed or may ridicule it and make ironical remarks. Do not criticise these people, but try to help them to overcome their inhibitions.

People who cannot appreciate themselves will have a hard time to appreciate others. Help them in the second part, when they have to write down their own positive qualities which they suppose others see in them. For many people it is a big step to write this down.

Also in the third step, when they read their cards aloud in front of the group, you will realise how difficult it is for some to say something positive about themselves. Encourage them to read their qualities loud with a strong and confident voice.

Acknowledgement of sources

Many years ago, I learned this activity from Bonnie Tsai (Thanks a lot, Bonnie!) www.new-renaissance.eenet.ee/bonnie/ I added the idea of the credit card as a lasting reminder later.

About *Madeleine Duclos*

– FlowChange

After her studies at the Universities of Berne (Switzerland) and Bordeaux (France), Madeleine began to specialise in holistic methods. Today she runs her own business in Switzerland. She develops and gives courses in communication, personal development, trainer trainings and leadership, always connecting mind, body and heart. For years, she has shown a profound interest in the latest developments in teaching, learning and change. Her strength is in running creative and active workshops and in coaching teams and individuals in change processes.

Business trainer and coach in communication, learning and development Cert. NLP Trainer, AL Trainer, Solution Focus, Systemic Constellations, Inner Game, NVC, Edu-Kinesiology

Address: Lerberstrasse 33, CH-3013 Berne, Switzerland
Phone/Mobile: +41 79 272 4775
e-mail: madeleine@flowchange.com
www.flowchange.com

Footsteps

Making progress one step at a time

Dominik Godat, Switzerland

Footsteps is an ideal activity at the end of a workshop, because it turns the results of the workshop into small and relevant steps that motivate the participants and give them more confidence, building a bridge into their everyday life. The activity is divided into two parts: first the participants plan their own next two steps. Then the other members of the group think of five resources for each step that make them confident that the participant will reach his goals.

Setting

- Part one takes 5 to 10 minutes and part two takes 10 minutes for each member of the group.
- Optimal number of participants: 3 to 6 people. If there are more participants, form several groups.
- Enough space for every participant to do the individual exercise undisturbed.
- Flip chart paper and a pen for every participant and one flip chart for the instructions.
- Preparation is minimal because the facilitator only has to prepare the work instruction and hand out the flip chart papers and pens.

Context and purpose

This activity is best used at the end of a workshop. It can easily be transferred into coaching settings with individuals or teams and can also be useful in team development processes.

The aims are to turn results of the workshop into relevant and realistic next steps and at the same time to increase the participants' motivation and confidence in their planned actions. It makes the results of the workshop more concrete and turns them into do-able actions.

Detailed description

Form groups of 3 to 6 people and give everyone a piece of flip chart paper. Tell them to draw two big footprints with five toes each on each. Then every participant takes five to ten minutes to think of the next two steps that he wants to take after the workshop.

The facilitator can introduce the activity with words like this:

For the next ten minutes, please find a quiet place and reflect by yourself about what you have worked on today and what you have already achieved. Then think about the next two concrete steps that you want to get done after the workshop. Please limit yourself to only two things that you can realistically do and which motivate you. You should be able to take the first step within the next 24 hours and the second step within the next 14 days. Please write each step in one of the footprints on your flip chart. If there is enough time left, you can think about your own resources that make you confident that you can accomplish these planned actions.

Then call the participants back in their groups and ask them to present their steps to the other members of the group. The others now talk about the presenter's resources that make them particularly confident that he will take his steps. For each step, the presenter writes down the five most useful resources that he has heard about – one into each toe. After this exercise every member of the group has two resourceful footsteps reminding him of his next steps.

Activity step by step:

1. Introduction
2. Organisation into groups
3. Handout of the flip chart paper
4. Drawing the two footsteps
5. Individual exercise: thinking of the next two steps and writing them down on the flip chart

6. Group exercise: presentation of the next two steps and reflection of the group on resources that give them confidence that the presenter will reach his plans, writing the most useful resources on the flip chart

What happens next

Because this activity is best used at the end of a workshop, the facilitator can continue with final reflections and questions and the closing ceremony.

Comments

- I realised that solution focused workshops are usually highly productive and the successes can easily be seen. But sometimes the participants don't write down the planned actions and after a short period of time they forget them. In addition, their motivation and confidence sometimes falls when they get back to their everyday life. I wanted an activity which would build a bridge to everyday life and support the next steps by increasing the confidence and motivation of the participants and thus the probability of success.
- I think it is important to do this activity in a solution focused way by limiting the number of next steps and focusing on small, realistic, and relevant actions and on resources that give confidence. Thinking of only two steps increases the probability of success – participants have to focus on small and realistic activities instead of a huge list of actions.
- The activity can easily be changed by letting the client think not only about his next steps but also about his own resources that give him confidence and letting him present it to a group or a single person (e.g. a coach). If you do it this way, it seems important to me that the client immediately gets a solution focused feedback (e.g. *I am impressed by ..., and it makes me feel confident that* ...) that increases his motivation and confidence. The playful and figurative representation of the next steps can easily be remembered. Participants often like to take home a picture of their plans.

Acknowledgement of sources

I developed this method inspired by several playful workshops, for example at the SOLWorld Conference in Interlaken, and by the desire to find a figurative representation of the next steps.

About *Dominik Godat*

As an economist, HR specialist and founder of Godat Coaching, Dominik Godat invented Random Coaching in 2006. He works mainly in Switzerland as a coach with profit and non-profit organisations helping them to implement solution focused management ideas. He also trains and coaches individuals, managers and teams who are looking for success in their private and business lives.

Address: Hechtliacker 44, 4053 Basel, Switzerland
Phone/Mobile: +41 76 420 19 18
e-mail: coaching@godat.ch
www.godat.ch

Team treasure chest

Josef Grün, Germany

The team treasure chest is an ideal exercise to close a workshop, team development seminar or longer working session in which the participants have developed new structures, processes or roles. The team collects concrete and personal contributions made by each one of its members to ensure the transfer and implementation of the workshop results. These contributions are the treasures that will encourage the necessary changes, especially when difficult situations occur during the transfer. This closing activity generates a high level of energy and commitment.

Setting

- 20–30 minutes depending on group size.
- Ideal for groups between 10–20 people.
- You need a box with a lid (possibly wrapped in nice paper). Finding an appropriate box could also be the team's task.
- Each participant needs a card and marker pen.

Context and purpose

This exercise rounds off a successful working session. Everyone sees and hears what the others are willing to do to ensure the transfer and implementation of the results. The treasure chest is a collection of individual, small and concrete contributions – not collective ones.

Detailed description

After the implementation project has been discussed and planned, the participants meet in a large circle.

The facilitator introduces the exercise by saying:

I am confident that you will successfully transfer what you have developed here today. I also know from experience that many tricky and challenging situations can occur during the implementation or transfer phase. In these situations, it is very useful to have a treasure chest! In a well-filled treasure chest, you are sure to find the right jewels or keys to master these challenging situations.

The facilitator presents the treasure chest (e.g. a shoe box, a wooden box, etc) and puts it in the middle of the circle. Cards and pens are then placed in the middle or on an empty chair (one card and one pen per participant).

This is going to be a team treasure chest just for your jewels and treasures. Please take one card and one pen each and write what concrete things you personally will do to ensure that the results of this workshop are realised. Take your personal strengths into consideration and be as precise as possible in describing how this specific action will be useful in the impending change process. For example: 'I will make sure that ...', 'I will speak to ...', 'I will support colleagues by ...'. These actions should be do-able by you without anyone else's support.

The participants write their contributions to the change process on their card (max. 5 minutes). When everyone has done this, the facilitator asks the participants to add the date and their initials to the card.

The participants then take their turn in reading out their cards and placing them in the treasure chest. Discussion is not permitted during this time. Some teams might spontaneously applaud, cheer or simply nod at every contribution.

When all of the cards have been presented, the facilitator ceremonially closes the treasure chest and marks the team name and date onto the box.

At the very end, the treasure chest is handed to one of the team members for safekeeping.

To do this, the facilitator can either:

– Ask who would like to guard the treasure. If more than one participant is interested, the team can decide.
– Offer the treasure to the senior or junior team member to strengthen acceptance in the team. In this case, the facilitator is using this closing ceremony as his last action.
– Hand the treasure chest to a sceptical team member, who will notice right away if the team lacks energy and will activate the treasures.

The facilitator hands over the chest to the designated team member and says:

You are now taking on the important task of ensuring that the treasure chest will not be forgotten. You can, for example, leave the chest in the meeting room for everyone to see, either on the table or on a shelf. As long as energy is high and the necessary changes are being made, the chest need not be opened. If you notice that the energy is dropping, ask the team to open the chest and find a contribution or two that will help boost the team's energy.

What happens next

The treasure chest is an uncomplicated and easy way of verifying how the transfer is going and maintaining the efforts towards change. The aim is to reactivate the team members in order to continually think of ways to keep up the change in progress.

Comments

- This exercise – which is commonly used amongst my colleagues – is ideal for ending a workshop as it:
  - can be done with little preparation
  - is short and activates every participant
  - is highly symbolic
  - motivates every member of the team to openly commit to the transfer
  - offers room for individual commitment
  - activates the team to think of solutions to tricky future situations

- offers positive associations (treasure hunt, treasure island, etc . . .)
- is interesting and fun
- ensures that the energy invested into generating the results is not lost.
- Possible difficulties in the implementation, such as decreased energy, loss of focus, etc. are considered normal components of a change or development process. In my experience, bringing up the topic of upcoming challenges and difficulties often has a prophylactic effect. Teams are prepared to deal with such situations as solutions have already been formulated and are available in the working environment.

Alternatives

- This exercise can be modified in many ways.
  - The participants can add their cards to the treasure chest without reading them out to the group. People might just guess what the others have written.
  - The treasure chest could be filled only with special treasures, for example referring to the workshop theme, concrete personal changes in behaviour, etc.
  - Many interesting interventions can be made in choosing the treasure keeper and defining his or her role.
- In a larger scale workshop, where many teams need to co-operate, exchange information and communicate effectively, the treasure chest could become a Challenge Cup. Once the group has decided which team will guard the Cup first, it is handed to a responsible member of that team. The facilitator adds the ceremonial words: *You are the keeper of this treasure and are responsible for ensuring the team's commitment to the changes agreed here. If you notice that another team needs support, then you will discuss the possible actions to be taken with this team and whether the Challenge Cup needs to be transferred. You can also offer your support in solving the issues.*

Acknowledgements

Inspired by the works of Rudi Ballreich and Matthias zur Bonsen in their seminar: From deep sources.

About *Josef Grün*

I have been working as a consultant and coach for profit and non-profit organisations since 1989. My main focus is on individual and collective learning in organisations: to clarify goals and structures and to support individuals in their roles at work. Key topics include developing guidelines and strategies in small and medium sized organisations, as well as team building and leadership coaching.

Address: Balthasarstr. 81, 50670 Cologne, Germany
Phone: + 49 221–973130–20
e-mail: josef.gruen@consultcontor.de
www.consultcontor.de

Perspective X

Resources and support for personal attitude and behaviour change

Josef Grün, Germany

Perspective X is a good closing activity for a workshop that focuses on improving social and communicative competences (e.g. high potential training). The participants are encouraged to speak about successful future changes from the perspective of their colleagues, employees or supervisors. This closing intervention consolidates the resources and efforts needed for the transfer phase into the job.

Setting

- 45–60 minutes depending on the size of the group.
- For groups between 10–20 people; ideally between 10–15 people.

Context and purpose

This exercise supports change and provides energy for the transfer by anticipating future success. Participants anticipate and talk about their behaviour change by stepping into Person X's shoes. In other words, they experience their own success stories.

Detailed description

The main focus is to answer the common question at the end of a workshop: *How will I transfer the competences I have developed or expanded here into my everyday working environment?*

The participants sit in a circle and the facilitator explains:

You will now imagine how the abilities and skills you have gained here can be applied and put to use in your everyday work. Person X, either a colleague, an employee or your supervisor, will probably be observing what you are doing differently or even better after this workshop. Think of someone who will be observing you most closely and supporting you in the implementation of these new skills.

When you have thought of Person X, take a few minutes to think of what concrete changes this person will notice in the next few days or weeks. Feel free to make notes.

When everyone is ready, everyone takes their turn to stand behind their own chair and take on the role of Person X. Each participant is asked to speak in the present tense and talk about the changes they have observed in behaviour, attitude, interactions, etc. They begin their sentences with: *I, as Mr./Ms. X, notice the following changes in my colleague's behaviour . . .*

It is important that the participants remain in Person X's role without slipping back into their own perspective. Once Person X has finished, the participant sits back down on his/her chair and after a short pause, the next person continues. The comments and observations are not discussed in the group.

When everyone has had his turn, the facilitator adds

Please turn around and silently thank Person X for their support.

What happens next

A short break should follow before entering the final evaluation round to wrap up the workshop.

Comments

- This exercise needs time and a calm atmosphere. The participants need to concentrate and take it step by step. They need time to find answers to the following questions:

263

- *Whose observations and reactions do I particularly appreciate and trust?*
- *Who do I choose for this exercise? Who is my person X?*
- *What exactly will person X observe and how can I describe it?*
- This exercise cannot be included spontaneously or quickly at the end when most participants are already thinking about leaving. It needs to be planned and even announced at the beginning of the workshop to ensure that enough time is dedicated to the exercise.
- Participants are not talking about intentions (*I want to ..., I will ...*) but rather about results, as if the intended change had already occurred. They are giving themselves feedback through a third person. They are talking about the solution that has already been implemented. It is therefore crucial to ensure that the participants are talking from Person X's perspective and not their own. A possible way of expressing it could be *As Ms. Brown's colleague, who has been working with her (pointing to the empty chair in front) for many years on many common projects, I have noticed that ...*
- As every participant expresses these observations openly, the other participants in the group often sense a certain obligation to support their team member in successfully realising these changes. If this is the first session of a series, the second session could start with the same exercise, Person X describing what has changed in the meantime and what should be focused on in this session.

About *Josef Grün*

I have been working as a consultant and coach for profit and non-profit organisations since 1989. My main focus is on individual and collective learning in organisations: to clarify goals and structures and to support individuals in their roles at work. Key topics include developing guidelines and strategies in small and medium sized organisations, as well as team building and leadership coaching.

Address: Balthasarstr. 81, 50670 Cologne, Germany
Phone: + 49 221–973130–20
e-mail: josef.gruen@consultcontor.de
www.consultcontor.de

The scaling party

Michael Hjerth, Sweden.

The Scaling Party is a wonderful way to end a conference, training or meeting. It extends the scaling walk to a party-like interaction about success and change, the future perfect and planning and committing to small steps. The facilitator acts like a toastmaster and invites the group to different activities on different positions on the scale: At 'now' and 'ten' the group mingles (with imaginary or real drinks or snacks) and talks about differences they see. At the final 'one step up', individuals decide quietly on their next steps, then they walk around the room to tell others about their step and to get good wishes and a handshake in return. Thus the activity ends with a playful commitment to new steps.

Setting

Allow between 15–30 minutes for the activity, depending on the size of the group.

The scaling party works in groups from 12 people upwards. I've done it successfully with groups of 180 people. If the room is good, with plenty of space to move around, I cannot see a reason why it could not be done with several hundreds. The participants should have some room to move, so a crowded meeting room is not the right place. If possible, move chairs and tables out of the way.

Context and purpose

The activity is a wonderful way to end an event. I have used it to end trainings, teambuilding days, conferences, planning sessions, etc. It is my standard way of ending a training session, to help it end on a high note.

The general purpose is to consolidate knowledge, decisions and ideas at the end of an event. An equally important purpose is to deepen commitment to change and the next steps.

266

There are several benefits and effects that can result from the scaling party.

1. It is done at the end of the day when everyone is tired of sitting down, and perhaps is low on energy. Standing and walking give a little extra energy boost, which helps end the day in good spirits.
2. The conversational quality and rules of a mingling conversation are different to a discussion sitting down. This gives an informal and creative touch to ideas or skills covered earlier in the event. Everyone knows that some of the most creative work at meetings actually happens at coffee breaks! The mingling conversations emulate that quality in the meeting room.
3. By moving physically along the scales, the brain's kinaesthetic resources are activated, which enhances the quality of learning, knowledge and ideas.
4. The hand-shake at the end consolidates decisions and steps since it is made public in a positive way.

Detailed description

Preparation
You might want to get some drinks and snacks ready beforehand. Champagne and nuts are great, but anything party-like is good. If this is not possible, you can serve imaginary snacks and drinks. This works just fine.

Make sure the room is set up right: you only have to make sure there is enough room to move around and that there is enough space at the middle and both ends of the room for the participants to gather there comfortably. It can be a good idea to ask the group to help you move tables and chairs out of the way.

Step by step procedure and suggested instructions
1. Ask the group to stand up and gather at one end of the room.
2. Introduce yourself as a toast-master whose job it is to host a scaling party to end the event.
3. Set up the room as a scale:
   Let us think of this room as a scale, this end over here is 0 and the other end over there is 10. 0 stands for this morning at 9 o'clock, when we started this meeting, and 10 stands for when we have arrived at our goals.

267

4. Ask the participants to silently choose a number on the scale:
So, on this scale where 0 is this morning, which could mean different things to different persons, and 10 is that we have arrived at our goals, which also could be different, where are you right now? Just think of your own number and don't tell anyone.

5. Gather the group in a row in the middle of the room, which stands for the number X. It is important that everyone stands on the same line, so as to avoid competition and debate about the individual numbers. The actual numbers do not matter in this activity.
So, let this line in the middle of the room be whatever number you have chosen. Please come and join me here.

6. Ask the participants to look back at 0 and consider changes between 0 and X. Ask for a few examples:
Now, turn and look at 0. It seems that we have all moved quite a bit during the day! Congratulations! What is different at X? What else?

7. Bring in the (real or imaginary) drinks and snacks and invite people to mingle:
So, it is my pleasure as a toast-master to offer drinks and snacks ... and while we are enjoying this, please mingle around and talk about what is different now we are at X and not 0. What new ideas do we have, what new skills, what new knowledge, what new contacts, etc?

8. Let the group mingle for a few minutes.

9. Invite the group to go to 10, the preferred future (ring a bell or tap a glass):
Ladies and gentlemen could I have your attention, please. It is now my pleasure to invite you to 10, the future where we have achieved our goals. [Gather the group at 10]

10. Set the mood of 10, get a few examples, and invite more mingling:
Welcome to 10, great to see you here, a miracle must have happened. All the stuff we have talked about is now reality! [You might give a few examples here]. What is different now, here? What else? Great, fantastic! I have some more refreshments here, and while we are having them, please move around and mingle with people chatting about what is different here in the future.

11. Gather the group at the middle of the room again.

    As the toast-master it is my unfortunate obligation to ask you to come back to now. [Let the group gather at X] Now that we've visited 10, what is different about standing at X? [Invariably people say things like I have a sense that it is possible, I feel motivated and want to get back there.] So, it seems that we want to be at 10 again? Can we just jump there? If not, what can we do? [Usually someone says: We must take a step] Ah, so we can take one step! Great idea! So let's all take one step. Next, ask them to move one step towards 10.

12. Ask the participants to silently figure out what the step they just took involved:

    So, I wonder what your step is. What will you do, as an individual, to take one step during the coming days? Just think quietly about this for a moment ... [Let people think for a minute]

13. Ask the participants to walk around the room, meet someone, say hello, shake their hand, tell them what they have decided to do, listen to what the other is going to do, congratulate them on their good ideas and decisions, and get congratulations back. They go on to meet someone else and do the same. The idea is to have people shake as many hands as possible, repeat their steps and get congratulations as many times as possible. A useful phrasing is:

    Now, at the end of the day it is time to say goodbye, so I'd like to invite you to move around the room. And, to the first person you bump into, shake their hand and say 'Hi! I've decided to do this and this as my next step'. That person will say: 'Congratulations! That sounds like a fantastic idea! Myself, I'm going to do this and that!' to which you reply: 'Wonderful! Good luck! Bye for now!' Then you move around and find another person. You can repeat the same step or tell them something else if you prefer that. Your job is to talk to and shake hands with as many people as possible during 5 minutes or so. Go!

14. End the activity by thanking everyone for a wonderful party.

What happens next

The scaling party is designed to work best at the very end of a workshop. I prefer to end after the activity, especially if we have real drinks and snacks, saving only things like filling our evaluation forms.

Comments

I first encountered the scaling walk in a workshop by Paul Z Jackson a few years back, and tried it out successfully right away. I noticed how differently people acted and how energised they become by working standing up. This led to the idea that this could be used at the end of a day, when people are tired of sitting down and talking and listening.

The idea to extend it to use mingling came from conversations with Eero Riikonen about the fact that most creative work at conferences and meetings happens at coffee breaks. I wanted to find a way to include that free quality in a regular meeting room. By supplying drinks and snacks, I also show my appreciation for all the hard work the group has been doing, and at the same time lighten the spirit and introduce a sense of celebration of work-well-done. I use the final shaking hands activity as a clear way to end the day. At the same time it deepens commitment by (1) stating decisions publicly several times (2) getting compliments and (3) using the handshake as a symbolic contract.

In a training situation, the activity also summarises the solutions focused model by illustrating change, future perfect and small steps.

This activity is also fun for the facilitator, who gets to play toast-master and can step out of the facilitator/trainer/leader mode. I usually become more lively and playful in the toast-master role play, to set a good spirit and to keep the party going.

Acknowledgements

I first learned about the scaling walk from Paul Z Jackson. Eero Riikonen's ideas about the usefulness of coffee-table talk has also been helpful as I developed the scaling party.

About **Michael Hjerth**

– SolutionWork

Michael Hjerth was born in Stockholm 1960. After a career as a musician and music teacher he studied psychology and philosophy at the University of Lund Sweden and graduated in 1991. Michael developed the PLUS-model of solution focus and Micro-tools: techniques to integrate SF-practice in the fast-paced worklife. He has been influenced not only by philosophy and language, but also by research into evolutionary theory, neuroscience and cognitive science.

In Sweden, Michael is highly sought after and well known for his combination of clear philosophy, scientific grounding and minimalistic practicality.

He is active internationally and has appeared in conferences in many European countries. He was the secretary of the European Brief Therapy Association and is on the steering group of Solutions in Organisations Linkup.

Address: Segelflygsgatan 39, 128 33 Skarpnäck, Sweden
Phone/Mobile: +46-703258837
e-mail: michael@solutionwork.se

My secret good resolution

Peter Röhrig, Germany

At the end of a workshop a secret good resolution will support participants in the transfer of their work back into their everyday surroundings.

Setting

- Participants: 3–30.
- Time: 15–20 minutes.
- Material: A flip chart or Powerpoint presentation with the instructions, paper and pens.

Context and purpose

The workshop comes to an end, results are documented and actions are agreed. This is a good time to focus participants' thoughts on the near future, when they are back at work. How can they personally make use of what has been agreed upon for their team or organisation? What small changes could they notice to show that they are on the right track?

The exercise works especially well with teams of people who work closely together and talk regularly about the progress of their work.

There are many benefits from running this exercise. It creates:

- Awareness that small, do-able and attractive tasks will suffice for successful transfer.
- Confidence that goals can be reached.
- Curiosity to notice things that work in the team.
- Incentive to talk more often about things they appreciate in their colleagues.

Detailed description

It is a good idea to have the instructions on a flip chart or a Powerpoint presentation.

Please think for a moment about the small changes in your workplace which could help you to see that you are on the right track. <Pause> What small first step could you contribute to make this happen? <Pause> What simple and unspectacular action can you do without help from others to increase your job satisfaction by just a fraction?

Get to work on something that you can do within the next three working days. Write down your good resolution on a piece of paper. Please do this so that nobody can see what you are writing. Put this resolution somewhere to remind you to check how you got on with it.

Do not tell anybody about your resolution.

And then try to find out during the next few weeks what other members of your team have decided to do. Notice positive change in your everyday work. In team meetings, regularly talk about the changes you have noticed in others and how this has affected you.

What happens next

No further discussion is needed after this and you can round up the workshop with an evaluation, for instance by asking for brief answers to the following questions:

- *What did I like best at this workshop?*
- *What suggestions do I have – for future participants, the facilitator, the venue?*
- *What affirmation do I want to give the team to take with them?*

Comments

This simple small task at the end of a workshop holds a special fascination. The clue lies in the secret that is made about the resolution. Participants are invited to bring to mind the direct benefit they could have from their collective work. It would be easy to tell everybody about their good resolution and use the power of witnesses for committing themselves. However, in teams of people who work closely together, the secrecy about the resolutions creates a starting point for a change in team culture. It arouses curiosity about other people's resolutions and offers many opportunities for mutual affirmation.

Furthermore this activity works with the idea of small steps. In the transfer phase, frustration often arises because the chosen tasks are too big. The old wisdom that even the longest journey starts with a first small step – or that an elephant can be eaten in very small pieces – helps here. If the first step is successful, the resulting confidence can cause a domino effect so that the next steps in the direction of the goal will succeed more easily.

I have worked with this activity for a long time. I show the individual steps of the exercise one at a time. I have the instructions prepared on a flip chart and fold it up and fix it with adhesive tape so that it is completely hidden at first. Then I introduce the first part of the exercise and unveil the poster as far as ... *that nobody can see what you are writing*. The later unveiling has something of a magic trick which is resolved nearly – not completely – at the end.

Some participants find a resolution quickly and others need considerably more time. It is worth being patient and supporting people with the hint that even a very small change might help to make a start. So far, all my participants have found a resolution for themselves.

Acknowledgement of sources

The basic idea stems from the Reteaming model of my Finnish colleague, Ben Furman. I have integrated it into my work in quality development processes.

About **Dr. Peter Röhrig**

– ConsultContor • Consulting and Coaching

Peter is an SF organisational consultant, facilitator and executive coach, born 1948, with two children.

- *Formal education as an economist and social psychologist*
- *Advanced training in epidemiology, organisational development, total quality management (EFQM) and solution focused consulting*
- *11 years as general manager of service companies*
- *Many publications, mainly about self-management, leadership and quality development*
- *Partner of ConsultContor, consulting and coaching, in Cologne, Germany*

Renate Kerbst, one of his co-partners at ConsultContor says about Peter:
Zeal for solutions is the name of an SF training series initiated by Peter, and this is a strong impulse for his professional functioning. His focus on practical resources and his attentiveness for simplicity are a solid foundation for his consulting and facilitating work. With subtle persistence he helps his clients to find surprising and furthering solutions.

As a recovering former manager he supports whole-heartedly people in challenging leadership positions – and people who want to create effective teamwork. One of his main working areas is quality development, with a special emphasis on the health and social sector.

Peter is committed to the international SOLWorld network and faculty member of the SOLWorld Summer University. He offers advanced training in SF consulting and workshop-design.

Mark McKergow says about Peter:
The biggest quiet style – a giant with velvet hands.

Address: Balthasarstsse 81, D 50670 Cologne, Germany
Phone: + 49 (0)228–34 66 14 Mobile: + 49 (0)179-523 46 86
e-mail: : peter.roehrig@consultcontor.de
www.ConsultContor.de

Taking it forward – from ideas to action

Janine Waldman, United Kingdom

This is a simple and effective process to pull together the key learning from a workshop and identify small actions for participants to take when they return to the workplace. This activity combines group work with individual reflection and builds individual commitment to taking action.

Setting

- Time frame: Allow 25–30 minutes.
- Optimal group size: 6–60.
- Flip chart with the respective questions for the groups.

Context and purpose

The aim of this activity is to review the course content and maximise the possibility of the skills, ideas and tools learned being transferred back to the workplace. By creating a positive future, the activity motivates people to apply what they have learned after the workshop. Participants are encouraged to choose small actions and to speculate on the positive consequences of taking those actions – and this too increases their commitment to using what they have learned.

The activity can be used towards the end of a workshop, and works equally well with teams that work together and know each other and those who don't.

Detailed description

Process overview
- Get participants into groups
- Collect ideas, concepts and tools covered during the workshop
- Draw a Future Perfect poster
- Individually identify small actions
- Share small actions with positive consequences

Activity
Start the activity by explaining that they are now going to explore how they will take forward what they have learned during the workshop – from this room into their jobs.

Get the participants into groups of 3–5.

NOTE: You can use coloured markers to form groups. For example, if there are 12 people in your group, have 4 red, 4 blue and 4 black markers. Invite the participants to take a pen and then find the other people with the same colour pen. Direct each group to a flip chart ... then ask them to take the tops off their pens, ready for action.

Show the instructions below on a slide or flip chart

Taking it forward

List all the ideas, concepts and tools covered in this workshop that you'd like to use in your work over the next month or so.

... and ask them to list all the ideas, concepts and tools from the workshop that they can think of. Tell them they have 2 minutes for this activity. They don't need to agree or discuss it at length. They all have a pen which they can use to write on the group's flip chart.

NOTE: If they are a bit slow getting started you might like to give an example of what you are looking for.

Call time after a couple of minutes. Ask the participants to tear the page off the flip chart and put it somewhere they can see it, such as on the wall, a table or the floor nearby.

Show the following on a slide or flip chart

> ### *Applications*
>
> Supose you are able to put all this into practice over the next 3 months . . .
>
> Together, create a poster that shows when and how you will be doing this.

Read the instructions to the participants and explain that a poster can be whatever they want it to be – it's a visual representation of them putting their learning into practice over the next three months.

Tell them they have 8 minutes for this.

NOTE: When they have completed the posters, you can take a photo of them to send to them after the workshop as a reminder.

Show the next set of instructions below

> ### *Small actions*
>
> Individually, pick one or two small steps with which you could make the maximum impact.

and invite the participants to sit at their tables, and say that now they have created a future perfect, the next thing to do is to pick some small steps that will make the maximum impact over the next days and weeks.

Invite them to spend a few minutes choosing their small steps and to write them down in their work books.

Good consequences?

- Share your small steps.
- Speculate about what beneficial consequences might arise from these small steps.

After a few minutes, show a slide or flip chart with these instructions and ask the participants to turn to the person next to them (working in pairs or threes depending on the number in the group) and to share their steps – those they are happy to share – and to speculate on the beneficial consequences that might arise from these steps ... what good things might happen as a result of them taking these small steps?

After a few minutes, check with the group that they all have a step that they can take.

If there's time: you can ask people to say, on a scale of 0–10 where 10 is you will definitely take this small step, and where 0 is there is no chance, where are they now? If everybody says about 8, 9 or 10, then move on. If any are lower, invite them to spend a few more minutes with their partner exploring what might increase the likelihood of the step being taken.

What happens next

As this activity is best positioned at the end of a workshop, it can be followed by an appropriate closing process.

Comments

This activity emerged as I looked for a simple, speedy and effective way of combining a review of workshop content and identification of action steps to be taken after the workshop. I wanted something that helped participants make more connections between what they had learned in the workshop and what they did at work.

I found that by getting the participants into groups using

coloured pens they were more likely to contribute to writing their contributions on flip charts. The fact that they don't necessarily need to have group consensus on everything that is written on the flip chart also helps with this.

The drawing of a collective future perfect facilitates a sharing of ideas and the creation of new applications. We have discovered that this works just as well with those who have never met before the workshop as with teams who work together all the time.

The sharing of small actions seems to have a large impact on the probability of taking the action, and the idea of checking the likelihood that they will take the step on a scale of 0–10 also models SF at work.

Acknowledgement

Thank you to Paul Z Jackson for his contribution to the development of this activity.

About *Janine Waldman*

– The Solutions Focus

Janine Waldman MSc FCIPD is an executive coach, consultant and facilitator who has trained numerous managers, in-house and professional coaches in the Solutions Focused approach worldwide. Her clients range from individual entrepreneurs to international organisations such as Beiersdorf (Nivea)

Address: 34a Clarence Road, St Albans, AL1 4NG, UK
Phone: + 44 (0)1727 840 340 Mobile: +44 (0)7786735945
e-mail: janine@thesolutionsfocus.co.uk
www.thesolutionsfocus.co.uk

CHAPTER 10

How was it for you?

SF evaluation   *Felix Hirschburger, Switzerland*

Progress monitoring as transfer assistance   *Susanne Keck, Germany*

The very act of asking questions about a workshop can reinforce the lessons learned.

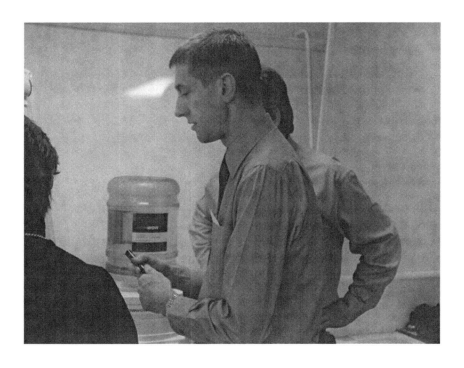

SF evaluation

... surprisingly simple and effective

Felix Hirschburger, Switzerland

This exercise makes it possible to reinforce the impact of your work while measuring its impact through evaluation. This SF way to wrap up your workshop focuses especially on things that already work and on potential for the future. Progress is initiated and reinforced.

Setting

- 30 minutes – 3 hours.
- 2–200 participants, sitting in a circle.
- Any room or a nice park bench in the sun can be used for the pairs interview.
- A flip chart.
- A camera.

Context and purpose

This exercise can be used for a powerful wrap up of workshops with small or big groups.

It evaluates your workshop in a way that reinforces things that already work as well as lessons learned; it finds potential for further development and it builds the platform for the transfer to daily business.

Detailed description

Introduction
I'd like to wrap up our work and take a close look at what has been helpful and what is still possible in the future.

In pairs, you can ask each other the following questions:

- *Tell me about the highlight of this workshop for you.*
- *If we met again for another workshop and you had 3 wishes, what would you ask for?*
- *What will be the first little sign tomorrow that tells you that helpful things happened in this workshop?*
- *And what else?*

Each pair has about 10 minutes for asking these questions (5 minutes each way).

Afterwards we share in the full group:

- *What were the highlights?*
- *What are the wishes for next time?*
- *How will people notice first signs?*

It's important to schedule enough time for that. Of course you can ask follow up questions like: *What exactly was so fascinating for you? What made this highlight possible? How will your boss notice that you made the next step* etc. In this way, you support the group in their creative and resourceful dynamic.

Work with scales is another option to show the impact of your workshop. For example you can ask: *On a scale from 1 to 10 where 10 means this workshop was absolutely perfect and 1 means a complete waste of time and money – where would you scale it?*

Let's suppose that the average scaling is between 7 and 8. Everything that is between 1 and 7.5 has been helpful. Between 7.5 and 10 is potential for further development – not to be confused with the negative aspects of the workshop.

What happens next

The question about the first signs of successful transfer connects what has been learned in the workshop with everyday life.

Comments

Appreciative, resourceful and solution focused attention results in a higher motivation and creativity. This activity also helps you to find out what already works and how you can make use of it in the future.

It is especially important at the end of a workshop to focus on things that are already working and to draw attention to areas where more of the same is wanted. Effectiveness becomes visible and is reinforced. In normal evaluations you ask: *And what were the negative elements?* With this approach we work with potential and wishes. Probably the most important part is the sharing of highlights. This reinforces learning and is an optimal platform for further success.

It doesn't matter whether the workshop went well or not. There is always something that worked and the spirit that emerges during the sharing of highlights is fascinating. It's also important to talk about potential for improvement. This gives helpful inputs and shows your neutral position. See that people give concrete examples when asking them about first signs of positive transfer. Encourage them through precise questions to make the picture as detailed as possible.

Acknowledgement of sources

It was Dr. Peter Szabó's idea to connect evaluation with a systemic solution focused mindset (de Shazer, Kim Berg). In 2003 we developed this idea together and put it into practice in post workshop evaluation interviews. We conducted 50 solution focused research interviews – with great success. On a scale from 1 to 10 (1 = this interview was useless; 10 = this interview was very helpful), the interviewees scaled an 8.6 on average. The main focus was on the word 'attention', asking questions like: *What happens if you pay attention to employees or trainees? What happens if you pay attention to positive things and things that work well?* The focus and quality of the attention you give make a difference.

This is one of the many ways that I work with groups. This approach was successfully introduced on the international SOL conference in Vienna 2006.

About *Felix Hirschburger*

– Resourcefulsearch

Felix Hirschburger holds an MA in economics and is involved in several solution focused projects. He works as an HR Manager for Losinger Construction AG, is founder of the Swiss-based company Resourcefulsearch and helps coaches, trainers, organisations and individuals to reinforce their success.

Address: Grossmühleber 222 / 3203 Mühleberg, Switzerland
Phone/Mobile: +41 01 534 59 69 / +41 78 778 18 09
e-mail: felix.hirschburger@bluewin.ch
www.resourcefulsearch.ch

Progress monitoring as transfer assistance

Susanne Keck, Germany

Progress monitoring is a structured interview held a few weeks after a workshop. It is designed to help the participants to appreciate and reinforce positive changes and resources in a solution focused way. It can be done by a short telephone call, by e-mail or through the company's intranet. The interview can be repeated as often as wished and can be continued by the participants (e.g. a team) themselves.

Setting

- Hardly any preparation time is needed if the interviewer has the questions for the relevant participants to hand. The questions are always more or less the same, adapted as appropriate to the group and situation.
- The questions are posted or e-mailed with an attachment to which the participants can respond directly, or alternatively telephone calls of approximately 10 minutes duration per participant can be arranged.
- If the interviewer wants to summarise the results and give written feedback to the client, this can take between 1 and 1½ hours depending on the number of participants.
- The number of participants is basically unlimited – the more participants the longer the summary takes.

Context and purpose

The exercise is suitable to reinforce the work of any workshop.

Progress monitoring supports the transfer back to the workplace. It doesn't matter whether this learning is behavioural or new content or whether the participants are one team or a mixed group of individuals. The objective is to strengthen the participants' sense of their own progress even if it may be small to start with or there are setbacks and frustration (which is often the case in change or learning projects). Moreover it allows additional success factors to be identified and it can stop modifications which did not turn out to be helpful in day-to-day work. It would be ideal if the participants themselves learned to apply this kind of progress monitoring on a regular basis.

Progress monitoring is an additional service you can offer your workshop participants to support motivation after the event. It is useful to address the subject of transfer during the workshop and possibly to do some exercises on successfully transferring results into day-to-day life. Usually, participants like the idea of being interviewed on their experiences some time after the workshop and you should set up this idea during the workshop. In my experience it is best to do the first monitoring 3–6 weeks after the workshop and by e-mail since this is the quickest and easiest way. If there is any concern about confidentiality in e-mail-transfer, you might consider encryption or other methods of data protection.

Detailed description

Possible questions for the monitoring could be (insert the relevant content in between the square brackets):

1 *Where are you now?*
   - *On a scale from 1 to 10 where 1 means there has been no progress and 10 means all your objectives have been achieved, where do you see [yourself, the team, subject xy ...] today?*

[If your answer is 1, you don't have to answer the following questions. And I admire the fact that somehow you are coping with the situation!]

   - *If there has been some progress, please tell me what lets you know that you have got as high as this.*
   - *What would it be like [at work, in the team, concerning subject xy ...] if you were one step higher on the scale?*

or alternatively:
- *What positive changes (large or small) have you noticed [at work, in the team, concerning subject xy] since the workshop?*
- *When have you noticed that [co-operation, team climate, subject xy ...] is going well? Or What tells you that there have been changes in your [life, everyday working life ...]? Please outline briefly the things you noticed.*

2 *How did that happen?*
- *What did you do to contribute to that? Or What did you do to make this possible?*
- *What would your [colleagues, team members, line manager, person xy ...] say you contributed? How would they have noticed that?*
- *What will you do more of in the future to encourage this positive development? How would relevant people notice that you want to encourage the process? Whose contributions of [your colleagues, line manager, the team, person xy ...] do you appreciate most?*
- *How do these people notice that you appreciate their contributions?*

3 *What else do you want?*
- *What has to happen more [at work, in the team, concerning subject xy]?*
- *When has this already happened, even to a small extent? What did you notice?*

Answering the questions alone is often useful in itself. It can be even better if the interviewer reads them out loud and makes motivating comments during the interview. Where there has been little progress, it is important to give compliments and perhaps ask some questions about how things could be changed or how to overcome the lean spell. It is important to notice and reinforce any small signs of progress, to notice and highlight strengths and resources and to take complaints seriously and give reassurance to stay on the track up the scale. Dissatisfaction, backward steps or obstacles can be reinterpreted as resources.

An example of reinterpreting dissatisfaction as a strength:

Dear team,
I am very impressed by the signs of progress in the important
subjects we talked about during the workshop. I was particu-
larly struck by keywords like (...) that appear in the lists of
what has been achieved and of the things that still have to be
improved (...) I am very pleased that some of you have
noticed some small but definite steps towards (...). At the
same time I understand that there may be impatience and frus-
tration with the time this is taking. Of course it is exhausting
to have to deal with (...) in addition to day-to-day-business.
Your frustration suggests you are still anxious to make
progress. This makes me confident that you will become a
very successful team.

This kind of monitoring can be repeated as often as wished.
Furthermore the participants can be motivated to apply the method
on the change project independently or on other subjects in the
future (e.g. on raising effectiveness of meetings etc.).

Comments

Because of its focus on the customer's goals and resources, the solution focused approach is already highly encouraging of transfer
back to the workplace. But the realisation of agreed measures is
often still a challenge. Day-to-day-business frequently lets us slide
back into familiar routines. Our ability to recognise the first small
successes of our new ideas can be overwhelmed by all the things we
can see that don't work. In this case, continuing support by the
facilitator can help participants to keep at it – without personal
contact or great effort on the facilitator's part.

It is possible to support our clients even after the workshop. Even
when things seem to be stuck, or going backwards, we can find
something that can be seen as a resource and confirmed encouragingly. This helps the clients to overcome obstacles. In the more
frequent case that there have been small successes the exercises
have a motivating effect and accelerate the process.

Acknowledgements

The idea of offering solution focused support to the participants after the workshop is not new. Felix Hirschburger's ideas of SF evaluation and the books of Daniel Meier T*eam Coaching with the SolutionCircle*) and Wilhelm Geisbauer (Ed.) *Reteaming – Methodenhandbuch zur lösungsorientierten Beratung* were very inspiring.

About **Susanne Keck**

– Solutionspace

I want to offer psychology as a service that creates lasting solutions. This requires an extremely good fit between the solution and the customer's goals, abilities and attitudes. Otherwise the solution will soon fall prey to the routines of everyday life. Systemic and solution focused approaches provide me with a tool to reach this aim.

Address: Schachnerstrasse 5, 81379 Munich, Germany
Phone/Mobile: + 49 89 38102661, +49 173 6911767
e-mail: sk@solutionspace.biz
www.solutionspace.biz

CHAPTER **11**

The next session

Starting the day   *Mark McKergow, United Kingdom*

Wouldn't it be nice?   *Peter Szabó, Switzerland*

Solution focused speed dating   *Penny West, United Kingdom*

What's better – focus on progress and success.

Starting the day

Connecting and building useful change in the middle of a workshop or process

Mark McKergow, United Kingdom

People pair up and discover both the things that have helped so far in the process and what might happen next. An affirming round can also be added.

Setting

- Allow about 15 minutes – or 10 minutes if no affirms are added.
- Works for any number of people.

Context and purpose

This activity gets people talking about the things they have noticed that seemed helpful so far – particularly in terms of their own contributions and behaviour. It can set a helpful context to the surrounding activities, as well as having people think about their personal contribution in the past and the future.

It is a great start to an afternoon or second day of a workshop – or any situation part way through a process where it might be useful to recap on what has happened.

Detailed description

Pair people up. Then say

OK, we're going to take a few moments to reflect on what's happened so far, and what's going to happen next. You'll have five minutes each way to ask your partner:

- *What were you pleased to notice about yourself yesterday. What else?*
- *What's better since we started? What else?*
- *What are you looking forward to catching yourself doing today? What else?*

Then the questioner offers two affirms to the partner – about what you have personally been impressed with in your partner's contributions and thoughts during this short discussion. Any questions? ... OK, go!

You may want to ensure that these questions are visible on a screen or flip chart for easy reference.

After five minutes, signal that the first round is coming to an end by ringing a bell or some such, and announce

OK ... the first round is coming to a close. Time to move on to the affirms, and then change over for the second round.

Watch how people are doing for time – if they don't seem to have changed over after a minute or so, ask quietly if they have changed over yet. They usually get the idea pretty fast.

At the end of the second round, follow the same routine and give people a couple of minutes to offer affirmation.

What happens next

Gather people back together and debrief. There are a number of ways to handle this:

- Just proceed with your next activity – the atmosphere in the room will be well grounded and more optimistic following this activity. It serves as a good way of re-focusing and settling down, so participants are ready to tackle whatever is to come.
- Gather some of the 'what's better' findings as an indication of how things are going, and to let everyone hear the different views about what's better.
- Maybe capture some of the things that people were pleased to notice about themselves yesterday – this can give people the chance to give themselves a small 'pat on the back'.

Comments

I based this activity on one devised by Guy Shennan at an accelerated learning course I was running a few years ago. It can serve as an excellent link on workshops or courses by having people take a moment to both look back and forwards, and can be used in many situations.

You may like to look carefully at the questions in the exercise – they look very simple but are carefully worded:

What were you pleased to notice about yourself yesterday is not the same as *what were you pleased with about what you did yesterday.* Noticing seems to me to be a more gentle and less deliberate process – as if you might have just noticed something that was not a deliberate intention, or even a hugely important aspect. However, as you talk about it, it becomes more important. De-emphasising the idea that things only happen because we deliberately make them happen, and emphasising instead the role of noticing when we do something useful by naturally responding to circumstance, are key elements of the SF approach.

Likewise, you invite your partner to *look forward to catching yourself doing something today.* This has a similar ring about it – you might catch yourself doing something, even if you had not intended or expected to do it. Although having talked about it, your chances may well increase ...

What's better since we started is a twist on a traditional SF question. It is of course different from *is anything better?* and also specifically refers to things that have happened *since we started.* This invites people to think carefully about what has happened since we started, and think about a whole range of things that might be better. It is not at all specific about the nature of these things – that's for the participants to work out!

Acknowledgement of sources

As mentioned above, Guy Shennan produced something like this on one of our courses. I tweaked it, used it and like it very much.

About *Dr Mark McKergow*

– The Centre for Solutions Focus at Work (sfwork)

*Dr Mark McKergow is co-director of sfwork –
The Centre for Solutions Focus at Work. He is
an international consultant, speaker and
contributor. Many people around the world
have been inspired by his work in Solutions
Focus – presented with his inimitable blend of
scientific rigour and performance pizzazz. He
has written and edited three books and dozens
of articles; was instrumental in the founding of
the SOLWorld organisation (www.solworld.org), and founded
SolutionsBooks with Jenny Clarke in 2005; their most recent
book is the case study collection Solutions Focus Working (2007).
He has presented on every continent except Antarctica, and is an
international conference keynote presenter.*

Address: 26 Christchurch Road, Cheltenham, GL50 2PL, United
Kingdom
Phone: +44 (0)1242 511441
e-mail: mark@sfwork.com
www.sfwork.com

Wouldn't it be nice?

Real and invented success stories

Peter Szabó, Switzerland

A plunge into team change! Participants share their success stories in small groups. As well as being fun, it provides everybody with the knowledge of what others are already contributing to the achievements of the team.

Setting

- 20–45 minutes.
- 12–100 participants.
- Flip chart with overview of Phases 1 to 3.
- Prepare flip chart with questions for Phase 2.
- Preferably the room should have movable chairs so that people can work in groups of 3 in Phase 2.

Context and purpose

This activity is a great start, especially for large teams and organisational units! It can be used to open up a team meeting, a specific workshop or team change project. It is also very helpful for follow-up meetings where you want to discover and enhance changes and successes in between meetings. It works well with soft topics, for example individual core competences or team communication skills.

In team change processes, it gives the group a chance to see what already works well and to build on examples where success is evident. Team members are challenged to spot how and what they have achieved individually and they can get in touch with their resources and competences and even tell about them in a fun and animated way.

As a side effect team members learn to ask each other solution evoking questions.

Detailed description

Phase 1: Individual preparation (5 min)

Each participant is asked to remember two recent examples of success, to which she has made a significant contribution. Pride and satisfaction in the personal contribution to the success may really shine through – wasn't it nice!

Participants have to make up a third example of success – an invented a story of a success she would have liked. Wouldn't it be nice?

The participant gives each example a catchy name. ('*The big dig or how we rejuvenated our archiving system*').

Phase 2: Exchange of the stories in groups of 3 (15–35 min)

Form groups of three. Person A tells the others the title of each of her stories – convincingly as if every story was true! B and C listen to the titles and choose two of the stories they would like to hear more about.

B and C ask questions to get to know more details about the stories they chose.

- *How did you do that?*
- *What has helped you?*
- *If I would like to do the same thing, what would I have to think about?*
- *What are you especially proud of?*

A answers with pride and conviction, regardless of whether the story really happened or not.

In turn B and C get to tell and be asked about 2 of their 3 stories.

If there is time, a round of resource gossip may be added. B and C talk about A. They exchange what impressed them that A did, to make the story come true. B and C gossip indirectly about A's resources, abilities, special behaviour etc. A leans back and quietly listens to the gossip, enjoying the resource shower. Then B and C get their turn.

You can choose whether or not to ask people to reveal which of the stories were true.

Phase 3: Debriefing (5–10 min)
There are two ways of debriefing:
1) Collect the most impressive, helpful success factors, so that the participants can profit from the variety.
   • *What factors might usefully lead to success?*
2) It is often very interesting to hear about the made-up stories. The facilitator may ask who was asked to tell one of those.
   • *What was it like telling about made-up success?*

Participants who told a true story can be asked:
   • *What was it like to get asked about true success stories?*

What happens next

When used as an opening exercise, there should be no direct connection with the content of the workshop ahead.

If it is used as a tool to check on a team's progress, it is useful to capture the steps the team has taken in the meantime and ask about how they can keep up what they have achieved.

If team-communication is the topic, it is very important to plan an additional 5 minutes for resource gossip after Phase 2. It is time well invested and may enhance an appreciative way of communication in a team.

Comments

• I was getting bored of always asking *what's better?* and asking about success stories. So I developed the idea about the made-up story. But what was meant to be just for fun turned out to make much more sense. The made up stories help participants to mentally act 'as if' and surprisingly often give them new ideas to find small steps towards a solution.
• There are two things I especially like about this tool:
  – When focusing on success, the level of energy and motivation in the group rises perceptibly almost immediately.
  – The discoveries made in the evaluation phase are a continual surprise to me. There are people who want to go and make their made up story come true right away. Others discover that what they thought was a fake story turned out to be surprisingly true already and became aware of lots of

achievements they had already made. And then there are those who just discover how simply being asked '*Wow, how did you do that*', or '*What helped?*' can be the best compliment they ever got ... and much more.

- Beware! Telling success stories can be addictive! This often leads to a loss of any feeling for time! I had groups I could only stop after 45 minutes in Phase 2. It helps to announce the end of the round after a third of the time is up.
- I leave it to the groups whether they come out about their 'made-up' story or not.

Acknowledgements of sources

The ideas for the tool were developed in discussion with Stephanie von Bidder. Other sources or further literature are unknown to me.

About *Dr. Peter Szabó*

– Solutionsurfers International

Peter Szabó is a Master Certified Coach with the ICF (International Coach Federation). In his private practice, he specialises in Brief Coaching. He has trained over 700 coaches for Solutionsurfers International and teaches post graduate courses in coaching at several European universities. He is asked to introduce the solutions focused approach to organisations all over the the world. With Insoo Kim Berg he is co-author of Brief Coaching for Lasting Solutions.

Address: Waldstätterstrasse 9, CH- 6003 Lucerne, Switzerland
Phone/Mobile: + 41 41 210 39 79
E-mail: peter.szabo@solutionsurfers.com
www.solutionsurfers.com

301

Solution focused speed dating

Penny West, United Kingdom

This is an energising exercise for the beginning of a second or third session when the facilitator wants to introduce newcomers into the group. It also allows the other participants to recall what happened previously in a non-threatening way. It is also a good warm up for the beginning or middle of a workshop.

Setting

- Timing: Allow 30 minutes. This works for a group size of 10 to 50. With a larger group of more than 25 people, you may need an extra 10 minutes to give them time to move around.
- You need a room in which chairs can be moved into a line or opposite each other in pairs in a circle.
- You also need a watch with minute hands to time the 2 minute speed dating slots and a bell, or a loud voice, for calling the end to the 2 minute slots – it can get quite noisy.

Context and purpose

This activity is great for getting the second or third session of a group started. It is useful for bringing to mind recent achievements and successes and for promoting both group and one-to-one inter-action. It is more effective than brainstorming which does not engage participants in this dynamic and interactive way. Newcomers are involved immediately by being able to ask *What was useful last time?* and *What else?* rather than sitting quietly hoping that they will gradually catch up.

It is good for integrating newcomers and reducing their anxiety if they missed a session used for team development, change work-shop, or action learning set. It is especially useful when there are several newcomers and the facilitator does not want to hold a boring catch up session.

It is also a useful way of energising a group, say in the afternoon, if the atmosphere is rather flat. It is great fun, very structured and a psychologically safe exercise for all types of groups, but is unusual in style, so may appeal to the innovative facilitator. It gives an opportunity to use solution-focused questioning techniques that will underpin the group's competence and allow them to uncover their resources.

This exercise always results in a positive and creative atmosphere that enables subsequent visioning, or other practical planning sessions, to be highly effective.

Detailed description

The facilitator tells people that they are going to have a speed dating exercise. This usually causes some laughter and ribald comments. The facilitator needs to model good humour and energy and to say that this is a warm up exercise so that the people who were not there last time can find out what useful things happened before. The facilitator, or the group, arranges a straight line of chairs paired opposite each other down the room, so that participants can sit facing each other: quite close together is best.

	Front of room	Back of room
Facilitator stands in front	GROUP A _ _ _ _ _ _ _ _ _ _ _ _ GROUP B _ _ _ _ _ _ _ _ _ _ _ _ Group B moves in this direction ⟶	

- The facilitator asks people who were *not* at the previous workshop – the newcomers (Group A for purposes of this explanation, but do not give them a group name) to sit down on one line of chairs and the people who *were* there last time (Group B) to sit opposite them. In spite of the title, this exercise is not divided on gender lines!
- The facilitator gives different tasks to the 2 groups:
  Group A asks *What was useful last time?* And follows this with *What else?* as many times as they like in order to get as much information as possible from their partner in the 2 minutes

303

available and Group B recalls something from the last session in reply to these questions.

- The facilitator checks people have a partner to talk to (and joins in if necessary if there is an odd number) and are clear about the task. If fewer than half the people are newcomers, ask some people to pretend they were not there last time to even up the numbers.
- The facilitator rings a bell to signal the start of the 2 minutes question and answer session.
- He carefully times the 2 minutes, then rings the bell to signal the end of the 2 minute session.
- The facilitator then asks the people in Group A to remain seated and Group B to move along one place – in the same direction at the same time – see diagram. This usually causes some confusion and chaos – which is all to the good, since it brings energy into the interaction! This means that the person at the back of Group B has to come to the front. People now get the idea that this exercise is a bit like a children's party game.
- Repeat the 2 minute session: same tasks, same questions with a different partner.
- Repeat about 8 to 10 times. For a change, to move things along or to add to the confusion helpfully, the facilitator could ask people to move up two, or three, places. By this time the newcomers will have a good idea – and different views – of what people got out of the last workshop: what had been useful or interesting experiences. They will have caught up. In addition the people who were at the previous workshop will have recalled what happened, thought about what was useful and got back into the spirit of the workshop. Everybody will now be in a better position to undertake the next stage of the workshop.
- The facilitator thanks everybody for joining in so fully and states that if it were a REAL speed dating session, they would all now choose who they want to see again. However since this is a change workshop (or whatever) ... *We will not do that part, but, of course, if people want to make their own arrangements* ... This usually leads to some laughter, as the facilitator asks people to move the chairs into position for the next part of the workshop. It may be appropriate to highlight the solution focused points of asking *What was useful?* and about the power

of *What else?* questions, or it might be better to not labour the point and move on using the energy this session has created.

What happens next

This exercise brings to mind useful content or achievements during a previous session. Afterwards, you can go on with your workshop programme.

Comments

This idea was developed after watching a documentary about speed dating and I tried it out during an Action Learning Set instead of the usual pairing and feedback. It will, of course, work with any simple questions and can be used to recall developments outside the sessions. In the Action Learning Set the questions were, *What improvements have there been on your ward since our last action learning session?* and *What else?* Participants were given two minutes each to ask these questions of each other and then one of the partners moved to the next chair until everyone had had a conversation with everyone from the opposite 'team'.

I also used it during a day workshop in which a chief executive had spoken for far longer than anticipated about the strategic priorities of the organisation, leading to a lack of energy in the room. After the tea break, I used this exercise to get some movement and involvement back into the room. The questions on this occasion were *From the chief executive's presentation, what is the key issue for action for you as a middle manager?* and *What do you need to take forward?* and *What else?* After the speed dating exercise, people were in a more creative state of mind to consider the miracle question and undertake some more traditional action planning. In effect they were speed coaching each other.

Speed dating is a simple concept, but not many people will have actually tried it. This makes the event memorable and fun: people go home and tell their partners they had been speed dating at work. However, the relevance of the questions is also quickly apparent and participants get a chance to have their voice heard in a safe (and often noisy) environment. It is important for the facilitator to take care in devising the questions so that they are simple and relevant to the aims of the workshop. Interestingly, people do not mind being asked to use the same questions, or giving the same (or similar) answers in this exercise.

This is a quick energiser needing limited preparation. It only requires clarity about the questions to be asked. These should be simple, relevant and solution focused. The facilitator needs to model having fun and use this exercise when they want to inject into the group a feeling of excitement, energy and creativity.

Acknowledgement

Devised by the contributor.

About **Penny West**

– Orchard Solutions

Penny is a consultant working mainly in mental health and older persons' social services in the UK. She trained originally as an occupational therapist and has an MSc from the London School of Economics and an MA from the Tavistock Clinic. She discovered solution focused approaches at the SOLWorld conference in Bristol in February 2003 and has since incorporated its thinking in all her work especially when facilitating awaydays, action learning sets and team development.

Address: 34 Orchard Road, Highgate, London, N6 5TR, UK
Phone/Mobile: + 44 7058 838 325
e-mail: pennywest@orchard-solutions.co.uk
www.orchard-solutions.co.uk

CHAPTER 12

How do you add solution focus to your toolkit?

Peter Röhrig and Kirsten Dierolf, Germany

We do not know if you talk to yourself when reading this book, but we hope that you couldn't help but sometimes exclaim *Now that's an idea. I could try this the next time I'm working with group XYZ!* And you may start by delivering the exercise exactly as described in the book, as if following a recipe. This would be a good idea for people who are not yet very familiar with solution focused work. Once you have more of a taste of solution focus, you will start to recognise and use more and more opportunities for using solution focused ideas.

Then you can start to vary the exercises in this book or invent new activities for yourself. For those of you who would like to start doing this right away, we have the following suggestions. Maybe you are simply curious or you are the type of person who would like to start trying out something new. Maybe you already have so much experience with solution focused work that you were only waiting for the opportunity to season a tried and trusted intervention in a solution focused way. In this case, you've come to the right place.

What is the difference between a group intervention and a coaching intervention?

There are many places and excellent books in which solution focused work and a face-to-face meeting between two people has been described – take for example Insoo Kim Berg and Peter Szabó's book *Brief Coaching for Lasting Solutions*. There are also very practical and inspiring publications about training the solution focused approach, for example Lilo Schmitz' collection 'Lösungsorientierte Gesprächsführung' (available in German).

What is special about the collection of exercises in this book is that it is the first to deal exclusively with interventions in teams and groups. What is so special about working with groups? What do we have to pay attention to if we want to apply solution focus in teams?

First and foremost, the facilitator of a workshop simply has to deal with more people than a coach in a one-to-one conversation. This usually means that you have to apply the solution focused tools in a different way. It may be attractive to ask a small team a miracle question just as you would in a coaching setting. If all the team members then speak about their future perfect, one after the other, they might identify ideas and steps for change. However, this is only realistic for groups of up to six participants. If the group is larger, there will be repetition and it can become long-winded and boring. Therefore, we have to find different ways of eliciting the rich images of the group's future which quickly lead to similar results. You can find many examples in Chapter 6.

Another important difference is the fact that in any group you will have people with different interests. In coaching, this diversity of interest exists only implicitly, for example when you are talking about the interests of a company or balancing work and family time. In group workshops, the interests of different group members or departments and the company are crucial factors which facilitators have to take into account. It may be necessary to start by making differences apparent and acknowledging them. Once a platform of trust has been established it is quite possible to work with different interests even if questions of power or hierarchy play a role. Solution focus helps facilitators not to be intimidated and to look at what the different people and different groups really want. SF facilitators are on everybody's side. As Matthias Varga von Kibéd phrases it, they work with 'multidirectional partiality'. If you see different interests as an expression of diversity and wealth, a resource oriented perspective can uncover previously the unexplored potential of groups. You can find examples in Chapter 5.

The examples in this book show how solution focused principles can be intensified by the group dynamic. The best exercises are those which make it possible to use solution focus in such a way that the special qualities and energies of the group multiply. There are good examples of this in Chapter 9 for the transfer of what has been learned and worked on. The power of witnesses when good intentions are voiced in a group increases commitment and thus sustainability. We often see how many voices can contribute to the intensification of appreciative remarks. Compliments have an effect even if the same thing is mentioned more than once. Recognition and appreciation of the group is especially strong and they contribute to the sustainable effects of the results of a workshop.

Finally, the principle of the client as expert can be implemented very well working with groups. Participants can build on what other participants say as well as on what the facilitator says.

The SF Excellence Triangle

At the first SOLWorld conference in Bristol in 2002, Peter Röhrig and Paul Z Jackson spontaneously developed the Excellence Triangle of solution focused work. Facilitators, trainers and coaches who work successfully with the solution focus have the following skills:

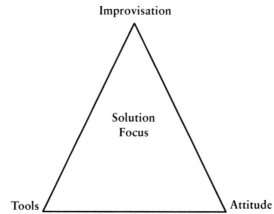

Excellence triangle of solution focused work

The tools
The structure and the tools of solution focused work are simple and easy to grasp. We would like to supplement Lilo Schmitz' overview:

- We ask open questions that are competency oriented and assume resources. They enable our clients to think about their goals and new ways of reaching them individually or collectively.

309

- We demonstrate real appreciation and recognition of resources. It supports and encourages our clients and is often combined with a new perspective, for example looking at problems as challenges or opportunities.
- Scaling helps to recognise differences and progress. It gives a vocabulary for talking about things that are not measurable, for example how the clients will recognise that he or she is one point ahead on the scale.
- The miracle question is a process, a sequence of questions and encouragement which helps clients to think about their own desires and their own picture of the desired future. It helps to release the creative potential.
- SF works with small and realistic steps which trigger change.

Attitude
The philosophy and learning theory of the solution focused approach is simple but not easy. This is especially clear when you look at the SIMPLE principles of the solutions focus as described by Paul Z Jackson and Mark McKergow:

- Solutions – not problems: a sense of what our clients desire (and not what they should do next). We discover this by being curious about all details of the desired future (future perfect) and about what has already been successful in the past.
- Inbetween – not individual. The solution focused learning theory assumes that people develop their skills in the interaction with others (and not from inside). This is why we use interactive language and look at observable behaviour avoiding mind reading.
- Make use of what's there – not what isn't. We work with what is already functioning, with what is working better and even with the things that stop things getting worse. In our experience, the building blocks for change can be found more often in the area of resources than in the area of deficits.
- Possibilities from past, present and future. We create hope and optimism from the possibilities and options in the past and future. Even in the past, there are often undiscovered opportunities which we explore by connecting them to what is desired in the future.
- Language – clear, not complicated. Our language is simple and

concrete and helps to describe daily life in detail. We do not use abstract and generalising language.

• Every case is different – avoid ill-fitting theory. We enter into every case with openness and an attitude of not knowing. We do not know what needs to be done next. This often helps to see things more clearly especially if the preconceived ideas of the consultant do not fit the experience of the client.

Improvisation

If we take the needs of our clients seriously, every workshop offers new challenges. We are not talking about creating customised processes as do many consultants and trainers to meet their clients' needs. What we mean here is an open and experimental approach, which helps us to support our clients and work on their issues in the way they need at this moment.

Many examples in the book show how successful exercises were created through improvisation – for example when Alasdair Macdonald was unexpectedly faced with 100 instead of 30 participants and was able to create an icebreaker which fit the situation perfectly.

The triad of tools, attitude, and improvisation is very helpful. We all know that even if perfectly planned, a workshop can take a completely unexpected direction. In such a situation, we demonstrate our professionalism and poise by being flexible and able to continue the workshop in a way that really fits the participants' needs. A quote attributed to Abraham Maslow is *'If the only tool you have is a hammer, you tend to see every problem as a nail'.*

Where do ideas for new interventions come from?

There are various ways to design solution focused learning and change processes. For example, you can find basic elements of the process in Daniel Meier's book *Team Coaching with the SolutionCircle* and the book by Louis Cauffman and Kirsten Dierolf *The Solution Tango.*

The following phases (which you can also find in the structure of this book) are usually involved, although not necessarily in this order:

➤ Exercises to start a workshop: getting to know each other, creating a positive work atmosphere, exploring the context.

➤ Goal definition: scope of the problem, clarifying hotspots and conflicts.
➤ Exploring resources: appreciating strength and successes.
➤ Future perfect: a rich picture of the desired situation, developing visions and strategies.
➤ Scaling: recognising differences and progress.
➤ Interaction: surfing on the surface.
➤ Exercises to end a session: identifying next steps, preparing transfer to the workplace.
➤ Continuing in the next session with *What is better?*

How do you actually do it?

If you want to turn an exercise into a solution focused exercise, it is a good idea to look at the different phases of the exercise. How can the exercise be made most useful for the clients when you are introducing it, during the exercise and when debriefing it.

Introducing the exercise
As usual, it is important to communicate the purpose of the exercise so that participants feel confident that this is a good use of their time, and to clarify the structure and time frame of the exercise. In addition, there are a few tricks that can help the participants focus on resources and success factors.

In the introduction, you can ask the whole group or individuals of the group to notice what is going well in the exercise. You can assign observer tasks and ask for specific positive feedback after the exercise. We try to identify what is working first and only then concentrate on what could be better following the solution focused tenet: *If it works, do more of it – if it doesn't work, do something different.*

During the exercise
During the exercise the SF facilitator is more of a coach uncovering resources than an entertainer running around in circles feeling responsible for everything that happens in the workshop. We assume that the participants are already experts in their own learning process and nurture responsibility and self-reliance in our participants. Our facilitation is simple, saves time and makes it possible for the participants to take an active part in the seminar.

The facilitator is the leader, but he or she steers lightly.

You will notice that SF facilitators give instructions for an exercise and then let the participants work on their own. Steve de Shazer said *There is no understanding, only more or less useful misunderstandings.* We assume that the participants will understand the instructions in a way that is most useful to them.

If conflicts arise between participants during an exercise, the facilitator's job is to have the different opinions perceived as complementary and as potential resources. We aim to help the group move from *yes but* and move into *yes and* and thus be able to develop new ideas.

Even if there is someone in the workshop who would be labelled 'negative' or 'resistant' by more traditional facilitators, a solution focused facilitator would assume that this person has good reasons for their behaviour. Their behaviour shows a solution focused facilitator that he or she has not established enough contact with that person. We try to find out what this person wants and what the next step could be toward reaching that goal. We do not feel personally offended (which is easier if we don't position and understand our role as entertainers or animators of the process).

Debrief

Where we set our focus is crucial in debriefing an exercise. We concentrate on the skills, the resources, the new ideas and the participants' a-haa moments. Usually, this means that the main points of the debrief come from the participants. In individual coaching, you only know what you asked your client when you have heard the answer to it. In the same way, you can only really say what the purpose of an exercise was after you've done it and heard what the participants actually learned from it. Therefore it is quite useful to start with very general open questions like *What did you notice?* or *How did that go for you?* We do try our best to find exercises that promote a specific learning effect and to ask questions that direct the focus and a certain direction, but the participants have to tell us about their experience of what happened first.

Next, appreciative questions about the resources uncovered in the exercise are very useful: *What does this exercise say about our strengths? Who contributed what to the solution? What would we like more of in our daily lives?*

Of course, it is important to transfer what has been learned into the participants' daily life. You can do that by looking for examples of the uncovered resources: *Where does something like that already happen in our daily lives?* or by thinking about new possibilities: *How can we take what we have learned here and use it in a different context?* You can also work with scaling questions: *On a scale of 1 to 10 where were you with regard to your topic in this exercise? Where are you in your daily life? How would you notice in your daily life that you had got one step higher on the scale?*

What are the limits?

Most exercises can be transformed into effective solution focused interventions if you use a few hints and tricks. Just occasionally, however, we have encountered exercises whose background is so different from solution focused thinking that we couldn't see how they could be reworked in a solution focused way.

Solution focused processes are always resource oriented. We aim at uncovering strengths and possibilities that our participants did not know – or had forgotten – they had. After a solution focused exercise the participants are positively surprised by their capabilities or by how easy it was to learn.

One big advantage of solution focused processes is that it is easy to create a positive working relationship between facilitator and participants and also positive, supportive relationships among the participants. Solution focused facilitators would not introduce an exercise which jeopardises this working relationship. Exercises which produce conflicts or embarrass participants fall into the same category. In a team workshop, there was one participant who regularly arrived late after the breaks. The other participants tolerated this and it was only after the facilitator mentioned the phenomenon that participants realised that the person who was late had been instructed to behave like this in order to show the impact of unpunctual behaviour. The aim of this kind of thing is often to demonstrate what is 'really' happening in the team. The facilitator wants to get to the root of the problem and get rid of it once and for all. A clear link between the problem (or even the problematic team member) and the solution is assumed. In a solution focused process, the goal would be different: to ask for the future perfect and for exceptions to the problem, to elicit the resources of the team and to define small steps toward the goal.

Applying instruments for team or personality diagnostics or personality typologies for individual or team coaching follows a similar logic. The goal is the development of the team or the resolution of a problem, and the first thing the facilitator does is look for the cause of the problem. Team members fill in a DISC profile or use the Myers-Briggs Type Indicator or a similar instrument. The results show where the team's problem lies and how it can be solved, for example by hiring a new team member who has the missing attributes.

When asked to work with organisations which use such typologies as a standard tool for human resource development, SF consultants can take the instruments as part of the organisation's grammar and start a solution focused process afterwards. You can ask questions like *What advantages and resources of your team are shown in the typology? Where do you see these resources having an impact in your daily life? If X is missing in your team, how have you so far coped productively? On a scale of one to 10 where you with regard to ...?* If used like this, these instruments actually provide good opportunities for interesting conversations and team or individual coaching.

If the instruments used are not typologies (like DISC or Myers-Briggs), but instruments to determine static characteristics of personalities, it becomes especially difficult for a solution focused consultant to continue the process. It is a basic tenet of solution focused processes that change happens constantly. It is therefore very difficult for us to work with instruments that assume an unchanging and unchangeable personality.

Some typologies, for example integral coaching or spiral dynamics (Ken Wilber) classify clients into developmental stages. There is a predetermined path for development from beige to green which also predetermines the development path of the client (or the client team). It is difficult to convert this into a solution focused process. We work with the goals of the client and cannot prescribe them. We would think it possible to use this diagnostic as a starting point for interesting conversations; however actively suggesting such methodologies for a solution focused process is hardly possible.

What next?

We hope that we have been able to encourage you to try something new with these hints and tricks. We know from our own experience that solution focus can really make our work as facilitators and team coaches light and effective. If we pay careful attention to our own responsibility in the workshop, we can concentrate on the process and how to keep it useful while the participants are working hard to achieve satisfactory results, as if by magic. As the world-famous cellist Pablo Casals said: *The most perfect technique is that which is not noticed at all.*

The best way to achieve such mastery is to practise. You can use the SOLWorld network (www.solworld.org) which offers various ways of swapping experiences and trying out new methods: there is an active mailing list, an annual conference and a Summer University. This international community continues to grow and it is increasingly gaining attention and recognition among customers and colleagues.

And, of course, you can also profit from the trainings and workshops of the authors' www.solutionsacademy.com and www.solution-tools.peter-röhrig.com. We are looking forward to getting to know you.

Bibliography

Louis Cauffman and Kirsten Dierolf: *The Solution Tango*, 2006, ISBN 3896706012

Paul Z Jackson und Mark McKergow: *The Solutions Focus. Making Coaching and Change SIMPLE.* Second edition, Nicholas Brealey 2007. ISBN 1–90483–06–5

Daniel Meier: *Team Coaching with the SolutionCircle.* SolutionsBooks 2005. ISBN 0–9549749-1-3

Lilo Schmitz: Lösungsorientierte Gesprächsführung. Trainingsbausteine für Hochschule, Ausbildung und kollegiale Lerngruppen. Brühl 2002, ISBN 3–00–010180–2

Peter Szabó and Insoo Kim Berg:, *Brief Coaching for Lasting Solutions.* Norton Professional Books, 2005. ISBN 978–0393704723

About **Dr. Peter Röhrig**

– ConsultContor · Consulting and Coaching

Peter is an SF organisational consultant, facilitator and executive coach, born 1948, with two children.

- *Formal education as an economist and social psychologist*
- *Advanced training in epidemiology, organisational development, total quality management (EFQM) and solution focused consulting*
- *11 years as general manager of service companies*
- *Many publications, mainly about self-management, leadership and quality development*
- *Partner of ConsultContor, consulting and coaching, in Cologne, Germany*

Renate Kerbst, one of his co-partners at ConsultContor says about Peter:
Zeal for solutions is the name of an sf training series initiated by Peter, and this is a strong impulse for his professional functioning. His focus on practical resources and his attentiveness to simplicity are a solid foundation for his consulting and facilitating work. With subtle persistence he helps his clients to find surprising and progressive solutions.

As a recovering former manager he supports people whole-heartedly in challenging leadership positions – and people who want to create effective teamwork. One of his main working areas is quality development, with a special emphasis on the health and social sector.

Peter is committed to the international SOLWorld network and faculty member of the SOLWorld Summer University. He offers advanced training in sf consulting and workshop design.

Mark McKergow says about Peter:
The biggest quiet style – a giant with velvet hands.

Address: Balthasarstsse 81, D 50670 Cologne, Germany
Phone: + 49 (0)228–34 66 14 Mobile: + 49 (0)179–523 46 86
e-mail: : peter.roehrig@consultcontor.de
www.ConsultContor.de

About **Kirsten Dierolf**

Kirsten Dierolf M.A., works as Executive Coach, organisational and human resource developer mainly for large corporations in global projects. In 2007 she developed several leadership development programmes, team trainings and human resource development programmes on intercultural communication, virtual teaming and communication. She regularly speaks at international conferences.

Address: Kalbacherstr. 7, 61352 Bad Homburg, Germany
Phone: +49 6172 684905
e-mail: kirsten@kirsten-dierolf.de
www.solutionsacademy.com

LaVergne, TN USA
18 January 2011
212917LV00002B/1/P